Praise for The Music Miracle: The Scientific Secret to Unlocking Your Child's Full Potential

Henriksson-Macaulay's book bursts with enthusiasm and a fantastic array of knowledge and suggested approaches for fostering the musical development of children. Her commitment to this cause never flounders. I applaud her.
Professor Lucy Green, Institute of Education, University of London

Never before have I seen such a comprehensive and in-depth review of the neuroscientific and psychological basis of the effects of music on young children. Parents and many others will be anxious to read it because of its very important message. Henriksson-Macaulay has blazed an important and pioneering trail for others to follow, and I wish this book every success.
David J. Hargreaves,
Psychologist FBPsS, Professor of Education, University of Roehampton

I am pleased to commend this is a very positive contribution to the public awareness of the power of music to transform children's lives. Every child is musical. By encouraging their children to make the most of their innate musical potential, parents can support much wider cognitive, emotional and social development as their children grow. Liisa Henriksson-Macaulay's narrative is engaging and full of rich personal anecdote, as well as a synthesis of key research findings and useful examples for parents of how music can be used successfully to nurture and strengthen children's development.
Professor Graham Welch, Institute of Education, University of London

Dedicated to Travis and our son Toivo Henriksson-Macaulay;
my parents; and Ken and Dom Stringfellow

THE MUSIC MIRACLE

The Scientific Secret to Unlocking Your Child's Full Potential

Liisa Henriksson-Macaulay

To contact the author of this work, please send your enquiry via the website contact form at www.moosicology.com

ISBN 978-0-9926643-0-5

Foreword

by David J Hargreaves, Professor of Education, London

Liisa Henriksson-Macaulay is a musician and a parent who is passionate about her message that musical training can promote children's development in many different areas, and that it can do so in ways that most other educational activities are unable to achieve. In this book she draws on an extremely wide range of scientific literature in the psychology and neuropsychology of music to make her case, and this literature is expertly reviewed. As an academic in music psychology myself, I think that the breadth and depth of this review is remarkable, especially since the author apparently has no training these areas: never before have I seen such a comprehensive and in-depth review of the neuroscientific and psychological basis of the effects of music on young children.

She describes the many benefits that early music training can bestow as the 'Music Miracle'. There are no miracles in science, of course, and no supernatural powers are actually being claimed here: rather, this is just a popular catch-all expression that the author has chosen to use to sum up the many benefits of music training. Whilst this is not a term that would be found in the scientific literature, I am nevertheless strongly in support of the point of view that Liisa Henriksson-Macaulay is putting forward: that early training in music can provide many developmental benefits, and that parents and others need to be made more aware of this.

She looks at some recent research on the effect of early music training on executive functioning and on later IQ levels, and relates this to research on developing brain function and structure in impressive detail. The neuroscientific literature emphasises that the brain exhibits plasticity at this early stage, such that early experiences of various kinds affect the ways in which the synaptic connections develop: this means that musical activity, which has been shown to draw on various areas of the brain simultaneously, can facilitate many different aspects of development that other activities may not be able to influence.

She then reviews a wealth of evidence which cover a wide range of phenomena and findings in early and later development, and on which I can only touch very briefly here. I think that it is useful to make the distinction here between what children learn in music and what they learn through music. By the former I refer, for example, to the phenomenon of 'communicative musicality', as it has been labelled by Colwyn Trevarthen and Stephen Malloch in particular: the basic idea is that early communication between babies and their carers is itself inherently 'musical' in that the relationship between the behaviour of one partner and the other in their verbal, visual, and other interactions is very precisely synchronized in the same way that that musical parts have to be for the music to succeed: this involves split-second timing and a powerful awareness of the intentions of the other partner. Babies and infants also demonstrate spontaneous reactions to music including rhythmic movement and dancing, which is also evidence of their inherent musicality.

This idea of children of children learning through music is the basis of this book: for example, research on mothers singing to their babies has shown how this can influence a number of different aspects of development including communication and language skills. Liisa Henriksson-Macaulay reviews the literature on learning through music in considerable detail, showing how it can promote a very wide range of behavioural skills and capabilities. These include physical health and fitness: memory capacity and skills; various aspects of language development including linguistic intelligence, pitch processing, syntactic abilities, semantic memory, the ability to learn foreign languages, phonological awareness and speech segmentation; mathematical skills and abilities; self-regulation and the expression of emotions, including aspects of self-identity, self-esteem, and personality development; the development of creativity and its relationship with intelligence, defined in terms of IQ as well as in other ways: and the growth of well-being and happiness.

If all this is true, then the educational implications are profound. Henriksson-Macaulay herself was brought up in Finland and describes how the early training that virtually all Finnish children receive in the Musiikkileikkikoulu (which translates as music playschool) - which is staffed by teachers with high levels of musical training and experience - enables them to learn musical concepts and skills in a child-centred fashion. This may be one reason, amongst others, why Finland has consistently gained first place in the Organization for Economic Development and Co-operation's (OECD) Programme for International Student Assessment (PISA) scores: educators from many other countries regularly visit Finland in order to find out what is the secret of this success.

Henriksson-Macaulay expresses some strong views about what she sees as some other myths and realities in music education: these include her rejection of the idea that children's music education should not start until age 7, which contrasts with her own view that the earlier it starts the better: she also takes some swipes at what she calls myth of the 'Mozart effect', suggesting that there are several different possible explanations for why it occurs in some of the empirical studies in the literature. She also suggests that music listening alone has very little effect on later development, but rather that children must be involved in active music-making in order to reap the developmental rewards that she adumbrates and advocates.

In conclusion, this book's basis in the research literature is exemplary: the review is deep as well as broad, and I approve the message that it conveys about the importance of early musical experience. I am naturally cautious about some of the generalisations from scientific evidence to practical recommendations, and I would also like to know more about what musical activities are actually involved in the 'Music Miracle'. These cautions aside, I would like to congratulate Liisa Henriksson-Macaulay on extremely impressive achievement in assembling all the evidence that is skilfully brought together in this fascinating book. Time will tell whether or not there is a single 'Music Miracle', and if so, what are the best ways in which it can be developed. She has blazed an important and pioneering trail for others to follow from both a scientific and an educational point of view, and I wish this book every success.

David J Hargreaves, Professor of Education
University of Roehampton, London

Like most Finnish children, I studied at the Finnish Musiikkileikkikoulu since I was a toddler. The playfully taught core music skills gave me a solid base upon which I started classical piano lessons at the age of five (here I am playing from notes while my friend watches). The Moosicology Method, which I started to devise after the birth of my son in 2007, is inspired by this Finnish way of fun but formal music training for babies and young children.

Part One
Introduction

Every parent knows that their children have come to them as gifts. But how many of us know that our children have inherent gifts of their own? Contrary to the old myth of talent being reserved for the special few, advancements in scientific research have made it clear that each and every child carries an astonishing amount of potential. This book is about how you can make your child's potential a reality.

A wealth of new scientific findings show that the key to unlocking your child's potential is one particular all-round brain fitness activity. All children are born with the capacity for this activity, and furthermore, they are born with the motivation for it, so no forcing is needed. Nor does it require hours of grueling, repetitive sessions that bring parents and children to tears. You will find that it is the only activity that is scientifically shown to increase your child's IQ, and in a significant way that leads to a statistically longer and healthier life.

But this is just the start. This brain fitness activity also makes your child more confident, emotionally intelligent and creative. It helps your child have better relationships. It boosts your child's learning skills, language abilities, literacy and mathematical reasoning all at once. It is also the secret behind most children's academic success[1] and all-round improved learning ability through the development of the brain's long-term memory, working memory, executive functioning and the processing of information as well as concentration skills.[2] It builds your child's self-esteem[3] – ability to value themselves – and empathy[4] – the ability to value others, at once.

What may at first seem surprising is that in a fast-paced era obsessed with flash cards, video games and other gadgets, the activity that actually advances a small child's development is no other than the time-honoured tradition of music training. Yet it is only through the recent technological developments in brain research that we have been able to see why this is so. Over the past 15 years, scientists have found that music learning activates practically all areas of the brain.[5] It engages all three ways of learning (the multisensory approach: auditory, visual and kinesthetic), and when started in the most crucial phase of brain development (roughly before the age of eight), it leads to a full brain development boost within your child.[6]

With music instruction alone, you can help your child enhance their development and success in practically all areas of life. In our achievement-obsessed culture, we are used to thinking of music as entertainment and, at best, an optional activity in the sidelines, reserved for the few children who are regarded as "musical". What is not as commonly known is that music learning is the secret behind the success of most doctors[7], Silicon Valley innovators[8] and scientists[9] alike. Einstein himself started playing the violin at the age of six and attributed his genius to his ability to play music.[10]

What the studies show most of all is that the brain of each small child carries an enormous potential just waiting to be realized. Far from having to choose between seemingly separate abilities, it is indeed possible to develop all these abilities simultaneously. Abilities such as academic skills *and* creativity, intelligence *and* social skills, as well as solid self-confidence *and* the appreciation of others were traditionally considered to be almost opposed to one another. Science, on the other hand, shows that the development of all these abilities through the study of music is easily within the reach of your child.

When our son was born in 2007, I soon found that everyone around us from relatives to neighbours had tips to share for the new parents. At first, I regarded it as helpful advice, but I soon noticed that many of these opinions contradicted each other like the concept of a square-shaped circle. My ideas of intuitive parenting went out of the window when my gut feeling could not be trusted to choose among all the various and equally strong views that were pulling me in different directions. I felt confused and worried. I wanted to do the right thing for my son, but I could not tell what the right thing was among all the well-intended yet contradicting advice.

Eventually, I found solace in scientific studies. For I realized that no matter how well a certain kind of upbringing, feeding or sleeping method works for some individuals, it is still not any more likely to work for others unless it has passed the rigorous procedures of science. Hence, this book is entirely based on the work of the incredible scientists of the last decades, especially those of new millennium. The studies that this book is based on adhere to the controlled and peer-reviewed procedures of scientific research and thus their remarkable results apply not just to some, but all children - including yours.

According to the studies, the brain upgrade from music training is available for every child, provided that they start early enough. What is especially surprising - and relieving to us parents - is that it does not require any hot-housing or pushy parenting. Chapter 1 is a general introduction to the topic of this book and why it matters now more than ever. In Chapter 2, we will see how children gain the benefits with less than an hour of music study a week, yet, as it emerges in Chapter 3, this is the real secret of successful children, even when success is defined by the most ambitious parents' standards of top-level achievement.

Chapter 4 is a brief overview of the history of the scientific research behind this all-round brain boost. These days, the scientific community is studying this music miracle at an ever-increasing pace, to the point where new research results crop up on a monthly basis. Some of the most recent highlights include the discovery that early music learning gives babies an advantage in mental age, communication and well-being[11]; that it develops the full-scale creativity of preschoolers[12]; and that it directly boosts their language abilities.[13] As for social skills, a study from the University of Cambridge is the most recent in many to find that it also boosts the empathy of children towards one another, enhancing the essential ability to put oneself in another person's shoes.[14] And for confidence an Australian 2012 study is the most recent one in a long line to show that music training increases the self-esteem of primary school aged children.[15]

The evidence keeps piling up, as now in 2013 the Journal of Neuroscience published the newest evidence that music training before the age of seven boosts the IQ of children.[16] This study was lead by Christopher J. Steele from the Max Planck Institute for Human Cognitive and Brain Sciences and gained nationwide fame when it was reported in the Daily Mail.[17] The original discovery of the IQ-boosting power of music was made by Glenn Schellenberg from University of Toronto nearly a decade ago, in 2004.[18] Slowly but surely, these important discoveries gather more space in the public consciousness. I want to congratulate you, the reader, for picking up this book and thus being a part of this change that is not just a transformation of what we know, but the transformation of the brain capacity of our children and what they can achieve.

Throughout this book, I refer to the all-round boost from early music learning as the Music Miracle. Science does not allow for miracles. And indeed, as you will find in this book, the Music Miracle does not require a supernatural leap of faith but is fully explained by the most recent knowledge on human evolution and brain development. But in my contention, what the studies reveal to us everyday parents is indeed miraculous, as parents are often desperate to make the right choices and find the time to do all the right things.

Chapter 5 looks at how the Music Miracle is explained in the light of brain science and child development, and Chapter 6 explores what the studies report on the critical age for achieving all these benefits. It is widely known that it's never too late to start music training. But all the studies show that to acquire the full brain boost your child needs to start early. To get the IQ-related boosts, your child needs to start at the latest age of seven[19] , and the age of eight tends to be the latest age to influence your child's language skills to the highest degree.[20]

Fortunately, music training at any age improves brain function. Studies have shown that it improves the memory of adolescents[21] and pensioners alike.[22] But what our culture has often got backwards is the idea that children need to be 'old enough' to start musical training. On the contrary, music training only produces the full brain boost when started young.

The Second Part of the book (Chapters 7-9) focuses on the benefits of music learning for babies and toddlers, and answers the question of how musicality and its brain boost can be unleashed even in the smallest of children who are not even old enough to hold or handle an instrument.

And music learning needn't be a chore. All children love music, and their brains are wired to learn it. Far from being a special ability reserved for the fortunate few, musicality is something that resides in all of us, just waiting to be realized. The Third Part of the book explores the many myths of music that hinder adults and their children from participating in this brain boost. The reasons why music causes such brain growth as well as pleasure are explained by evolution and are the focus of Chapter 10. Chapter 11 explores the widespread myth that listening to Mozart produces an intelligence boost.

Even though listening to music is not enough to produce the brain boost, it has benefits that we will explore in Chapter 12. However, it is only music training that will unlock your child's brainpower. In Chapter 13, we will examine the most harmful music-related myth of all, namely, the myth that musical ability is only reserved for a selected few. This belief has no scientific backing; on the contrary, research shows that we are all born musical. Recent neuroscience has established that even newborn babies' brains are programmed to recognize all the core components of music, from beat and rhythms to pitches and whether a sound or musical piece is in tune or out of tune.[23] We will also look at the psychological harm that is caused by the widespread assumption that some people lack musicality - such as the phenomenon entitled 'musical restriction'.

In the Fourth Part of the book (Chapters 14-21), we will look at the incredible IQ-raising power of music training for children that was only first researched in 2004 by Professor Glenn Schellenberg from the University of Toronto. This, like the other recent findings on the benefits of music on the brain, has since attracted a lot of attention from neuroscientists and educators alike. We will also look at the Multiple Intelligences framework formulated by Howard Gardner and see how music training boosts all of your child's multiple intelligences, from mathematics to the bodily-kinesthetic intelligence that predicts better fitness ability and health. The Fifth Part (Chapters 22-25) is dedicated to the vastly expanding research on how early music training unlocks your child's genius for language in all its forms (including the syntax, semantics and foreign languages). In the Sixth Part, 'Don't Believe the Rhyme: Music skills as the route to literacy' (Chapters 26-29) we will see how it is training in music rather than rhymes that helps children acquire reading skills, and why music skills predict reading skills even better than abilities in phonics. We also look at the surprising new research onto the shared neural networks between dyslexia and inadequate musical skills.

The Seventh Part (Chapters 30-35) is dedicated to emotional intelligence, social skills, well-being, empathy and self-esteem. You will find how you can boost your child's all-round abilities in all of these areas with the simple activity of music training. The Eight Part is dedicated to the much-needed new learning abilities for surviving in today's information overload. It also shows how creativity is the most valued asset of successful CEOs and how you can maximize your child's genius creativity – or rather, sustain it until adulthood. This part also explores the most recent studies on the intriguing finding that formal training in music increases creativity in general – not just in terms of artistic creativity, but equally in all other areas, including technological and entrepreneurial innovations. The Ninth Part of the book explores what precise elements of early music training are essential to ensure your child makes the most of their potential in all areas of life.

The very last chapter of this book is dedicated to nothing less than the meaning of true happiness as researched by acclaimed scientists such as Mihaly Csikszentmihalyi, as well as the classic philosophers. We will look at how the Music Miracle promotes all the different ingredients that are crucial for a happy, productive and fulfilled life.

Your child is gifted. Now, let's get unlocking their full potential.

Chapter 1

The Chance

At the moment, only a minority of children get to benefit from the Music Miracle. A 2010 survey commissioned by BBC Worldwide found that the amount of children under 18 in the UK who have played an instrument is half of that of their parents' generation.[1] There is some reassuring irony in that the same technological advancements that made it possible for children to play video games instead of instruments have also brought forward the solid scientific evidence on how music training transforms the brain.

Like most parents, I had never heard about the brain benefits of early music learning, despite having engaged in music training since toddlerhood to the point of eventually becoming a musician. I first saw a passing mention of it in a parenting book I read in late 2007, some weeks after my son was born.[2] This mention concerned a groundbreaking study by the Harvard neuroscientist Gottfried Schlaug and his research group that found that music learning before the age of seven helps connect the left and right sides of the brain.[3] It does so by enhancing the neural connections in the corpus callosum, which is the 'brain bridge', the main connection between our two otherwise separate hemispheres of the cerebral cortex – the so-called left and right brain.[4] For reasons that will be explained later on in this chapter, I was so struck by this piece of information that I started to look for more.

At first, the information was hard to find. No other parenting book would even mention the importance of music. But when I started researching scientific journals - the ones that publish leading, cutting-edge reports on new findings of science - I came across a wealth of incredible research results. I found that since Schlaug had first made his discovery in 1995, other scientists had discovered that learning music at an early age boosts the language and reading abilities of children, their mathematical understanding, memory, emotion recognition skills, self-confidence and school success, just to mention a fraction of the benefits.[5] The first controlled study that assessed whether music learning resulted in a full-scale IQ increase had been made by E. Glenn Schellenberg in 2004, and the results had identified early music training as the best IQ-boosting intervention ever (we will discuss this in Chapters 4 and 14).[6]

Thus, the academics knew all about the Music Miracle. Yet none of this research was brought into the attention of parents. Aside from the mention of Schlaug's study in the book I came across by pure chance, I could not find other parenting books that addressed the importance of music learning. On the contrary, when looking for more information, I was surprised that none of the books for parents that focused on early years' development mentioned music at all. Or if they did, it was in the context of the myth that listening to Mozart makes a baby smarter (more on this false, yet persistent myth in Chapter 11).[7]

The more I dove into the research, the more I realized that we were completely off base when it came to children and music. I would talk to parents who assumed that children have to be old enough to learn music, whilst other parents thought that their child was born unmusical, a belief completely disputed by scientists (see Chapter 13). I would talk to professional music teachers who taught preschoolers and during their impressive careers had never heard that they were actually building up not just their little pupils' musicality but their whole brain capacity.

In fact, these teachers that I met seemed, at best, mildly amused by my enthusiasm concerning its brain benefits. Music educators, quite rightly, are passionate about music and consider it crucial for its own sake. But the flipside to the passion that us music makers feel is that we forget that our appreciation of music for music's sake is not shared by most people. There are a multitude of hobbies parents can choose to encourage their child, from swimming and ballet to art, crafts and drama, yet every family only has a limited amount of money and time. Whilst all children love music, only a fraction of them get the chance to learn music at the age where it matters the most. Thus, I ended up writing this book for the parent who wants to support their child's full development, yet lacks the information on how easy it is with just one activity: the early learning of music.

One of America's leading music educators, Edwin E. Gordon, the developer of the foremost musical ability test for children used worldwide, calls the lack of early musical guidance that is so prevalent in today's world the 'music abuse' of children.[8] He argues that the value of music is inherent and does not need external validation from its general brain benefits.[9] He states that every child should be allowed to develop their musicality for its own sake.[10] Whilst most people who have received the gift of early music learning can sympathize with Gordon's indignation concerning the loss of musical potential, one could equally argue that we all suffer from 'golf abuse' because we were never allowed to develop our full golf potential in the same way as Tiger Woods, whose father started his training at the age of eight months.

Music is important for its own sake, but so is golf, along with ballet, football, chess and every other domain of the human culture. Specifically in today's world, there is an ever-increasing amount of different skills that one can choose to master, yet there is only a limited amount hours in the day and resources in a family to invest in the hobbies of its children. Therefore, I believe it is important for parents to know the scientific facts that transcend the matters of opinion. Early music learning is not just for future musicians. It has crucial, life-transforming benefits for each and every child. Compared to any other activity, music training is a full-brain workout the benefits of which extend to all areas of human life and give your child a chance to unleash their multiple academic, social and emotional gifts.

What is widely known is that to become a top-level classical performer, a child needs to start young, just like with other domains that require technical precision, such as ballet or athletic sports. But from this, our culture has made the erroneous assumption that early music learning is essential only for those children who aspire to be classical top-level performers. Hence, most children miss out on the most effective brain boost available, one that they could achieve with less than an hour of music training per week.[11]

Yet, when looking into having instrument lessons for my son (before I started the Finnish Musiikkileikkikoulu-style Moosicology classes which he now attends), I would often come across music teachers' websites that said that children could not start learning music before the age of seven. As the studies in this book will show you (see Chapter 6 on why an early start makes a difference) the truth is exactly the opposite. The sooner a child starts learning music, the greater the benefits they gain.

The first cut-off point is likely to be the age of seven: no studies have shown that any amount of music learning after the age of seven will produce the IQ enhancement.[12] This observation corresponds with studies that have found that after age seven, a person's IQ is generally set for life, with rare exceptions.[13] Similarly, increases in spatial-temporal intelligence have only been shown for children who take up music at the latest at seven, and no later.[14] It has also been found that increases in the corpus callosum size, which is crucial for abilities relating to learning capacity and general creativity, only happen when a child takes up music at age seven or before,[15] and the same finding has been reported for many other regions of the brain, as we will see in Boxes 1 and 2 on pages X and Y.

All parents who want their child to learn music would be better off starting as soon as possible, when the child can still gain an all-round boost in their abilities. This is what gives the child unlimited options in later life to use their potential for whatever they wish. From engineering inventions and scientific discoveries via entrepreneurial creativity and academic success to emotional wellbeing and the ability for better relationships, the world is the playground of the brains that engage in music training. Parents who have not considered the importance of music would be better off in looking at the incredible effects it is shown to have in every area of human achievement, when started early enough.

My Chance: The Finnish school system and how to survive it

A few hundred years ago, it would have been inconceivable to think that every child should – or even could – learn the basic levels of literacy and mathematics. Now those skills are regarded as essential and their instruction to all young citizens is regarded as a benchmark for a civilized society.

In contrast, most children who have an early introduction to music do so by chance. Maybe their parents are musicians, or wanted to learn music themselves but never had the possibility, or just happened to decide that their child could benefit from music instruction. To this day, most children do not get the sufficient opportunity to bring out their inner musicality and the all-round brain boost that it nurtures, presumably because people still think that early music learning is mainly for the future professional musicians. However, music learning turns out to be the key to success in any type of learning – crucially, even those all-important areas of literacy and mathematical reasoning.[1]

When my parents were born in the aftermath of the Second World War, Finland was still a developing country. My mum always wanted to learn to play the piano, but her parents had barely enough money for food and housing, let alone an instrument. But changes were in the air: my parents' generation was the first one in Finland to benefit from free education, and it grabbed this opportunity with both hands. By the time I was born, Finland had risen to the level of affluence of a first-world country, largely due to the changes in the educational system.

For several decades now, since the development of Organization for Economic Development and Co-operation's (OECD) international student assessment named PISA, Finland has baffled education experts worldwide. Students in the Finnish state school system have consistently had top scores in literacy, mathematics and scientific skills on the PISA exam. The OECD reports: 'Since the publication of the first PISA results in 2001, Finland is now seen as a major international leader in education ... for these reasons, Finnish schools have become a kind of tourist destination, with hundreds of educators and policy makers annually travelling to Helsinki to try to learn the secret of their success.'[2]

Sure enough, my Mum wanted to give me the chance she never got, and I started my piano lessons at the age of five. However, I was well on my musical journey by that time since my toddler years, due to the development of the Finnish custom of Musiikkileikkikoulu – the music playschool – that ensured that practically all Finnish children learned musical concepts and core music skills as babies and toddlers. I started at the Musiikkileikkikoulu after I turned two. Most Finnish children have some experience of the Musiikkileikkikoulu which, despite its name, is not centred around play but a child-centred pedagogy that teaches music concepts and skills in an age-appropriate, educational way. As the studies reported in this book have discovered, these are exactly the skills that promote the literacy, mathematical and scientific thinking of any small child.

Musiikkileikkikoulu is not, contrary to its name, an all-day playgroup but instead it consists of just one regular group music training lesson a week, each lasting between 45 and 60 minutes. Coincidentally, studies show that this little time is all that is needed to produce the full Music Miracle. Practically every musical institution, organization or conservatory in Finland has an active Musiikkileikkikoulu teaching the little ones, and many non-musical organizations have also acquired a music playschool of their own by hiring highly trained music educators.[3] Learning music is considered the birthright of every child.

With regards to the research that you will read about in this book, it could be suggested that the Finnish custom of early music training may just be the real secret of Finnish students' school success. After all, Finnish pupils only start school at the age of seven, when the watershed age for the kind of crucial brain development that boosts the underlying abilities for mathematics, literacy and science – the skills that the PISA tests measure - has almost come to an end. Either there's something in the Finnish breast milk or it's the custom of Musiikkileikkikoulu.

Aside from Musiikkileikkikoulu, if there was a country I would need to ascribe my school success to, it would be Italy - although not the traditional mainstream Italian schooling system but the world-famous Montessori Method of child-centred education. Maria Montessori was born in Italy in 1870 and she was the first female in Italy to qualify as a physician. She developed an educational method for children from three to seven that centred around the revolutionary idea that a child is born curious, wants to engage learning, and is able to learn all the important skills through self-initiated playing with age-appropriate materials. Montessori developed a wealth of educational materials that the children were to use according to their own wishes, and she theorized that this was the key for autonomous learning instead of the standard school system in which the curriculum is initiated and executed by the teacher.

The Montessori method was shown to be a success. The Montessori children developed skills in reading, mathematics and thinking long before their peers, and these results still hold true today. Montessori students are shown to do better in maths and reading than children from the standard school system.[4] Their brains also have a highly developed executive functioning, which results in better study skills, social ability and creativity even when they have graduated from Montessori.[5] What's more, the children from those Montessori schools that include a music programme are shown to outdo even the other Montessori students in areas such as study skills and mathematics.[6]

By chance, the apartment where my parents lived and where I spent my earliest childhood years was situated right opposite one of the first Montessori schools in Helsinki – a music-enhanced school where the children had a small amount of individual instruction in music theory on a weekly basis. When I turned three, my mum enrolled me. Before I turned four, I had learned to read, like several other pupils my age, and I pursued writing with passion. I started writing stories at the age of five and by the time I entered the Finnish school system at the age of seven, I had written several 100-page novels (because the journals my mum bought for me had exactly 100 pages in them, and I kept developing the stories until the pages were finished).

Writing stories was just something that I did naturally; it was only 15 years later in a university class on primary teaching that I learned that every seven-year old child who can confidently write a two-page long story from their imagination is 'gifted'. When researching this book, it has become all the more apparent to me that giftedness is something inherent to each and every child, but it requires the right environment for the giftedness to shine through and develop into an unstoppable force. It is more than likely that if I had not started music learning and gone to a music-enhanced Montessori school, I would not have learned to read and write with ease – at least not at such a young age.

My parents never thought that my abilities were the result of Montessori methods or music; they just regarded it as a curiosity. All they knew was that they had not taught that to me at all. As a child, I didn't ponder such questions. I was just writing with the same passion and ease as I played with my toys or the garden swing. But when my son, who did not attend a Montessori school, turned four, I was surprised that he had not automatically learned to read. Then I realized that giftedness tends to appear and flourish where it is intentionally nurtured.

I am not saying that all children are gifted in the same way, nor that they should be. I am not saying that all children need to learn to read at the age of three. Finnish is a phonetically regular language, which makes it easier to learn to read than other languages. If I had been born in an English-speaking country, I may have learned to read at around the age of five, or possibly four, but probably not three. The exceptional fact of the Finnish language is even mentioned in the National British Curriculum when emphasizing the importance of phonics for reading.

Coincidentally, phonetic ability is more related to music skills than phonetic skills themselves,[7] which would make the early acquisition of music skills even more crucial for non-Finnish, non-phonetic languages such as English. We will talk more about language and reading in the part 5 of this book. For now, suffice to say that a child's learning skills are radically enhanced with optimal learning tools.

More often than not, the discovery of these beneficial tools happens by chance. Shortly after my son was four, a distant relative gave us Jenga bricks as a Christmas present. These plain wooden bricks are all the same size and shape and are meant to be used for a particular game. But before we knew it, our son had adopted the Jenga bricks for his building purposes.

By the time December had turned into January, our son spent hours at a time building from them, always coming up with something new. I was gobsmacked seeing his concentration and the architectural innovations that bore a strong resemblance to the architectural styles of Ancient Greece and Rome. Without instruction or intervention, he came up with the idea of building from Jenga bricks, as well as what to build and when. It struck me as a model example of spatial-temporal intelligence, the kind of intelligence that architects and engineers demonstrate to a high degree. If we had never gotten the Jenga bricks by chance, our son's spatial-temporal ability would have remained hidden, and quite possibly vastly underdeveloped.

Coincidentally, spatial-temporal intelligence has been one of the first scientifically studied benefits of early music training. Research since the late 1990s into the benefits of music has shown that early music instruction increases the spatial-temporal intelligence of children, whereas other activities, such as drawing or computer training in spatial skills, do not.[8] Early music training is at least one thing I have been able to provide for my son, and it is reasonable to assume that it has brought out his spatial-temporal intelligence to the point where he felt compelled to grab the building bricks.

It was by chance that I had such an advantageous early childhood. And it was equally by chance that it all took a turn for the worse in a matter of weeks after I turned nine. I started at one of the schools that my parents considered to be the best in the area; one of the handful of state schools in Finland that chose its pupils based on an entry exam instead of household location. To make a long and winding story short, a few of the pupils got beaten up in class on a daily basis by some of the most domineering pupils, and our class teacher, for whatever reason, never did anything about this. I soon ended up being one of the victims. I did not tell my parents about this, as they had made it clear that I had to be a good student and do what the teacher said. It is hard to understand from an adult's perspective, but when something like this happens to children, they really do not have much to compare it to, and therefore they make the logical assumption that it is normal.

I felt ashamed and afraid, and assumed that it was all my fault. It felt arrogant to assume otherwise, as I was made aware that I was the worst of the worst. Soon even the nice pupils in class knew not to associate with me (other than in an unfriendly way) in order to avoid being treated with the same fate. I did not know about 'student rights'. I assumed that because all was fine according to the authority (teacher), I deserved to be treated like this.

By the time I was thirteen, it had become obvious to my parents that something was wrong with me. They nagged at me for being lazy at school and only making minimum effort; when my grades dropped from A+ and A to the forbidden combination of As and – shock horror – some Bs, they were enraged. They kept pushing, saying I could do better, and of course, I knew I could. I barely spent any time studying as it was. At school I was mainly trying to not exist, and at home I tried my best not to think about school and focused on writing songs instead of homework.

I did not understand the purpose of school. I simply kept showing up, because to not do so would have resulted in an aggressive conflict with my parents. (I tried it once, so I knew.) Despite being depressed to the point of considering suicide, I remained a school success, gaining acceptance to Finland's most competitive sixth form (which corresponds to the grammar schools of England) and graduating with a string of As. I applied to university because of further parental pressure and got accepted as one of the 5% of applicants into the government-sponsored University of Helsinki degree in Philosophy.

On my first week at university, a group of friendly, older student mentors gave us a two-hour talk that emphasized the emotional support available for students. When they started telling that there was a zero-tolerance policy on harassment, that the university had its own department to deal with any bullying or insults, and that we should report if anyone ever harassed us in any way, I started to feel sick. I went to my student flat and spent the next week crying to the point of vomiting, not showing up for lectures. My world was turned upside down. For the first time I had learned that what happened to me at school was not my fault, and that it should not have been allowed. I was eventually diagnosed with depression.

I started my treatment with the assumption that once my depression was cured, I would be able to finish my degree. But instead, I gained the confidence to drop out and pursue my dreams. Since I was eleven, I had been obsessively writing songs, yet I had mostly kept it a secret from my parents and peers, only occasionally daring to play pieces to a few close friends, even eventually to my sixth form music teacher who exclaimed that I was a young genius. But it was only with my therapist whilst at university that I gained the understanding that I did not have to keep building my life around trying to please other people whilst sacrificing my calling. A few years down the line, I decided to not complete my degree, and went on to pursue where my music, wherever would take me.

I was told that it would not take me anywhere. Instead, I ended up getting the support of the Finnish rock legends of 22-Pistepirkko, who recorded, produced and promoted my music for a few good years. During that time I also met my English partner Travis while he was living in Helsinki, started a family and moved to England. I tried working with various producers in England before plucking up the courage to contact my all-time favourite singer-songwriter Ken Stringfellow, an American producer living in Paris, who is widely known for working with bands such as REM and Big Star as well as founding The Posies. It was my wildest dream when he said he loved my songs and wanted to work with me, and since 2010 we have been recording what is to be my first solo album – the one I had dreamt of making since I was eleven.

During this time, I have been bringing up my son and formulating

Moosicology, a new research-based music education method for children. As I found that the artistic and intuitive way of life had its downfalls when it came to getting clear answers for burning parenting questions, I started to appreciate the world of science more than I ever did at university. What started as a personal passion – reading up on the studies on the benefits of music – soon became a compulsion to get this information out from the academic ivory towers into the world of real families so that all the knowledge could be put to good use. This book was born out of the ethos of making this wealth of life-changing information more accessible outside the academic community, so that parents – and most importantly, their children – can benefit from it.

Amongst the research on the benefits of music, the researchers are often quick to emphasize that music is valuable in its own right and should not be regarded as a panacea, a cure-all. I am the first one to agree. But I am also the first to say that school success is less of a cure-all than music learning. I can say with confidence that as opposed to the top grades I gained at exams and reports, it is music learning that has given me great advantages in life – advantages without which I might not be here today: it has allowed me to become emotionally stable again and to use my brain to engage in meaningful work, not to mention start a family and look after my son.

For the parents who want to enhance their children's school success, music learning provides the best proven way, but my wish is that no parent becomes so obsessed with their child's external success that they disregard what else could be going on in their lives. I believe children are capable of much more than they are normally given credit for, or indeed, even the chances to demonstrate, and studies confirm this. I have also learned the hard way that parents can easily be misinformed on what their child really needs to flourish, as in my case. My formal academic success could never compensate for the damage of the abuse I was receiving in the same environment.

As parents, we must constantly remain aware of what is really happening in the lives of our children and seek real knowledge instead of holding onto anything as a cure-all, be it school success, external validation or indeed, music learning. I believe our job as parents is to do the best we can for our children, but we must be careful in how we define what the 'best' is. Here scientific studies can point the way.

In life, it would be unrealistic to expect any one thing to be a cure-all to all the problems of human life. But it would be equally silly to not try and do the best we can to help our children flourish. Parenting requires practical answers, and early music learning gives our children the best opportunities of all: better general intelligence, school success, mental and emotional wellbeing, empathy and creativity as well as an enhanced learning capacity and better memory. These are gifts that every child is shown to gain from music, and these skills are truly transferable. They are useful for everything our children ever decide to do in the course of their lives, even when life throws obstacles in their way.

Unfortunately, the wealth of the scientific research has not yet reached families. I still find it hard to believe that I had engaged in music since my first years of life, yet I had never heard about these benefits until I, by chance, saw them being referred to in a context that was rather poignant to me personally. The parenting book I came across as a new mother and that lead me to these studies was What Every Parent Needs to Know by Dr Margot Sunderland, and it recommended music practice as a remedy for, out of all things, the brain damage that results from being bullied.[9] My first shock was the finding that bullying causes damage to not only something as invisible and often undervalued as human feelings, but to the physical brain itself! (Nobody told me this, either.) More specifically, 'an underdeveloped corpus callosum inhibits communication between one hemisphere and the other. As a result children could end up "residing" in one hemisphere rather than moving rapidly and easily from one to the other', as Sunderland quotes the Harvard-affiliated neurologist Martin Teicher.[10]

I had my second shock straight after when Sunderland mentioned the research pioneered by Gottfried Schlaug: that the best way to re-build the connections between the two sides of the brain was early training in music.[11] It dawned onto me that music training might just have saved me in more ways than I ever could have imagined.

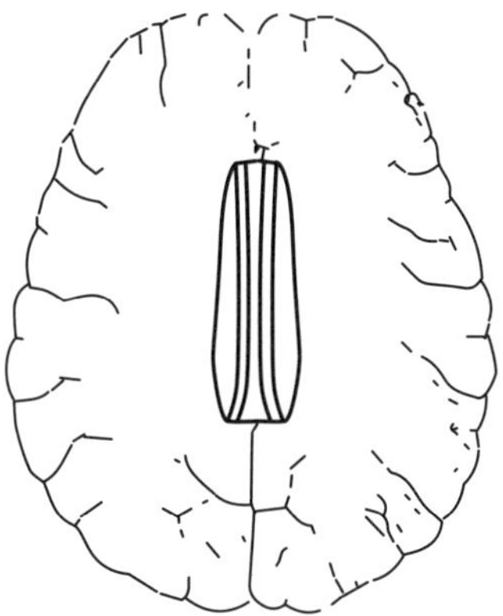

Box 1: The music boost for the corpus callosum

The corpus callosum is the brain's largest nerve tract. The outer layer of the human brain, neocortex, is divided into two separate hemispheres (the so-called 'left' and 'right' brains) and the corpus callosum is responsible for relaying information from one side to another, connecting the two distinct halves.

Better hemispheric interaction via the corpus callosum results in various advantages such as higher intelligence[1] and higher creativity[2]. Music training that is started in early childhood (at the latest at the age of six or seven) is found to increase the size of the corpus callosum[3] as well as hemispheric interaction[4], which likely plays a part in why early music training also boosts both intelligence[5] and creativity[6].

An underdeveloped corpus callosum is not just a small problem. It is, even without psychiatric disorders, linked to significantly decreased learning ability, attention-deficit disorders and lack of normal development in communication.[12] Alongside bullying and other forms of child abuse[13] (including verbal abuse alone[14]– so much for the old adage 'sticks and stones may break my bones but words can never hurt me'), the corpus callosum may be damaged by other factors, such as environmental toxins. But what the studies show is that whether or not your child develops under the lucky stars, their giftedness can be brought to life with music training. Even when a child has a normally-developed corpus callosum, it has the capacity to grow significantly – but only through music training.

I would not even want to imagine where I could be if it wasn't for the rebuilding of the corpus callosum that making music gave me. Especially during my teenage years, I contemplated suicide every day, and it was only since I fully pursued my musical path that I was able to recover, be productive and most importantly, have the loving relationships I had always dreamt of, with my partner and my son, who have been my dreams come true. I could not have written this book without the hope and will to live that they have given me. And without the power of music, I would not have been in a position to have stable relationships at all. Furthermore, I am grateful that I never lost my academic skills to the depths of depression. Now that I have recovered, those skills have been invaluable to my pursuit of meaningful work to help others – the research behind the Moosicology method being one example – and this book being another.

When I talk about success, I am not making the assumption that every child must gain the top grades, nor that they must compete with one another. Look no further than my own story to see how empty academic success can be. But if we want to understand what enhances children's brain development, we must look to scientific studies that compare the performance of children with and without early music education - properly controlled studies that take into account other possible factors such as the level of ability the children start from and their families' socioeconomic status.

These studies have unequivocally shown that children given one hour of musical instruction a week – even over a short span such as four months or a longer span of a year or two – have intellectual advantages over children who do not have music education. Before these studies, 20th century experts in child development assumed that the success of music students was just a by-product of coming from a family with academic and financial advantages (as they were more likely to afford music training), but 21st century research shows otherwise.

It is well known that children from affluent families have multiple academic advantages compared with children from poorer backgrounds.[15] But hundreds of controlled studies during the past decade have shown that the Music Miracle is available for every child. Perhaps the most illuminating example of this is that children who come from financially disadvantaged homes but engage in music training end up surpassing, with regards to school grades and academic success, those children from wealthy families who do not engage in music training.[16] The fact that the Music Miracle beats the multiple effects of poverty on school success is nothing short of a miracle in itself.

Ultimately, what everyone wants is a good, happy and healthy life. My experience shows that we should not leave the development of our children to chance, and scientific studies show us how we do not need to leave it to chance. We simply need to notice what is proven to work, and do it.

Chapter 2

The Music Miracle: why it matters now more than ever

Every parent knows the story: our children are born into a world that is changing faster than ever. Leading education experts state that the school system is not enough to prepare the new generation for the challenges ahead.[1] New, previously unimaginable professions emerge as traditional jobs are being automated. The economic system, as well as the environmental, are under severe changes and no one quite knows where it will all lead by the time our children are grown.

In short, nobody can foresee what particular skills will be useful in fifteen or twenty years' time. A few generations ago, learning the basics of literacy and mathematics guaranteed you a job, and excelling in the narrow domain of these core subjects paved the way for a well-paid career for life. Now unemployment among university graduates is blossoming, to the disillusionment of many.

Parents have responded to the world's increased competition by becoming more competitive themselves and have created a whole new phenomenon known by alternative names such as Pushy Parenting, hot-housing, helicopter parenting and Tiger Motherhood. This new breed of parents plays Mozart to their child before birth, teaches them reading from flashcards as a toddler and at school age, ushers them from a class in Mandarin Chinese to an extra-curricular advanced science and mathematics class to an evening occupied by homework. Pushy Parents try and ensure their children, even as babies and toddlers, are ahead of the developmental milestones of their peers who represent the dreaded 'average'. At school age, excelling in competitive extra-curricular activities is as much of a demand as the unquestionable position at the top of the class.

This is different from the dilemma of many modern parents – the recognition that there are endless fun activities that your child could engage in, yet there's only a limited amount of time. Pushy Parenting flourishes in a culture that focuses on competition, fear of failure and the comparison of children against one another. The most telling example is Amy Chua's best-selling book and media sensation *The Battle Hymn of the Tiger Mother*, where she gives a ruthless account of coaching her two daughters to always get the best grades, to gain awards and to practice their classical instruments rigorously from a young age. In her own words, she set the target of bringing her children up as winners, not losers.[2]

Only a small minority of children, such as Chua's, start learning music before the age of eight. Yet the recent decades of scientific research have shown that early music learning is the key to success in most areas of human achievement. Practicing music has shown to be the secret behind most high-flying entrepreneurs and engineers,[3] doctors[4] and scientists[5] alike. The prototypical genius Einstein took up violin at the age of six and attributed most of his discoveries to playing his instrument.[6]

But what struck me when I was first acquainted with the studies was how simple it was for any child to gain these brain benefits. It turned out it does not require the stress and sacrifices of Amy Chua's Tiger Mothering. As long as children start music training before the watershed age of eight, they only needed to engage in music study as little as 40 to 60 minutes a *week*, less than the time it takes to give them a bath.

Yet this modest amount of music learning is enough for their brains to soak in the full benefits. The hundreds of studies that form the scientific essence of this book have shown that it takes less than an hour of music learning a week to restructure the brain for a significant IQ increase, better language skills, reading success, school success, mathematical understanding, creativity and the all-important measures of social success: self-confidence, better relationships and empathy.

Some intriguing results were first established in Germany in 2003. Scientists studied the mental abilities of three types of young children: The first studied music rigorously on a daily basis to gain professional classical playing ability, the second didn't study music at all and the third studied music as a hobby, averaging on little less than an hour a week. The scientists found that both groups of early music learners had a highly significant advantage in mental age and thinking speed as opposed to the children who did not learn music.[7] What they were surprised to find that hot-housing in music practice did not increase these benefits in children. The laid-back little music learners gained *exactly the same brain boost* as the children who practiced intensely for several hours a day.[8]

The secret to the gains is that music training, unlike any other activity, engages practically all areas of the brain.[9] It builds up large areas on both sides of the brain – the 'logical' left side and the 'holistic' right side, as well as building up the brain bridge between them (see Box 1).[10] Furthermore, music activates the emotional regions of the brain,[11] which could well explain the emotional skills that are amongst the benefits of music training. During the 21st century, the leading neuroscientists have labelled musically trained brains the 'perfect model' for studying how the human brain can be positively restructured through learning, especially when the training is started early on.[12]

In brain imaging studies, it has been found that children and adults who have started music training at a young age have significantly larger neural networks than non-musicians in practically all areas of the neocortex. The neocortex can be said to be the most 'human' part of the brain, in that specializes in activities such as thinking, planning, attention, emotional intelligence, language and mathematics as well as the processing of auditory, visual and kinesthetic information. All these areas are enhanced by early music training (see Box 2). In addition, early music training boosts brain regions such as the hippocampus (which deals with memory and spatial orientation) and builds better neural connections even down to the brainstem (where the brain connects with the spine) and the corticospinal tract (through which the brain gives orders down to the spinal cord and the rest of the body). (See Box 3.)

These enhanced neural connections result in an overall better functioning brain, which leads to higher general intelligence, faster and more accurate processing of information,[13] better long-term memory[14] as well as a better short-term memory,[15] better working memory capacity[16] and better thinking ability.[17] Additionally, music training boosts connections below the cortex such as the hippocampus which specializes in memory (see Box 3). Better connections in all of these areas are shown to boost general intelligence,[18] which likely explains why music training increases the IQ - and is the only activity to do so.

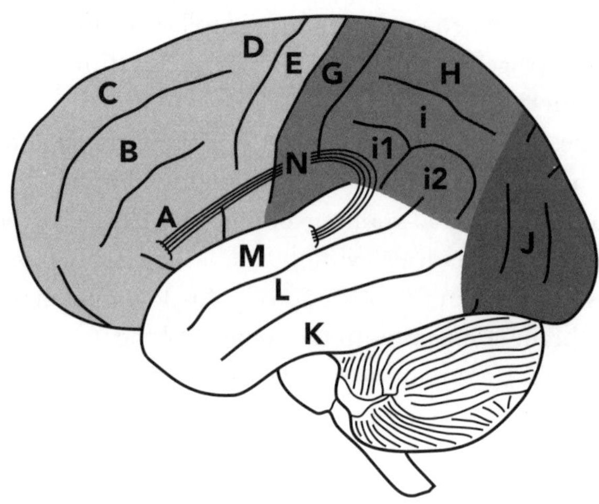

Box 2 - Regions in the neocortex where neural networks are enhanced by music training

a. Inferior frontal gyrus – involved in a wide range of crucial 'human' tasks such as language production and understanding, social communication, self-regulation (a key component of emotional intelligence), empathy, attention and deliberate planning of action. This area is boosted by music training that is started before or at the age of seven.[1]

b. Medial frontal gyrus – associated with executive function (more on this in Chapter 37), episodic memory (memory of one's own life events) and decision making. This area is enhanced by early music training.[2] This may explain why musically trained children have better executive function (as we will see in Chapter 37). Furthermore, neural connections in this area decrease when a person ages, which leads to age-related memory loss – with the incredible exception of musicians and music hobbyists. Music training that is started at an early age (before seven or eight) protects from this phenomenon, as it is found that those who played music in childhood display memory and neural networks equivalent to those of the non-elderly.[3]

c. Superior frontal gyrus – involved in a myriad of tasks such as self-awareness, self-regulatory function (such as reducing cravings), working memory, spatial cognition and directing complex movements. This area is enhanced by music training in children[4] and even in adulthood.[5]
d. Premotor cortex – deals with action-related cognition, such as observing and recognizing actions performed by other people via the mirror neuron system (more on mirror neurons in the intro to the Part Seven.). In a proper 'weird science' way this area also deals with recognizing tools and using action-related language such as verbs. It is enhanced by music training.[6] Furthermore, it activates in all humans when they hear music with a beat, but musically trained people exhibit more activation in this area and its connections with other areas of the brain.[7]
e. Precentral gyrus – includes the primary motor cortex which (together with the central sulcus) directs voluntary movement. This area is enhanced in children who start music training at the age of seven or earlier.[8]
f. Central sulcus – includes the primary motor cortex (together with the precentral gyrus) which directs voluntary movement. Music training is found to balance the left and right sides of the central sulcus, whereas in people without musical training it is imbalanced towards the left side.[9] This music boost of the right side appears also in other parts of the brain and may explain why music training is found to boost creativity (see Chapter 39).
g. Postcentral gyrus – the primary somatosensory area which deals with information related to touch and bodily sensations.

Music training in childhood enhances the function of this area and its within-brain links with the auditory areas.[10]

h. Superior parietal lobule – deals with multisensory information (such as touch and vision) as well as spatial orientation and working memory. This area is enhanced by music training even in adults[11] and may explain why musically trained children have better spatial-visual skills than their non-musically trained peers.[12]
i. The inferior parietal lobule consists of two regions:
   1. Supramarginal gyrus – associated with perceiving and processing language in a multitude of ways such as spelling, word recognition and phonological awareness (more on phonological awareness, a critical component of learning to read, in Chapters 26-29). This area is enhanced by musical training.[13]
   2. Angular gyrus – associated with a variety of tasks demanding higher intellect, such as reasoning and problem-solving, understanding language and abstract numerical concepts, spatial skills, memory, attention and recognizing emotion. It is also a "cross-modal hub" that processes multisensory information – visual, auditory and kinesthetic.[14] As music training is a multisensory activity like no other, this area of the brain is, as one can expect by now, found to be enhanced by music training.[15] It is also one of the essential regions f the brain that deal with reading musical notation.[16] Additionally, the inferior parietal lobule is found to be enhanced by mathematical training, as academic mathematicians have bigger volume in these areas as a function of how long they have been dealing with higher mathematics.[17] The fact that music training enhances these very same areas could explain why musically trained children have better mathematical skills than their non-musically trained peers.[18]

j. Occipital gyri – area dedicated to processing a wide range of visual information, including reading and (visual) working memory. This area is enhanced in musically trained individuals, presumably due to music reading activity.[19] It is also found that musically trained people are able to engage this visual area in other tasks such as memorizing words[20] – a finding which may explain the established finding where music training gives a brain boost for memory.[21]
k. Inferior temporal gyrus – processes visual information related to complex objects, facial expression and recognizing numbers. This area is enhanced by music training,[22] the suspected reason being that playing music from notation is a complex visual activity that exercises this area and thus forms better neural connections in it.[23]
l. Middle temporal gyrus – deals with a myriad of tasks such as semantic memory (which is memory of one's knowledge of the world), recognizing faces and understanding language and people's actions. It is also a key area for understanding music.[24] When experiment participants are played music, the brains of the participants with musical training activate more,[25] but it remains to be studies whether this also implies a brain boost for musically trained people outside the context of music.
m. Superior temporal gyrus – contains the primary auditory cortex that processes information related to sound, and deals with tasks requiring auditory working memory. This area also processes language (it contains Wernicke's area which deals with the meaning of language) and social information, such as recognizing emotion in facial expressions. This area is significantly enhanced by early music training,[26] which could explain why musically trained children have better working memory[27], language skills[28], recognition of emotion

in faces and speech[29], as well as enhanced social skills and empathy.[30]

n. Arcuate fasciculus – this pathway connects the two areas of language processing, Wernicke's and Broca's areas which deal with semantics (the meaning of language) and syntax (the structure of language, including grammar) respectively. It is enhanced by music training[31] and is likely to play a part in explaining the music boost for language skills.[3]

Box 3 - Other notable areas of the brain that are enhanced by music training

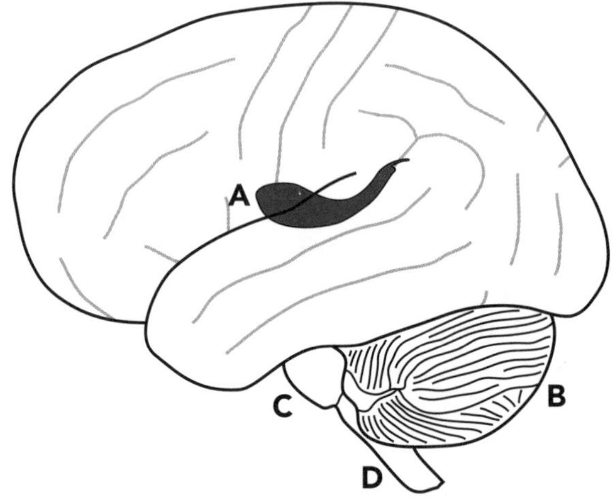

a. The hippocampus specializes in memory and spatial orientation. It is enhanced by music training,[1] which likely explains the music boost for both memory and spatial-visual skills.[2]

b. The cerebellum was traditionally thought to only guide movement, but has more recently been found to also play a crucial part in a variety of higher functions such as attention, working memory, executive function, language, learning and emotion.[3] It also is involved in perception of both rhythm and melody.[4] It is significantly enhanced by music training.[5]

c. The brainstem sits right on top of the spinal cord and is the gatekeeper between information coming to the brain from outside the brain, and vice versa, and it regulates the central nervous system. Musically trained people (again only those starting at age seven or before) have been found to process sound better already at the level of brainstem,[6] which may explain many of the auditory advantages of early music training, from reading (phonemic skills) to emotional intelligence (recognizing emotion in speech better).
d. The corticospinal tract relays information from the brain to the spinal cord, directing action and movement. Music training enhances the myelination in this area, which increases the speed at which the information travels, and it is enhanced more the sooner the child has started music training,[7] and might explain why music training leads to faster reaction times[8] which, in turn, is linked to faster information processing and higher IQ,[9] both of which are also the fortuitous results of early music training.[10] It has been found that children who started music training at the age of eight or later have not received the boost in this area.[11]

Early music learning also benefits your child for the decades to come, protecting them from age-related cognitive deterioration such as memory loss and the slowing-down of thinking abilities. Musically trained people are found to *not* experience the cognitive decline that other aging humans do. This is why both the American Psychological Association[19] and leading neurologists such as Harvard's

Gottfried Schlaug[20] have recommended music training as a tool for preserving the brain's abilities in old age.

In a 2011 study published by the American Psychological Association, neuroscientists Brenda Hanna-Pladdy and Alicia McKay from the Emory University School of Medicine compared the cognitive abilities of three types of elderly people (aged 60 to 83) and found that those who had played an instrument in early childhood had significant advantages in brain function compared to the elderly who had not played an instrument.[21] Hanna-Pladdy states: 'Based on previous research and our study results, we believe that both the years of musical participation and the age of acquisition are critical. There are crucial periods in brain plasticity that enhance learning, which may make it easier to learn a musical instrument before a certain age and thus may have a larger impact on brain development.'[22]

Hanna-Pladdy continued to research the topic further, comparing music training to other general lifestyle activities. A 2012 study reported on the findings: these brain benefits were specific to music training and not to other activities.[23] She concluded, 'To obtain optimal results, individuals should start musical training before age nine, play at least 10 years or more and if possible, keep playing for as long as possible over the age of 60'.[24]

Thus we can see that the study of music trains the brain like nothing else, and the gains last for life. In contrast, when Pushy Parents are attracted to music training, it is usually because of the highbrow status of classical music and the competitiveness of the domain. They're oblivious to its brain benefits and how little effort they could expend to achieve them. Amy Chua writes that she wanted her children to take up classical instrument instruction because it was a domain in which she could, with her willpower, train them to surpass other children and thus excel in yet another discipline beside school. And she did. Her daughters gained several classical music awards and gained a proficiency in the piano and violin. This required her supervising her daughters' instrument practice several hours a day, shuttling them from one music class to another, and writing them detailed schedules and practice notes on how to practice minute by minute.[25]

Many parents think, like Chua, that if a child wants to take up music learning properly, they need to start young. And they are right. Just like the top athletes need to start young to compete in the Olympics, so do classical musicians if their dream (or that of their parents) is to play in the New York Metropolitan Orchestra. The domain of professional classical playing is indeed highly competitive and demands rigorous practice to gain the required technical proficiency.

But because of this, many parents make the assumption that early music learning is only for those children whose parents are serious about them becoming the next Mozart (or, rather, the next Mozart soloist). Contrast this with sports. We all know that exercise is crucial for our children and that we need to let them run around and play outdoors. We don't make the assumption that we either have to force our child to become the next David Beckham or just give up and tell them to sit down all day. We take our children to parks, to our garden patches and to indoor play areas where they can run around and climb. Alongside this, our children get a good amount of exercise on an average day simply by accompanying us when running our daily errands in town by foot.

While exercise is crucial for physical fitness, science now knows that the ultimate way to achieve brain fitness is by music training. And to gain its benefits, a child doesn't need to be locked in a dungeon to practice for several hours a day. Yet they *do* need to *learn* music, as simply listening to music or playing games to music does not count.[26] Your child needs to learn the music concepts of rhythm, melody and notation to gain the brain benefits.[27]

Studies show that each and every child can gain the full brain boost as long as they start before the age of eight – but as it stands, too many children are missing out on this unique opportunity. The good news is that these skills can be taught to children even before they start playing an instrument. In fact, the earlier a child starts learning music, the bigger benefits they gain. Far from classical instrument playing being the only way, child-friendly music activities crucially benefit babies and toddlers who are too young to even hold an instrument. Babies[28] and toddlers[29] alike show more developed thinking ability, brain development and emotional wellbeing than their same-age peers who do not learn music, even when they are at the same level of development before starting the music training.[30] Due to the increases in wellbeing and patience (see Chapter 8), they also behave better, making music learning a parent's dream inoculation against the 'terrible twos'! Rated independently by parents and teachers, children who have engaged in a music training programmes have shown to significantly improve their behaviour as a result.[31]

The bad news is that not everything that claims to teach music actually does. For instance, non-educational music games do not promote a child's intellectual development – only the learning of music does.[32] Comparative studies also show that music appreciation classes such as traditional school music lessons or sing-along baby groups alone do not provide the brain boost.[33] Rebecca Asher poignantly describes an experience familiar to many new mothers in her book *Shattered,* 'activity existed in the main simply to fill the time. I went to a parent and baby group and found myself singing nursery rhymes with other grown women as our tiny children lay impassive on the floor'.[34] Username 'MarshaBrady' on the Mumsnet discussion forum echoes the same sentiment: 'My bête noire was wind the bobbin up on a mat at music class. I think I had some existential crisis right there, and avoided it like the plague for the second child'.[35]

To gain the full brain benefits, listening to music is not enough. Even when the babies listened to the same amount of music at home – a remarkable 15 hours or more a week – only those who engaged in music training (for just an hour a week) experienced the boost in their mental and social abilities. The babies whose music group consisted of listening to classical music did not experience these benefits.[36]

Circulating amongst well-meaning parents is the rumour that playing Mozart, or classical music in general, to a child makes them more intelligent. This myth is, despite its popularity, completely debunked by scientific study.[37] Yet as a parenting myth it persists, which is why I have included this discussion in Chapter 11. Putting on a Mozart record or going to nursery rhyme classes can be fun activities, but it is only a developmentally appropriate and emotionally engaging music training programme that produces the brain benefits. Just like your child will not get fitter by watching athletes on television, it is hardly a surprise that they do not become more intelligent by simply listening to music that portrays the image of intelligence.

But here we must not take up the hot-housing 'no pain, no gain' thinking. Music learning needn't be a chore. All children love music, and their brains are wired to learn its skills. Babies naturally try to match the music they hear with body movement, and when they gain better rhythm skills, their faces light up and they feel pleased with themselves.[38] Studies show that preschool children are more engaged in music learning than video watching.[39] Even more surprisingly, when studies have been made on free playing with toys as opposed to guided music making, it has been found that children prefer music training.[40] One study that compared the amount of smiles of hospitalized children as a measure of happiness found that the preschoolers smiled an astonishing 300% more in music therapy than in play therapy.[41] The reasons why music causes such pleasure are explained by evolution and will be touched upon in Chapters 7, 10, 12 and 35, among others.

But hot-housing must make the child more successful, right?

Wrong. If only it did, for the sake of the childhood that the hot-housed children must sacrifice at the altar of formal education. Recent research has found that Pushy Parented children, even at the verge of their adulthood, still suffer from the long-term harmful consequences such as increased stress, mental illnesses, anxiety and addiction to medication.[42] In recent years, reports of cases where some hot-housed children have become murderers, often of their own parents, have come to light even in mainstream media.[43]

Pushy Parenting also trades the child's time for free play for formal learning, and in excess, this has detrimental consequences for their learning skills.[44] It is well known that children need free play to learn about the world in their own terms. With free play, children become more independent at learning and more resourceful at coming up with solutions to challenges and problems.[45] These are crucial skills that a child who is pushed into full-fledged, full-time formal learning will not be able to develop.

In a longitudinal study published in 2002, Professor Rebecca A. Marcon from the University of North Florida investigated the long-term effects that different methods of preschool learning have on the children. She followed up a large sample of children who had started going to preschool at the age of four. Some of their preschools were child-initiated, consisting mainly of free play, and others were academic, emphasizing formal education. Marcon's study found that 'by the end of their sixth year in school, children whose preschool experiences had been academically directed earned significantly lower grades compared to children who had attended child-initiated preschool classes. Children's later school success appears to have been enhanced by more active, child-initiated early learning experiences. Their progress may have been slowed by overly academic preschool experiences that introduced formalized learning experiences too early for most children's developmental status'.[46]

Thus it is ironic that even with regards to formal learning skills, most of the methods that Pushy Parents use do not actually work. This book shows you what does. You will learn why early music learning is a better way to teach reading skills than flashcards or phonics. It is a better way to increase performance in mathematics and science than more courses in mathematics and science, and it is the real secret to success within all school subjects. Most importantly, it does not require any counter-productive hot-housing but instead provides your child with higher levels of emotional and social well-being - whilst leaving plenty of time for free play.

Chapter 3

What the Pushy Parents Don't Know: The Real Secret of Successful Children

The Pushy Parents are right about one thing: children need a nourishing environment to flourish. All children's brains contain the potential for multiple talents, but without the opportunity to develop the neural networks, the brain areas and the corresponding abilities do not get to develop.[1] Even if the school system was wired up to maximize our children's all-round talents and intellectual ability, there would be crucial potential lost, simply because the crucial age for brain development is in most cases from babyhood to the preschool and the very earliest of school years.[2] But as we found out in the previous chapter, most formal learning at this age does not actually boost your child's development. So what does?

Studies have shown that music skills acquired before school directly affect a child's school readiness. In a groundbreaking study from 2002 that since has become legendary in the academic circles, Sima H. Anvari, M.Sc., and her research group from McMaster University in Ontario, Canada, studied a hundred 4- and 5-year-old children and found that the better a child's music skills were before they started school, the better reading skills they developed.[3] In 2009, a study led by Professor Graham Welch from the University of London studied a sample of more than 1200 British children and found that children who have a high level of musical skills are more likely to have fulfilling social relationships than the children who lack them.[4]

Even more recently, a 2011 study led by Professor Warren Brodsky found that the level of musical hand-clapping skills your child has at kindergarten age reliably predicts their academic success at school. According to the researchers, 'the findings confirm that when a child does not have exposure to these types of activities [handclapping songs], he or she is more vulnerable to develop dyslexia and dyscalculia'. On the positive side, the researchers found that a short period of rhythm training helped children catch up with their more advanced peers. 'Within a very short period of time the children who, until then, hadn't taken part in such activities caught up in their cognitive abilities to those who did'. They also found, like the researchers before and after them had, that the brain boost only occurred to children who took part in music training. The children whose classes instead consisted of listening to music and a standard school music curriculum did not gain developments in their intelligence.[5]

Despite the unquestionable brain benefits that have come to light, the vast majority of schools do not yet include music in its core subjects. The small amount of music instruction that is present at school, as Edwin E. Gordon points out, often consists of just listening to music rather than learning it.[6] Children are taught to recognize instruments, not musical concepts. The music 'lessons' are regarded as recreational, not educational.[7] This, as we have already touched upon, does not provide the brain boosts that music training offers.

Even though music is not regarded as a core subject, studies show that it is the key to excelling in all the traditional core subjects: mathematics[8], reading[9], language skills[10] and science.[11] The children who are lucky enough to have either parental support for learning music or access to good quality music education at school reap the benefits. Recent research, such as the 2009 study led by Dr. O.E. Wetter from the University of Zürich, has shown that the children who engage in music instruction have significantly higher grades than the children without music instruction in all school subjects except sports, where the performance is equal. The music learners had significantly higher grades even when their family's income levels were taken into account. Wetter's study determined that the effect was in music itself and not an enriched environment due to a higher family income level.[12] This research result follows in line of many others, such as a similar 2006 study made in Ohio by Dr. Kate R. Fitzpatrick that found that the pupils who learned music outperformed their non-music leaning peers 'in every subject and in every level'. When the effect family income was accounted for, it was found that music students from poorer family backgrounds had surpassed their non-music students from wealthier families by the end of compulsory schooling.[13]

A common phenomenon in America for those who study music is what is called the 'pullout music lessons'. In the pullout lessons, the students who opt to get private music tuition can do so during their school day, while missing out on some of the lessons the rest of the class participates in. Studies have found that the academic achievement of the pullout music students tends to be the same or, in most cases, *higher* than that of the students who engage in all of the standard curriculum but no music tuition.[14]

In line with this finding, one exceptional experiment taken in several Swiss primary schools in the 1990s went as far as to replace a substantial amount of weekly academic core lessons with music lessons. Regular measurements found that despite the lesser time dedicated to core subjects, the students of the music programme did equally well in mathematics and even better in reading than the students from the schools outside the experiment.[15] The first American study along these lines was done in 1996 by Dr. Martin Gardiner and his research group. The results showed that children who previously lacked behind in maths soon not only caught up with the normal-achieving pupils when they took up music learning, but even surpassed them.[16]

For children about to start school, better music skills directly predict better school readiness.[17] And the effect of first grade success lasts throughout their academic years right until adulthood.[18] Curiously, Wetter's study from 2009 found that music is the cure for the phenomenon that has long worried education experts: the phenomenon of student grades falling during and after the fourth year at school. This phenomenon, which in America has been dubbed The Fourth Grade Slump, surprisingly does not happen for the children who study music. In fact, the study found that for non-music children, the deterioration of school success actually starts to happen at year three instead of four, and continues dropping over the next four years. In contrast, the music learners do not drop their grades, and keep on being successful students.[19]

Many Pushy Parents would undoubtedly love to see their child become someone with a highly respected and highly paid position in society: ideally, a doctor. An American study by physician and biologist Lewis Thomas found that majoring in music at college is much more likely to open the doors to the medical school than majoring in any other subject. A full two-thirds – 66 percent – of music majors pass the admissions tests to medical school. The second largest group, those majoring in biochemistry, are much less likely at 44 percent.[20]

In the United Kingdom, medicine is likewise one of the most popular and competitive university courses to get into. While the admissions procedures differ substantially from one university to another, top grades in several Science A-levels is an essential requirement as well as previous school success as demonstrated by the GCSE (General Certificate of Secondary Education) scores, and many universities also want the candidates to exhibit a 'well rounded personality'.[21] As an example of the latter, candidates are commonly guided to express their musical background in the personal statement part of the application form, in a kind of decorative fashion. Yet the actual advantage of music learning is more than putting it on your CV: the full-scale brain upgrade that gives rise to exceptional school success, as well as a multitalented, authentically well-rounded person.

Chapter 4

The History of the Music Miracle in a Nutshell

In the late 1960s and early 1970s, scientists started noticing that musical skills could be beneficial for not just future musicians, but all children. There had already been a wide interest in the links between musicality and intelligence for the preceding 50 years, but that this research was interested in whether a high IQ was crucial for musical excellence.[1] Research of that era examined those links and concluded that musical ability was not determined by IQ or other intelligence markers.[2]

Something quite opposite started to emerge over the next decades of research. It was noted that musical learning seemed to cause improvement in various intelligence-related areas of life. At first, it wasn't clear which was the chicken or the egg. Many researchers suspected that because musical activities are expensive and only the wealthier families could afford such training, the music boost could be just a coincidence. They theorised that as highly educated parents were more affluent and more able to offer an overall enriched environment, they would prioritize cultural activities such as music education and that this compound effect was the real reason behind the seeming benefits.

But in the 1990s and early 2000s, more results started coming in from scientifically controlled experiments that assigned children randomly into music groups and control groups. In these studies, everyone in the groups started from the same level, but only the children in the music groups experienced the learning enhancements. The control groups did not get musical training and showed much slower development compared to the music groups.

It was noted that children who learned music early on were more successful at school in areas such as mathematics[3], reading[4] and the science-related spatial-temporal intelligence[5]. These results were generally found for children who started training before the age of seven or eight.[6] In 2004, Schellenberg and his research group published the mother of all studies with groups of six-year-old children: music learning boosted the full-scale IQ.[7] To this day, music learning is the only hobby that is shown to increase the IQ of children.

Science in the past decade has shown a growing interest in the effects of music learning on the brain. Gottfried Schlaug, today a neuroscientist at Harvard Medical School, lead the research group that discovered in 1995 that musicians who started playing an instrument before the age of seven had significantly larger corpus callosums.[8] The corpus callosum is the brain bridge that connects the two sides of the brain – left and right. This makes the brain more integrated and effective: a thicker corpus callosum is linked to higher intelligence and better verbal skills.[9] Conversely, children with learning deficits are often found to have an underdeveloped corpus callosum. These deficits can range from ADHD to poor reasoning ability and inferior social skills.[10]

In 2009, Schlaug and his large research group verified in a controlled study that a thicker corpus callosum and the other brain effects visible in brain imaging studies were not a pre-existent marker of musicality.[11] The scientists placed randomly selected children of less than eight years old into groups of music instruction and control groups. When the children's brains were measured two-and-a-half years later, only the musician children had developed these parts of their brain.[12]

Thus, it has only recently been scientifically verified that it is music training that boosts the corpus callosum and other parts of the brain. Now we know that these benefits are available for every child who takes up music training before the age of eight. Music training is a truly democratic opportunity that unlocks the potential of every child who engages in it. In the next chapter, we will look at what explains this hugely significant phenomenon.

Chapter 5

How is this possible? The scientific explanation behind the Miracle

The underlying reasons for the Music Miracle in young children are found in modern research on brain development. At birth, a baby's brain contains a hundred billion brain cells called neurons. This is the same amount of neurons that are found in the adult brain. What happens during human development is that the neurons adapt to their specific environment by forming connections between each other.

These connections are called synapses, and during the first years of life, the baby's brain goes through an explosion of new synaptic connections based on the stimuli that the environment is offering. This is how we learn vital skills such as our mother tongue – and, if our environment offers it to us, music skills. The ability of the brain to adapt to its environment is called *plasticity*.

The plasticity of the young brain is never matched in an older one. The young brain is quick to form synaptic connections, but it needs to maintain them with some regularity. If they aren't reinforced, the brain will discard about half of its earlier synaptic connections by puberty. This makes the brain more efficient with its remaining connections, but it also narrows down the scope for developing the brain. Early music learning is unique in its ability to spread the neural networks far and wide, to allow for maximum efficiency in the brain that enters puberty. Your child's brain has the magnificent opportunity for supercharging their networks, but 'use it or lose it' literally applies here.

What differentiates music skills from other abilities is that by practicing music, your child is developing their whole brain and all its abilities. As we see throughout this book, by learning music, your child builds up neural connections in the same areas that the brain uses for other domains such as language, listening, mathematics, higher-order thinking and emotional skills. This phenomenon is called *transfer.* But why does music learning build up all these various areas in the brain?

Practicing music uses both the left and right hemisphere of the conscious human brain (cerebral cortex) and builds a better connectivity between the two through the corpus callosum (the brain bridge). It involves various networks related to language skills[1], mathematics[2] and higher-order thinking.[3]

And this is not all. Beyond the conscious human brain lies the mammalian 'emotional' brain (limbic system), with its parts such as the amygdala, the management of which Daniel Goleman, the author of Emotional Intelligence, has branded as crucial for human success.[4] The mammalian brain is the basis on top of which the conscious human brain has evolved. In recent years, neuroscience has shown that music taps into the amygdala[5] and other parts[6] of the emotional ('limbic') brain. Beyond the limbic brain, in turn, belies the basal ganglia, the 'reptilian brain', the most basic yet the most essential brain component of life, relating to motivation and sub-conscious planning of action. Music taps directly into the basal ganglia[7], which is just one piece of the evidence pointing to the evolutionary necessity of music for humans (and also some other animals). We will look at the evolutionary basis in Chapter 10 and see how nature has programmed us to be musicians.

And it doesn't end here. Music training also boosts the brain regions that are responsible for movement -- the cerebellum, known as the 'little brain'. Children who start music training before the age of eight are found to develop bigger cerebellums as a result.[8] The benefits of this are numerous, as better rhythmic movement abilities translate not only to higher rhythmic skills[9] but also school success.[10] Conversely, children with learning difficulties are often found to have lesser rhythmic motor skills.[11]

The Music Miracle: Easier than a second language

Learning music bears similarities to learning a second language. Both music and language consist of a hierarchy of auditory and written sounds and symbols, and brain research shows that the areas for music and language overlap in several the brain. This allows for the transfer to occur and explains why children gain a better command of their language and verbal intelligence, as well as a greater ability to learn foreign languages, just by studying a modest but regular amount of music (see Chapters 22-25).

Early exposure to two languages – being bilingual – has been shown to result in some IQ-enhancing benefits, namely that of the brain's *executive functioning*.[12] The executive functioning relates to higher-order thinking and scientists suspect that when a child has to balance several language systems due to developing more than one language, they need to exercise their higher-order thinking.

This hints at why music learning boosts intelligence. The brain of a child with just one mother tongue and who learns music is similar to a bilingual child's brain. But curiously, studies by the leading researcher on bilingualism, Ellen Bialystok from the York University in Canada, reveal that while bilingualism only causes a modest increase in executive functioning, music learning produces the same executive functioning increase plus a full-scale IQ increase as well as a boost for other crucial neural networks.[13] And music works its miracle with much less effort than learning a second language at childhood. Studies show that just an hour of regular music learning a week produces more IQ benefits than daily exposure to two mother tongues.[14]

But the benefits of music learning do not stop at language and intelligence. Music study also involves learning logical patterns like those of mathematical concepts such as fractions, and it engages emotions to the point where music is often called 'the language of emotion'. This could explain why early music learning builds up neural networks that the brain needs to use for mathematics, emotional intelligence and social skills.

Music learning is a multisensory experience which involves all three ways of learning: auditory, visual and kinesthetic.[15] Recent research has pointed out that the brain is a multisensory organ and this could partially explain the remarkable benefits of music learning to all areas of life.[16] It is visibly such a big brain-booster that it has become the scientists' model for studying brain plasticity and transfer in general.[17] So at a young age, the little ones can literally restructure their brains with music learning, forming new connections between different parts of the brain, even if they do not have access to a second language.

The Auditory Scaffolding Hypothesis: The realm of brain is ruled by the ear

Recent research also indicates that there is something special about hearing as the mother of all modalities. The developers of a new theory on how children learn called the *Auditory Scaffolding Hypothesis* have found that auditory deprivation impairs learning in deaf children for visual modalities, too. The Auditory Scaffolding Hypothesis has been developed by a group of scientists from various American universities and it has only come to light in 2009. According to the Hypothesis, the ear is the way to access the realm of all higher thinking in general.[18] Other recent studies have shown that children who have had music training have become better at recognizing and analyzing patterns in not only sound but other modalities, which supports the premise of the hypothesis.[19]

Indeed, music training boosts the processing of both auditory and visual information.[20] The reason for this is not known, but it is interesting to note that hearing is the first sense to develop in a fetus and newborn baby, and generally the last sense to deteriorate in a person's final days. (At least, this has been the case before our noise-polluted culture and music blasting through iPod earphones!) Indeed, the gradual loss of hearing with age has been found to be the main reason behind the often-observed cognitive impairments of the elderly. It turns out that their reasoning, as such, is not worse -- it is their hearing! [21]

There is also evidence that auditory training alone is as effective as multisensory training that comprises the auditory, visual and kinesthetic equally. Diane Cummings Persellin from Trinity University in Texas has researched the effects of different modalities in music training for children. She found that when teaching rhythm, multisensory training is the most beneficial for school-aged children, although smaller children learn better through the auditory and kinesthetic modalities than the visual.[22] When examining the effects of different types of music training onto four- and five-year-old children, the results showed that the children who were taught either the multisensory way or just the auditory way learned better skills related to rhythm and singing in tune than the other children. Interestingly, the kinesthetic training alone was the least successful for this age group.[23] These results further highlight the importance of early ear training. Auditory training should be the centre of effective multisensory training, as visual and kinesthetic learning alone do not produce the music skills needed for the Music Miracle. After all, music is first and foremost the art of the ear.

Thus, the evidence is building up that the brain is the realm of the ear. A better listening ability on the level of the brain's neural connections has been found essential for abilities such as memory, and recently it has been found crucial for avoiding learning difficulties for children at school.[24] Music training has been found to boost the brain's auditory abilities on both cortical and subcortical level[25], and if the Auditory Scaffolding Theory is correct, then it could explain why music training has been shown to make children's brains think faster and more accurately. The elderly who have a better hearing ability have been found to have the same cognitive abilities as those who are their children's, or even grandchildren's age.[26] This could explain why elderly people who have engaged in music training in childhood still retain cognitive functioning at a much higher level than their peers who have not practiced music.[27]

Chapter 6

The Music Miracle: Why an early start makes all the difference

Part of a Pushy Parent's anxiety stems from the idea that there is an optimal window of time for infants and toddlers to build essential brain connections, and if that window closes without the proper stimulus, all is lost. It is true that the children in their earliest years are in the midst of exponential brain development that is never repeated in their lives, but there's also plenty of good news. Music education benefits brain development of people of all ages.

However, research shows that there are critical ages for brain development – time windows when the synapses need to be established, or otherwise they will never be built.[1]

Studies on hearing-disabled children with *cochlear implants* provide evidence for the critical age. Thanks to this invention, children who are born deaf can these days have this device inserted into their ear(s) that translates sound vibration into their brain and makes them able to 'hear'. Research has established that children who receive cochlear implants at the latest at the age of seven can develop hearing skills to practically the same level as their normal-hearing peers. Doctor Hamid R. Djalilian, director of the Neurotology and Skull Base Surgery at the UC Irvine Medical Center, has remarked: 'There is a time window during which [children who are born deaf] can get an implant and learn to speak. From the ages of two to four, that ability diminishes a little bit. And by age nine, there is zero chance that they will learn to speak properly. So it's really important that they get recognized and evaluated early.'[2]

In contrast, children who have received implants within their first, second or third year of life, develop their hearing, speaking, language and reading abilities practically to the same level as their normal-hearing peers.[3] Research led by Dr. Anu Sharma, Professor at the Institute for Cognitive Science at University of Colorado at Boulder, concludes: 'Our data suggest that in the absence of normal stimulation there is a sensitive period of about 3.5 years during which the human central auditory system remains maximally plastic. Plasticity remains in some, but not all children until approximately age 7. After age 7, plasticity is greatly reduced.'[4]

As music training relies first and foremost on the ear, these results may explain why it is only during the younger years that children have been found to get the maximum brain boost from music training. Therefore, to get the optimal results, children should start music training during their first few years of life, but at the very latest at the age of seven. Increases in full-scale IQ[5] and verbal intelligence[6] as well as spatial-temporal[7] and mathematical reasoning[8] have only reliably shown for those children who start at the latest at the age of seven. The children who have started after the age of seven have not gained the same benefits from music study.[9]

The results from studies of physical brain development correspond to this evidence. Only the children who start music learning before or at the age of seven, but no later, go on to develop a bigger corpus callosum[10], which is linked to increased intelligence[11] as well as better social and emotional well-being.[12]

And an earlier start makes a difference. A US study on a large sample of 200 preschool children and mathematics skills showed that the children who took part in a six-month music programme at three performed even better than their peers who took part in it at age four, and those four-year-olds performed better than children who went through the course at age five. Compared to the other children, all the music training groups performed better than the control groups after a modest six months of one-and-a-half hours of weekly music training, so every music learner gained benefits. However, the effect on the younger brains was striking and shows that the earlier your child begins their Music Miracle, the better.[13]

If your child is older than three or four, don't despair. Studies have shown that children up to eight years can gain crucial benefits from music learning. For children even older than that, self-esteem benefits have been widely reported, and one recent study showed that 10- and 11-year-old children who take up music learning significantly improved their memory as a result.[14]

These timescales correspond to evidence from language learning. It is widely shown that humans cannot learn a language at a native level if they haven't started learning it before the age of 12.[15] This matches the age when puberty starts and by which time the pruning process has finished by getting rid of 50% of the brain's synaptic connections.[16]

But if you've missed that window too, there is still hope. Music learning is widely recommended as a tool against memory loss for even the oldest of us. A study from 2007 found that when elderly people aged 60 to 85, who had never previously engaged in music training, took up intensive piano lessons for 6 months, they developed their working memory and motor skills compared to the control group who didn't learn music.[17] Following these types of discoveries, both the American Psychological Association[18] and leading brain researcher Gottfried Schlaug now recommend music as a brain fitness tool for old age pensioners.[19] As Schlaug puts it: 'Music-making places unique demands on the nervous system and leads to a strong coupling of perception and action mediated by sensory, motor and multimodal integrative regions distributed throughout the brain'.[20]

Interestingly, even stronger effects have been found for those pensioners who played music at a young age, yet stopped playing decades ago. This been found in the studies lead by the American neurologist Brenda Hanna-Pladdy and her research group. Healthy elderly adults with varying musical and non-musical backgrounds have been studied and those with a musical background in childhood still have a better memory and faster processing speed of information. The scientists concluded that both the age of musical learning and years of training had made a positive difference to the brains of these pensioners, even when they had long since stopped practicing. Thus, the brain boost of early music learning lasts all the way through the golden years.[21] This effect was specific for music – no other activity caused the brain benefits.[22]

The human brain always retains some plasticity, and anyone at any age can take up an instrument. But it is clear that only the smallest of children get the full brain benefits. This is because their brains are forming neural connections at a pace that will never be matched in an older brain. Yet, as Hanna-Pladdy's research shows, the effects of this early training never end - even when the training itself has ended decades before. The Music Miracle is the true gift for life.

Part Two

Music Miracle for babies and toddlers: Gains for the baby's brain, boost for the family's mood

While the studies on the amazing benefits of music show that there is a deadline for the full brain boost to take place, there is no lower age limit. Even babies and toddlers, who are too small to even hold an instrument, can start music learning and gain incredible benefits from it. The key is to engage them in an age-appropriate pedagogy. We must remember that all children are born musical. They do not need to be pushed to learn, just given the tools that they naturally seek out for to display their musicality. In doing this, they are building their brains.

Babies are precious and bring indescribable joy. At the same time, caring for a small baby can be one of the most stressful phases in a healthy adult's life. I have all sympathy for parents who have just welcomed their new offspring into the world, and I understand that Pushy Parents aside, most normal parents just want to survive the unpredictable daily routine, the sleep deprivation, nappy changes and feeding concerns without the additional hassle of becoming the baby's first personal brain trainer. I felt the same way. It was just by coincidence that my son got some introduction to music as a small baby. Whenever he was content to listen to me play the piano, I grabbed the opportunity as a sudden full-time Mum just to preserve some of my old familiar life.

In retrospect, I could have done much more. With what I know now, I would have made every effort to introduce short periods of music training just a few times a week into the routine. That said, the research was not even available at the time. The first fully controlled study onto the Music Miracle for the babies was only published in 2012.

But my keenness to engage my baby in music training, if I could go back in time, would not be motivated solely by the brain benefits for my son, but also for purely selfish reasons. It turns out that when you take the time and effort to engage your baby or toddler into music training for as little as one hour or less a week, they become calmer, more emotionally stable, more patient and ahead of their peers in mental development. Thus, they become more balanced and mature. Not only do they gain brain benefits for life, but their parents gain precious sanity. Babies and toddlers look angelic, but music training brings out the angel in their character, too!

Chapter 7

Your Baby's Brain Craves for Music Training

With regards to the importance of early influences, it should not come as a surprise that the first years of a child's life are considered the most crucial for the type of brain development that affects a child's IQ. Studies have found that the initial brain size of a baby at birth surprisingly does not predict their future IQ – it is the brain growth from birth onwards, throughout early childhood, that affects it. Babies whose brains grow faster than their peers' end up having higher IQs than their peers even throughout adulthood. The brain responds to correct stimuli and the results remain for life.[1]

So how can we best nourish the brains of babies? Recent discoveries show that music training is the best way to advance the IQ-related mental advancements in babyhood. The very earliest music learning increases your baby's mental age, communication skills and language development.[2] What's more, the better a baby is at jigging along to rhythms, the more they smile[3] and the higher their level of emotional well-being.[4]

The pioneering study on the benefits for babies, published in 2012 by researchers from McMaster University in Canada, compared six-month-old babies who attended weekly music classes to children who didn't. It was the first fully controlled study to assess the effects of music training on babies. The babies in the music learning group and the comparison groups (one of which revolved around listening to classical music, but did not include the learning component) were randomly assigned to their respective groupings, tested before the study and were found to be on the same level of development. Within four months of treatment, when the babies were tested again, the babies in the music group were significantly more advanced in communication and social skills. The babies also had a higher level of emotional wellbeing than the babies who missed out on the music learning. The real learning of music was found, once again, to be significant. The group of babies that simply listened to classical music without instruction did not gain any development benefits compared to the control group with no treatment.[5]

This astonishing finding affirms studies that show that toddlers who learn music develop skills that help them in the years to come to succeed at school above the level of their non-music learning peers.[6] They are also more able to manage their emotions in situations such as waiting.[7] These benefits relate to a psychological ability called self-regulation, which links to emotional intelligence and is shown to be developed in even in tiny toddlers who study music.[8] The significance of self-regulation is not just that it makes life easier for parents (fewer tantrums!), but it also improves the wellbeing and life skills of their little ones. These skills, in turn, are considered by teachers to be an even more important component of school readiness than early academic skills.[9]

Even more surprisingly, a better self-regulation ability in the early years is linked to sustained willpower throughout life, resulting in many crucial life outcomes. The famous marshmallow study by Walter Mischel in the late 1960s measured the self-regulation ability of four-year-old children. In the test, each child was given two options: to eat one marshmallow now, or two marshmallows after a ten-minute wait. Only a minority of the four-year-olds were able to wait for ten minutes to double their marshmallow dose. Over the decades to come, when these children had grown up, researchers discovered that the children with a higher level of self-regulation, those who had been patient enough to wait 10 minutes, were now adults who had a higher educational and career attainment, a better ability to cope with stress, better physical health and less addiction related to drugs or overeating.[10] In 2010, a study found that toddlers and preschoolers who had gone to group music lessons had a significantly better level of self-regulation, including tests that mirrored the marshmallow study setting. The results showed that the longer these children had participated in music learning, the better their self-regulation levels were.[11]

The lesson we can learn from this is that self-regulation is not a given, but can be unlocked in your child through musical instruction. Mischel's studies also show that a high level of self-regulation in childhood predicts equally high levels in adulthood, so it's yet another Music Miracle investment for life.[12] As a longitudinal study published in 2011 lead by Terrie E. Moffitt of Duke University reports: 'Following a cohort of 1,000 children from birth to the age of 32 years, we show that childhood self-control predicts physical health, substance dependence, personal finances, and criminal offending outcomes, following a gradient of self-control. Effects of children's self-control could be disentangled from their intelligence and social class as well as from mistakes they made as adolescents. In another cohort of 500 sibling pairs, the sibling with lower self-control had poorer outcomes, despite shared family background'.[13]

The younger a child starts learning music, the bigger benefits they gain – and with the least effort. A 2011 study by Toronto neuroscientist Sylvain Moreno and his research group on 4- to 6-year-old children showed that those who learned music skills related to rhythm, notation, melody and basic music concepts for just 20 days (2 hours a day) significantly improved their verbal intelligence and thinking skills. Another group of children in the same study studied visual arts with the same method and did not experience these benefits.[14]

Music instruction for toddlers and infants can seem impossible, since babies and very young children cannot hold or use an instrument. And it is true that just singing and shaking rattles to songs does not pass for learning content. But core music skills such as rhythm, melody and notation can be taught in an age-appropriate way even without regimented instrument tuition. The methods of Kodaly and Suzuki as well as the Finnish Musiikkileikkikoulu have successfully been doing this for decades. Rebecca Ann Shore writes in Music and Cognitive Development: From Notes to Neural Networks: '...sustained music lessons or training methods that increase in complexity over time can positively affect cognitive development. For comparison, consider preschool and elementary school instruction in numeracy and literacy. Children do not learn number identification and continue to recite numbers year after year. They learn numbers and then the addition of numbers, subtraction of numbers, and so on, increasing in complexity over time. (...) Simply singing the same song at calendar time every Friday may not glean the possible cognitive benefits that music has to offer the early childhood environment, albeit including songs for fun and community building is an important role for music as well. Incorporating a systemic program that is sequenced in complexity is needed to build denser neural networks for higher cognitive performance and should be a criterion for high-quality early childhood music instruction'.[15]

Similarly, both the Finnish Musiikkileikkikoulu tradition and the Moosicology method combine the playful teaching of notation with core music concepts such as major and minor, pitches and chords, scales and note value. These basic musical concepts are indeed possible to teach to babies and toddlers who are very responsive to them.

It's these basic concepts that are at the heart of any kind of real musical learning, yet it's only a minority of adults themselves who know such concepts. Hence the commonly noted problem of music education in nurseries and schools is that even the instructors themselves do not have the knowledge to teach music, so they resort to teaching *about* music instead. Unfortunately, as we see throughout this book, teaching about musical genres and instruments does not produce brain benefits -- only real musical learning does.[16] As for the difference between children's music education programmes, many of the popular franchises require from the instructor, at most, the ability to sing in tune, whereas the teachers of Kodaly, Suzuki and Musiikkileikkikoulu are required to have a deep understanding of music. In Finland, the music teachers of toddlers are required to be professional musicians as well as music educators. As one would expect, studies have found that Musiikkileikkikoulu significantly improves the language skills, communication skills, social wellbeing and confidence of the smallest of children.[17]

The improvements in the children have also been reported by the parents and daycare professionals who look after the children for the lion's share of the week, as the Musiikkileikkikoulu activity only takes up an hour or less of the children's weekly routine.[18] Many parents may feel that it's too ambitious to try to attend music lessons in the midst of feeding, sleeping and nappy changing routines. But all evidence shows that if a new parent can muster to access real musical learning for their baby just once a week, they will soon find that they're rewarded with a happier, more relaxed and more patient little one. This alone produces visible improvements to the stress potentials of family life, not to even mention the fact that this paves the way to learning success and the avoidance of pitfalls such as learning deficits.

Chapter 8

Harmony in the Household

When my son was born, I, like many other new mothers, found myself singing songs that otherwise were too simple for my taste, making new silly songs up as well as singing 'Twinkle Twinkle', 'Incy Wincy Spider' and other musical standards of childhood that I had previously deemed as boring. Suddenly these tedious and simple tunes had a whole new shine to them – the shine of my son's face lighting up.

I thought I must have been imagining things. How could my baby be so visibly delighted by a simple tune? Yet, as I was to find out, science shows that babies actually prefer singing to speech.[1] Furthermore, out of different singing voices, they prefer most of all the voice of women, especially that of their own mother.[2] As if that's not astounding enough, recent research shows that babies also prefer rhythmic music recordings, such as uptempo pop or children's songs with drums, to speech.[3]

What's even more significant, at least to those of us who have suffered from baby-induced sleep deprivation, is the finding that distressed babies calm down with a 94.5 percent success rate when they are being sung to – much more that when they're being comforted by other means, such as cradling and cuddling.[4] Even when recorded music is played, 4 out of 5 crying babies calm down and get happy almost at the press of the play button![5]

Our son was a bad sleeper during his first year, waking up on average seven times a night, and a lot of the time his father Travis and I were desperate to try and comfort him by carrying, hugging, having breast on tap (feeding on demand) – anything for peace and rest. In the middle of the night, the last thing I felt like doing was singing jolly songs – I just wanted to sleep. As we took turns attempting to comfort our precious little one, I did not want to further disturb Travis' sleep by joining in with my son's vocalization. I thought I was doing the right thing keeping quiet a lot of the time, simply cuddling our baby and whispering to him. Now, when I think about the missed opportunities to sing him to sleep, I would be tempted to take my turn in crying. Music would have been the ideal method of surviving the stressful baby phase, whether in singing, playing records or both. It's a win-win as both singing and listening to records are a stress-releasing activity to the parent as well!

It turns out that the love of song is biologically wired in babies. Already at birth, babies' brains recognize whether the sounds they hear are consonant and in tune with each other or dissonant and out of tune.[6] Just like with rhythm and intelligence, this melodic processing serves as a building block for a set of crucial skills beyond the mere musical ones. Melodic processing is the foundation on which babies build their language skills, understanding of speech, the learning of vocabulary, and the ability to eventually learn to read and communicate effectively. Recent research has found that not only do the abilities for language and music develop simultaneously and indistinguishably in a baby's brain[7], but that the brain develops its musical understanding before its language comprehension.[8] Hence, it is commonly found that gaining music skills facilitates the baby's learning of speech and language.[9]

It's not all about singing and lullabies either. Recent research by Dr Marcel Zentner from University of York and Dr Tuomas Eerola from the Finnish Centre of Excellence in Interdisciplinary Music Education in the University of Jyväskylä in Finland has identified that rhythm is the element that makes babies spontaneously try and move to the beat of the music.[10] The rhythm makes the babies spontaneously develop their rhythmic movement skills[11], and these skills in turn are strongly linked to academic excellence in the years to come.[12] The lack of them is, in contrast, linked to future learning deficits.[13] As your baby is programmed to develop their motor movement, giving them the stimulation from songs with drums or percussion is as simple as it is fun a method to boost their brain development. Indeed, not only do babies prefer rhythmic music to speech -- the better they get at jigging to it, the more they smile![14]

In everyday life, parents often feel overwhelmed with balancing each day's unrelenting demands: looking after the children, working, keeping the house tidy, managing the finances, having time for the spouse, and possibly, at some distant point, even some me-time. This is the modern parent's dilemma, further strained by the unpredictable future, which breeds hot-housing on one hand and negligence on the other. What I find so useful about the Music Miracle is that everyone's a winner. Unleashing your child's intelligence and multiple talents takes an hour or less a week, and it benefits the parents as much as the children. By engaging in early music learning, the family is most likely to avoid future time-consuming problems such as failure at school, low self-control, low confidence, learning deficits and problems that result from sub-optimum social skills, just to name a few.

There are also immediate benefits. A baby with better emotional wellbeing makes the parent's job easier, less worrying and more rewarding, since a small child with better self-regulation is more mature, better at patience and less prone to tantrums. Surprisingly, studies even find that parents of children who engage in music have less stress and better mental health after the start of the music activity. A 2008 study led by Jan M. Nicholson from Griffith University in Australia investigated the effects of a 10-week parent-and child music program on children aged between 0-5. The results were nothing short of amazing. 'Participants were 358 parents and children from families facing social disadvantage, young parents or parents of a child with a disability. Significant improvements were found for therapist-observed parent and child behaviors, and parent-reported irritable parenting, educational activities in the home, parent mental health and child communication and social play skills.'[15] Another study from the Florida State University compared the interactions of 0-2-year-old children with their parents, and found that those children who had participated in developmental music training exhibited better parent-child interactions in toy play in everyday life than the families whose babies and toddlers did not participate in music training.[16]

A baby with better emotional wellbeing makes the parent's job easier, less worrying and more rewarding, since a toddler with better self-regulation is more mature, better at patience and less prone to tantrums. With regards to this scientifically proven payoff, a short weekly music training session achieves the whole family a level of ease and wellbeing that no money can buy.

Chapter 9

And Your Baby Can Sing: Unleashing your baby's inner vocalist and wordsmith

'A child's first words are eagerly awaited not only as a cognitive milestone, but as a bond with the adult world – one that heralds the full measure of human thought and expression. But that is not how language cognition begins. For the first year of life, babies hear language as an intentional and often repetitive vocal performance. They listen to it not only for its emotional content but also for its rhythmic and phonemic patterns and consistencies. As Newham says: "… whereas the verbal infant will later organize such sounds according to the rules of the dictionary, the baby, not yet familiar with such a scheme, arranges them according to an intuitive, creative, and innate sense of pitch, melody, and rhythm in a fashion directly akin to the composition of music."'

Brant, Gebrian & Slevc, Music and Early Language Acquisition (2012) [1]

The Italian researcher Johannella Tafuri's longitudinal study of babies' musical development, published in 2008 and translated by the London Professor Graham Welch, is nothing short of astonishing. Tafuri compared newborn babies who took part in a weekly music training class and whose parents were instructed to sing to their babies on a daily basis – as well as keep log of these activities – to babies who did not get this treatment, and found that the music babies developed vocalizations at a rate previously unimagined by developmental psychology researchers themselves. What is even more surprising is that these babies sang – they responded to mothers with singing-like sounds more often than had previously been assumed in research.[2] Based on her wealth of research, Tafuri found that 'even a child of six to eight months creates his/her little song, as we heard in some of the recordings. (...) Everyone, or perhaps we should say, most people, start of musically "gifted", that is to say, they possess "normal" genetic endowment for music. However, only those people who have been facilitated with a very positive and stimulating interaction with the environment, with education, and with many other factors including above all interest, are the ones who fully develop their potential skills'.[3]

Tafuri's research followed the musical development of children starting from their babyhood - more specifically, the music training started during the last trimester of pregnancy! Unsurprisingly, the babies became much more musically advanced than their peers in the control group.[4] But Gerry's study from 2012 is the pioneering study that shows that these musical skills, gained early on, have significantly wider effects beyond their blossoming musicality.[5] Little wonder as babies learn from singing at least as much as from speech if not more[6], and out of these they strongly prefer singing.[7]

It is interesting that the connection between singing and speech has not travelled from the academics to families. I myself would have loved to know about it when my son was just a baby so I could have made the most out of it. However, the midwives only emphasized talking to the baby and engaging with him in other ways than music. Music seemed optional, and as a sleep-deprived new mum, I sadly bought into their attitudes. I didn't know that such a simple thing as singing to your child and playing them vocal music from recordings would be so beneficial for their wellbeing – and the wellbeing of the parents too.

Edwyn E. Gordon remarks that in our culture, every parent places great emphasis on their baby's early attempts at talking but less so on their equally frequent attempts to sing and make music.[8] This is emphasized in how often babies get exposure to speech and how little to song. The first words are considered crucial landmarks on every parent's memory lane, and nursery caretakers place great emphasis on the small child's language development through words and speech. The focus on music is neglected, even though that would be at least as effective in developing a baby's language skills than speech.

Crucially, the most recent research has come to suggest that music could even be more important to the baby's brain than speech altogether, because it is through music that babies learn to distinguish components of speech.[9] In a recent (2012) overview of the wealth of studies so far, American neuroscientists Brandt, Gebrian and Slevc state that 'spoken language is introduced to the child as a vocal performance, and children attend to its musical features first. Without the ability to hear musically, it would be impossible to learn to speak. (...) Rather than describing music as a "universal language," we find it more productive from a developmental perspective to describe language as a special type of music in which referential discourse is bootstrapped onto a musical framework'.[10]

Along similar lines, Stephen N. Malloch from the Macarthur Auditory Research Centre in Sydney wrote already in 1999: 'A mother and her young baby are playfully interacting. We hear the mother speak in short bursts, talking in an inviting sing-song manner, and the baby occasionally "answers back". It appears that communication is taking place, but communication based in what? The baby cannot understand the meaning of the words the mother is using, and the baby often answers in "gliding-type" sounds. The communication must be "held" by means other than lexical meaning, grammar and syntax.' He describes a situation so familiar to all of us parents, yet precisely because of this familiarity we may easily regard the interaction as mundane or unnecessary. But Malloch examined the interaction between mothers and babies using computer-based analysis of their voices. His research found that 'communicative musicality is vital for companionable parent/infant communication.'[11]

Indeed, parents and other grown-ups naturally tend to interact with a baby in a 'musical' rather than a 'linguistic' way. It's easy to notice that all that cute cooing clearly gets a better response from even a newborn. The scientists have named this 'baby talk' *motherese* or, in the name of gender equality, *parentese*. Curiously, the rising and falling musical intonations stem from the very heart of music making, the root that like all other roots is often unseen: emotion. Malloch writes: 'Communicative musicality (...) is the vehicle which carries emotion from one [person] to another. When our ability to share emotions is impaired, it appears that the elements of communicative musicality change in ways that make them less "musical".' [12]

Malloch's analysis found that musicality stems from emotion. A year after his study, a group of scientists lead by Professor Laurel J. Trainor from the McMaster University in Canada made a discovery that I found incredibly enlightening. The scientists recorded and analyzed the speech of adults to each other and compared it with how they talked with babies. As was expected, the adult-to-adult speech was vastly less 'musical' whereas the speech directed at babies sounded exaggerated, more rhythmic and higher-pitched with a larger melody range in comparison. The surprising discovery was quite something else: when the scientists put the adults in situations where they were expressing emotion to each other, the sound analysis showed no difference from the baby-directed parentese. The researchers concluded that parentese itself 'is not special. What is special is the widespread expression of emotion to infants in comparison with the more inhibited expression of emotion in typical adult interactions'.[13] In other words, parentese doesn't actually exist – what exists is nothing more than emotional expression, whether it is directed at babies, your spouse, other adults or your dog and MacBook. It is just that we adults express emotion so rarely to other grown-ups that naturally parentese was thought to concern only the interaction with babies and other cute creatures.

Thus, the main gift of Music Miracle for your baby may not even be the fantastic advancements in speech, vocabulary and communication. Rather, it may provide crucial emotional stability, as shown by the aforementioned facts that babies prefer singing to speech and that when upset, they are better soothed by singing than any other means. As we will see in the Part Seven of the book, The Sense of Sensibility, music is the 'language' of emotion and this produces all the emotional benefits from a higher self-esteem to a better understanding of others' emotions.

But for the intellectual benefits alone, is amazing to see how little time and effort it takes for music to positively affect a baby's development. As Tafuri's research shows, the babies developed the language-related music abilities at a much more advanced level than the babies whose parents sang to them only sporadically. Yet the mothers in Tafuri's research were far from superhuman singers; many of them only managed to sing to their baby once or twice a week. Yet the results were astonishing. Perhaps crucially, the babies also attended an academically designed music education class every week and this early learning may have played and even more important part in their development of not only music, but its associated benefits. A little becomes a lot in early learning, as long as it is done on a consistent yet realistic basis.

Part Three
The Many Myths of Music Education

Something that immediately strikes the person who encounters the scientific study on music for the first time is how little accuracy the widespread, everyday myths about it contain. Real evidence can rip these commonly held beliefs to shreds in mere minutes, but most people have not been likely to come across the research unless they have specifically studied it.

As music is a widespread phenomenon in itself, it is understandable that everyone has opinions on some aspects of it. Contrast this with brain surgery or medieval history. Most people would not confidently profess to any view on these domains unless they knew they had acquired specific knowledge on them.

As opposed to those domains, music seems easily accessible. While its accessibility is crucial for humans, as we see in the following chapters, it also results in many popular myths related to it.

Before Galileo, the world was believed to be flat and the sun was considered to orbit the earth. Galileo's discovery was possible due to the development of technology, as the telescope allowed him to look into space. It has taken further centuries for us to develop the technology that allows scientists to see what is right inside of us – the brain imaging technologies.

Over the past ten to fifteen years of research, scientists have uncovered facts amidst the popular fiction relating to music. But outside the immediate academic world of music research, many highly educated people still believe that listening to Mozart can raise a child's IQ; that classical music is 'intelligent' and genres like alternative rock aren't; that listening to instrumental music improves intellectual tasks; and that only a selected amount of people have 'got what it takes' for musicality. We will investigate these myths in this part of the book.

One of the most widespread and harmful myths, of course, is the belief that music training is just a hobby with insignificant benefits; a option for the laid-back parent who naively thinks they can afford to spend resources on something besides hot-housing in the academic subjects of literacy, mathematics and science. The rest of the book, like its beginning, shows how you can use music as the scientifically proven key to unlock your child's full potential. But first, there are the hurdles we need to jump through: the misinformation on music that you are likely to have encountered and may even have, like the rest of us, been convinced to believe.

Chapter 10

The Culture Myth – Tuning into Human Nature

'Music is a biological adaptation, universal within our species, distinct from other adaptations, and too complex to have arise except through direct selection for some survival or reproductive benefit.'
Geoffrey R. Miller, Evolutionary Psychologist[1]

Despite being a musician, I had never though of music as anything other than a cultural, man-made phenomenon. I was surprised to find out that these days, scientists consider music as being deeply rooted in our biology.

And in the face of evidence, there is no reason why they wouldn't. Every human culture that has ever existed is known to have music as a central part.[2] New research has shown that even animals such as birds like to move themselves to the beat of music,[3] so it's not just humans who have musical ability: it is central to the biology of many a species. Even fireflies are found to show a consistent 'beat' with their flashing.[4] Thus, along with many other species, making music is biologically inherent to humans. Even though the style of music varies from culture to culture, the use of music in itself is a necessary phenomenon in our lives, one that has survived millions and millions of years of evolution.

Music from different cultures than one's own can often sound so unusual that it is easy to overlook the universality of the core component of music. Researchers Erin E. Hannon from Harvard University, US and Laurel J. Trainor from McMaster University, Canada write: 'Across all cultures, pitches whose fundamental frequencies stand in small integer ratios (e.g. octave, 2:1 ; perfect fifths, 3:2) form consonant intervals, and elicit more positive affective responses than pitches whose fundamental frequencies stand in more complex ratios (dissonances: e.g. tritone, 45:32)'.[5] The researchers note that the universal preference for consonance could be due to inborn mechanisms of the hearing system, as not only all humans but also many nonhuman animal species have a preference for consonant intervals.[6]

As a subtitle to those of us who haven't studied Music Theory with Physics, the researchers are saying that the pleasant-sounding notes that form music in all cultures are not random, but they represent regular physical relationships. Just like all right-angled triangles adhere to the Pythagorean Theorem, so do the melodies and accompaniments of all music share predictable relationships with one another. (The exception is noise music, the little-known genre of experimental music which deliberately breaks these musical laws. But as an illustrative consequence of breaking these laws, it really does sound like 'noise' and not 'music'.)

There is something almost magical in the fact that the physics of our world align with pleasant-sounding combinations of notes. Humans did not invent music. At best, they discovered it; it was already implied in the mechanics of our world.

Acclaimed brain researchers Anne J. Blood and Robert J. Zatorre from the Neurological Institute at the McGill University in Montreal found out in 2002 that listening to music activates the same reward mechanisms in the brain as food and sex, causing intense pleasure.[7] In other words, evolution has made our brains crave for music. The researchers note that hard drugs such as cocaine are so powerful because they also manipulate the same reward mechanisms.[8] We all know that hard drugs are addictive, and addictions for sex and food have become widely publicized, but why music?

This finding is rather more significant than simply finding out scientific evidence for the popular question of whether something is better than sex. The researchers of the study pointed out that these reward mechanisms in the brain that music, sex and food activate are the basis for evolutionary survival.[9] If the human brain didn't feel exceptional pleasure related to sex, we would have all stopped existing a long time ago. And if the brains of humans before us hadn't felt exceptional pleasure with regards to eating, it would have had the same effect. All human cultures, historical or present, no matter how different they are on the surface, have music as a central feature of life. Could music be as evolutionarily necessary for human survival as sex and food? And if so, why?

One possibly explanation could be, quite simply, survival of the fittest. Members of the human species would have had an evolutionary advantage with all the skills that the Music Miracle provides. A higher level of general intelligence as well as faster brain processing of stimuli[10] would have helped early humans perceive predators and other threats faster and more accurately. It would have also helped them find food. Spatial-temporal intelligence would have been crucial to making tools that would have helped humans to acquire food more efficiently.[11] A better memory would have helped them remember where food was found and what the signs of a previously experienced threatening situation were.[12] All of this would have contributed to better survival.

The founding father of modern biology himself, Charles Darwin, was inherently passionate about music and wrote that music 'gave me intense pleasure, so that my backbone would sometimes shiver'.[13] His wife Emma was a musician, and according to research by Julian Derry in the Institute of Evolutionary Biology at the University of

Edinburgh, music influenced at least two of Darwin's key evolutionary theories.[14] Naturally, Darwin was pondering what purpose music might have served to have survived as an essential component of the human species throughout evolution. His answer in 1871 was sexual selection: musical ability was a signal of higher reproductive fitness and humans made music because it attracted higher-fitness members of the opposite species to them.[15]

Darwin wrote his hypothesis over a century before the brain imaging technology was developed and the brain benefits of music making came into light. Sexual selection may surely play a part in the popularity of music making, as demonstrated by the teenage boys' sudden interest in grabbing the guitar and becoming a local rock star, as it is a common finding in 'How did you get started?' music interviews to hear a famous male performer say they initially just wanted to get 'chicks'. But this does not, according to the modern evidence, summarize the core biological importance of music making.

Biologists know that a wide variety of activities can be used as a means for improving one's chances for sexual selection (often unconsciously, of course, as we conveniently forget we are still an animal species). From all sorts of sports activities to intellectual games to visual arts, any kind of special ability could be equally argued to be a status signal to attract the opposite sex. So why, out of all activities, would music be a special ability to improve one's sexual selection? In my opinion, the sexual selection hypothesis becomes circular reasoning. Either everything humans do is a status display motivated by reproduction, or then music is an especially good way of attracting mates. If every activity is a status display, we have no explanation for the special place music has within the biology and evolution of human species. And if music is an especially efficient way of displaying status, we can only ask: why?

If we assume that Darwin was right, why would humans have been attracted especially to the musical abilities of the opposite sex rather than other activities? Why would music skills have been prioritized to survive as an inherent biological component of humans? Darwin himself wrote that music skills are a prime way of expressing total fitness.[16] According to Darwin, as music making involves abilities of rhythm, movement, voice control, voice aesthetics and complex coordination between different fingers and limbs, this is what made music such an all-round display of an individual's reproductive fitness.[17] But you could equally say that sports skills demonstrate all-round fitness, or any other complex skill that requires coordination, like juggling. It is rather that music skills, produce early on, *produce* all-round fitness for survival rather than *display* it for sexuality. This fitness relates more to the better survival of the individual than to the passing on of genes who cannot inherit any of these acquired music skills.

Now we know that musicality is inborn in all humans, and it is a matter of early exposure and life-lasting practice what makes musicality flourish (See Chapter 13 for more information). Our genetics have made us all musical, but it is our environment that determines how musically able we become. As skills are never be passed on to the offspring like genes are (as every individual has to go through their own skills learning from scratch), and as the Music Miracle can only happen in early childhood – years before the individual even enters adolescence and the reproductive age – my contention is that if Darwin was alive today and making his brain imaging discoveries, he may well have realized that sexual selection alone does not explain *why* music has such a special place in human evolution.

It is significant to remember that recording technology has only been available for a fraction of human history. Now we can get by putting on a record made by other musicians at another point in time. Little more than a hundred years ago, it wouldn't have been possible to listen to music without participating. If early humans wanted a brain high from music, they had to create it themselves by singing, playing an instrument or both.

Indeed, recent research from 2012 confirms this hypothesis. A study lead by R. I. M Dunbar from the University of Oxford found that it is the specific activity of *making* music that triggers the happy chemicals, endorphins, in the brain. Listening to music did not release endorphins, except in rare cases.[18] As we will see in the next chapter, these rare cases were likely due to the music selection happening to match the personal preference ('musical taste') of the test participant, and this is indeed what Blood and Zatorre had used to identify the stimulation of the reward centres. Whereas active music making produced endorphin release in practically every test subject in Dunbar's test, listening to music only did this sporadically.[19]

Even before the first primitive instruments were made, humans would have been able to make rhythms and beats with sticks, tree trunks or other elements of nature, or even just by clapping their hands. Research over the past ten years has shown a surprising link between rhythm skills and general intelligence[20] and handclapping skills in early childhood are associated with excellence in academic subjects years down the line, as just one evidence of higher intellectual ability.[21] In the chapters following this myth-busting part, we will discover more of these incredible benefits that each individual can gain from music training early on. But the full benefits only come to those who are not yet the initiators but the very recent end product of sexual selection: our children.

Chapter 11

The Mozart Myth: Why listening to a genius will not make your child one

With the help of modern technology, we now have the ability to stimulate our brain's reward mechanisms with music without any effort from our part. Unfortunately, music listening does not have the same brain-boosting effects as music learning.

The so-called Mozart Effect became a widely publicized media phenomenon in the 1990s. It started from a study in 1993 that showed that listening to Mozart before an IQ test raised the adults participants' IQ scores for 15 minutes.[1] Many similar scientific experiments soon followed, yet most of them couldn't replicate the Mozart Effect, and those follow-up studies that could were found to be incorrectly designed.[2]

The incorrectly designed research compared participants who listened to Mozart to participants who, as Glenn Schellenberg – the original discoverer of the full-scale IQ boost from early music training – notes, had to sit in awkward silence for 15 minutes before the test.[3] When compared with stimulus instead of silence, it was found that the Mozart Effect was due to something other than Mozart.

Indeed, it was found that listening to music boosts the mood rather than the brain. Enhancing mood, whether by listening to Mozart or the 90s chart-topper Mark Morrison, was shown to slightly increase intelligence test scores for a brief period of 10 to 15 minutes, but even then it only worked relatively to the control groups' conditions and what music each personally preferred.[4] The same mood-boosting effect was also created by playing the participants a Stephen King story before the test if they preferred Stephen King to Mozart – what Schellenberg sarcastically dubs 'The Stephen King Effect'[5] – or by simply giving the participants a sweetie treat just as they were about to take a cognitively loaded test.[6] Indeed, as Blood and Zatorre observed, music and food cause the same pleasure to the brain[7], and any mood boost is what causes people to perform better than they otherwise would.[8] However, this effect is short-lived, lasting only 10 to 15 minutes.[9]

Even though the Mozart Effect does not actually exist, the myth around it persists. When you mention music, children and intelligence in one sentence, many parents immediately think of playing classical recordings to their newborn. The irony is that it is often the best-educated parents who fall for the Mozart Effect myth. As an example, the 2012 bestselling parenting book 'French Children Don't Throw Food: Parenting Secrets from Paris' by Pamela Druckerman, writes: 'We play Mozart as background music constantly, because we've heard it will make her (Druckerman's baby) smarter'.[10] Unfortunately, listening to a genius composer does not a genius child make. This myth is yet another distraction for well-meaning, caring parents who would probably otherwise be signing their child up for music learning and get the scientifically proven brain boost for their little one.

Even the researcher Frances Rauscher from the original Mozart Effect study describes her horror at the media frenzy that ensued, and states: 'The original research report (...) received a disproportionate amount of attention from the popular press. To our horror, the finding has spawn a Mozart Effect industry which includes books, CDs, web sites and all manner of hyperbole. (...) Far from no one doubting it, there is no evidence for the claim at all that listening to classical music CDs improves children's spatial-temporal reasoning or any other aspect of intelligence (...) The scientific reports made no claims about general intelligence, SAT scores, or babies'.[11] Yet the initial media storm hit so hard that even the Georgia Governor Zell Miller made it compulsory for the state to send a CD of classical music to the household of every newborn child.

Many parents still think that listening to Mozart must benefit their child because of the highbrow status of classical music. But this myth isn't based on reality. Actually, studies have shown that listening to children's songs enhances the short-term creativity of small children, but classical music listening does not produce this type of creativity boost.[12] This result, of course, is also linked to the mood-boosting effect and the fact that most children prefer children's music to classical compositions. (The preference is not inborn, either, but due to musical enculturation, which we will discuss in Chapter 12.)

The Mozart Effect took a hit in 1996, when Susan Hallam from the University of London conducted an extensive experiment with the help of the BBC.[13] Over 8000 schoolchildren aged 10-11 were randomly placed in three groups in their classrooms, all listening to a different BBC channel before moving on to take a problem-solving test similar to the one used in the 1993 study that launched the concept of the Mozart Effect into fame. One channel played a Mozart sonata while the others played either a spoken conversation or three songs that were at the popular music charts at the time (the songs were 'Return of the Mack' by Mark Morrison, 'Stepping Stone' by PJ and Duncan, and 'Country House' by Blur).

When the test results came in, the researchers found that neither the Mozart composition nor the conversation had increased the intellectual capabilities of the schoolchildren, but the chart pop did. It wasn't Mozart that made children intelligent, it was 'The Return of The Mack'. The study report, called 'The Blur Effect', concluded that the cognitive benefits of listening to music were simply a manifestation of the happiness effect.[14] Indeed, in the control groups in the studies that have replicated the Mozart Effect, the participants were exposed to either sitting in silence for 15 minutes before the test – as Schellenberg noted, this has an effect of making the participants feel awkward and thus lowering their mood – or, rather more horrifyingly, to white noise, which sounds like fridge buzz magnified.[15]

Even in the early 2000s, I remember my mathematics teacher bringing in a CD player and playing classical music, telling us that it would improve our problem-solving abilities. It is thus ironic that since 2010, scientists have found that it is music with a drumbeat that activates babies. Listening to a drumbeat activates the babies to move rhythmically,[16] which in turn has been found to play a part in their intellectual development.[17] Dr Marcel Zentner from the prestigious University of York says: "Our research suggests that it is the beat, rather than other features of music, such as the melody, that produces the [rhythmic movement] response in infants."[18]

Yet the highbrow status of classical music persists in people's minds as intellectually superior to other music. Listening to classical music may be a shortcut to portray the image of an intellectual, but scientifically speaking, it has nothing to do with actual intelligence. In fact, a 2012 study from the London School of Economics, tentatively titled 'Why more intelligent individuals like classical music', actually found that people of higher IQs are as likely to equally prefer singer-songwriter music, jazz or even distortion-filled alternative rock such as Nirvana and the Sex Pistols as classical music.[19] (So much for the idiocy label that punk often gets!)

Similarly, it wasn't found that listening to any particular type of music would boost anyone's IQ. On the contrary, the researchers Kanazawa and Perina concluded that high-IQ people are more likely to understand more 'evolutionary novel' types of music and thus be more likely to have a preference for them. That said, the study found that high-IQ people are as likely to also appreciate simple chart pop music as anyone else.[20] To appreciate a musical genre, one must be able to understand it, but understanding a genre does not yet imply a liking for it. And no amount of appreciation can magically turn a genre, no matter how 'cultivated', into a shortcut that boosts your – or your child's – brain by simply listening to it.

Background music or music background

In the Mozart Effect studies, people listened to music *before* taking an intellectually challenging test. But how about listening to classical music *while* taking a test?

Contrary to popular belief, research has found that background music does not enhance intellectual performance. The effect is quite the opposite.

Studies have found that any kind of background music, even when it is on a low level of volume, significantly disrupts performance.[1] Granted, music with vocals such as pop music and opera is even more disruptive than instrumental music such as a concerto or a film score because the brain is wired to give even more attention to the human voice than other instruments.[2] But both are detrimental to the brain's working memory, which is the short-term memory that is needed to hold and analyze mental information.[3] Even when a person is not focusing on the music on a conscious level, their brain takes it in, which in turn uses up the brain's short-term memory resources.[4]

However, as we will see in Chapter 36, the Music Miracle significantly improves working memory, allowing the brain to hold larger amounts of information more accurately at any one time. Ironically, music learning also protects from the detrimental effects of background noise.[5] It is clear that we must engage in music learning instead of simply music listening to gain the brain-boosting benefits. Even with the Music Miracle there's no such thing as a free lunch, but at least music produces the same happiness effect as one's favourite food.

Chapter 12

When Listening Helps: The four exceptions

There are a few cases when the mere act of listening to music can be said to have extra-musical benefits.

Early Enculturation

Edwin E. Gordon notes that during the first year of a child's life, listening to different types of music is crucial in order to build the baby's 'musical vocabulary'. Gordon does not mean that a child should listen to different genres, such as classical, chart pop and children's music. Instead, he talks about the importance of exposing the baby to conceptually more varied songs and compositions, no matter what the genre.[1]

Gordon essentially has put to words what any parent with a musical background soon observes in a mummy-and-baby sing-along group. All the children's songs are composed in the common time (the 4/4 time signature) and in the major key, following a common misconception that babies only understand simplified music. This presumption is commonly seen in many Western baby products, and, on closer look, it implies a patronizing misunderstanding of a very young child's real brain capacity.

This misunderstanding is especially ironic if the product claims to be educational. Research on infants has shown that babies understand complex music as well as or better than adults. The same applies to language: babies benefit from hearing complex language and they can even learn two or three separate mother tongues. I once met two preschool-aged boys in Edinburgh whose mother was Finnish, father was French and the language in their daycare was English, with the result that these boys, aged only three and five, fluently spoke three languages.

Studies show that children who only have one mother tongue benefit from hearing more complex vocabulary in their parents' and caregivers' speech as well as in books, poems and songs. Research has found that all babies vocalize about 150 times an hour up until the age of 36 months – after this, their levels of vocalization start to resemble that of their parents' vocabulary and its complexity more than any general developmental guidelines, for better or worse.[2]

Within music, neuroscientists Lauren Stewart and Vincent Walsh from University College London report that based on current studies, very young babies understand complex rhythms equally well as simple ones.[3] Yet, babies measured after the age of seven months had generally lost the ability to understand complex rhythms.[4] However, babies who regularly hear music with complex rhythms manage to completely retain this ability.[5] This is scientific evidence for what Gordon has been arguing for decades: that babies and children are in danger of 'music abuse' when they are not given the proper tools to develop their blossoming musical potential.[6]

Babies understand and benefit from complexity, but do they enjoy it? Surprisingly, studies on infants show that at least in the domain of music, small babies enjoy complex music even more than most slightly older children.[7] This is due to the phenomenon called *enculturation*. Newborns and small babies are open to all musical influences and enjoy all music genres as well as all levels of musical complexity equally. For instance, it has been found that even though the understanding of rhythm is inborn, the preference for the common 4/4 time isn't. It is a result of repeated exposure.[8]

The power of early enculturation. My dad was a true fan of 60s music, and the music of Elvis was always played in my childhood home. Even as a baby, my Dad would ask 'where's Elvis', to which I had learned to respond by pointing at Elvis' profile on the wall, as shown in this picture. Obviously, I still believe Elvis is the King of Rock.

Ironically, some music classes for babies have been shown to limit small children's musical preferences. A study found that the children that had gone to one popular baby music franchise that focuses on the simple duple-metre of 4/4 (and its sibling, the march beat 2/2) preferred this simple rhythm to more complex ones even sooner than babies who hadn't gone to any music classes. They had less of an ability to engage even in another core musical metre, the 3/4 (which is commonly referred to as 'waltz beat').[9] This points out the importance of introducing different time signatures in early music training – especially the waltz beat which is the second-most common time signature in classical and popular music alike.

Yet, in early childhood, a child's musical tastes are still forming. One study compared two randomly selected groups of kindergarteners, one of which played musical games to classical music once a week for 10 months while the other group did not participate in this. Before the experiment began, all the children enjoyed classical music as much as popular music. However, at the end of the study, only those children who were in the classical music listening group still maintained their equally distributed preference. The children who had not been exposed to classical music now liked it significantly less. Both groups of children liked popular music equally.[10]

Again, the preference for classical music does not make anyone more intelligent. Yet this example shows the incredible openness of small children to adapt to any forms of culture that they are given access to, whether simple or complex. By this I don't mean to imply that classical music is complex and popular music is simple, as many forms of popular music such as singer-songwriter music and alternative rock can easily be musically more complex than many standards by Bach and Mozart. A sample of Tori Amos' albums such as *Boys for Pele* (1993) and *From the Choirgirl Hotel* (1998) demonstrate this poignantly, as well as Ken Stringfellow's albums *Soft Commands* (2003) and *Danzig in the Moonlight* (2012).

The finding that our musical tastes are largely based on what we are familiarized with in childhood may be rather surprising for parents to hear. Studies show that family enculturation is astonishingly influential, as the musical tastes of parents successfully predict the musical tastes of their offspring. Even in adolescence, when teenagers are seemingly drawn to preferences of their peers over those of their parents, science shows that teenagers in fact favour their parents' musical taste over that of their peers.[11]

I did not know this. Yet, in the light of research it seems obvious that my teenage obsession with 90s Britpop was a continuation of my Dad's constant playing of the Beatles and the Kinks during my baby and toddler years. As for American music, I have never found anything to surpass Elvis. I received training for this from a young age. There's a picture of me laying on my tummy on the living room floor as a 6-month-old baby, holding my arm up and pointing to the Elvis memorial plaque on the wall, in response to my Dad's question, 'Where's Elvis?'

Conversely, even as a child it felt alien to play classical piano, as it never was a type of music I had heard much. It could be safely assumed that my parents would have been more successful in motivating me to play classical piano if they had played more classical music in the household. Apart from some occasional Mozart or Tchaikovsky, our household environment was taken over by popular music of my Dad's generation, and while I have been successfully indoctrinated into believing that it is the best type of music, I now know that it this is likely to be a consequence of early enculturation.

In this sense, a parent wishing for their child to play classical music would be wise to introduce classical music into the household early on. In this indirect way, it will help in learning the classical genre. On another hand, regardless of whether you have a preference for classical music, listening to music with a drum beat is crucial for your child right from babyhood, as scientists have found that without a rhythmic accompaniment, the music does not promote the rhythmic movement of your child[12], the importance of which has been strongly linked to academic and intellectual success.[13] We will further examine the surprising link between rhythm and intelligence in Chapters 17-19.

Songs as learning tools

Whereas listening to music, classical or popular, does not produce educational benefits as such, songs as learning methods tell a different story. Studies have found that learning through songs is one of the best educational methods available.

Listening to songs in a foreign language helps a child learn that language better, particularly with extending their vocabulary and learning grammar rules.[1] One 2008 study from the Mediterranean Cognitive Neuroscience Institute concluded that '(...)the present results show that learning a new language, especially in the first learning phase wherein one needs to segment new words, may largely benefit of the motivational and structuring properties of music in song'.[2] This knowledge has even spread to mainstream education to some degree for more than a decade now, as I remember that my English language books in my last school years suddenly featured interesting pop songs in them. Even before that, I was just one example of the many non-native speakers who had learned their English from pop songs, to the point where I drove my English teacher insane by achieving an A+ in every exam despite refusing to do homework.

It turns out that songs are one of the best methods for teaching just about any subject imaginable, from science and mathematics to history and political science.[3] Songs have even been shown to help school-aged children to master educational content better to the equivalent degree of gaining an additional 10 to 15 IQ points in the subjects that have been taught through songs.[4] This is separate from the permanent, full-scale IQ increase that music learning produces and is restricted only to the subjects where songs are used as teaching methods. Nevertheless, it shows that learning through songs gives a child or student an unprecedented advantage in mastering whichever subject is being taught.

I experienced this at the age of fifteen when I got my hands on the album *The Holy Bible* by the Manic Street Preachers, a little-known piece of work compared to their later hit albums. The lyrics of *The Holy Bible* consist of an overwhelming amount of references to the history of the past century, from the Second World War and the Holocaust to 20th century dictatorships, American politics and Thatcherism. The album changed my non-existent interest in the subject of history overnight, to the point where I seriously contemplated studying political history at university in order to write songs as great as those on *The Holy Bible*, whose lyricists Richey James Edwards and Nicky Wire both had history degrees. The vibrant music did what none of my history teachers had ever achieved or even attempted to. It often seemed like they found their subject uninspiring, and their pupils picked up on the vibe. But studies show that this effect of songs is not just my personal observation and can be used to perk up any student's interest in any topic.

Even before I became an anguished teenager who found solace in listening to *The Holy Bible* and its grim details of what the historians have widely described as the most destructive era of human history, I had a personal tradition of making up songs based on whatever I needed to master to succeed in a school exam. At age 11, I made songs on geography, as the subject did not motivate me and I needed to get a top grade to get my parents off my back. I succeeded, and continued to write songs whenever I needed to learn something new in a hurry. My invention of composing songs to teach music theory, which eventually led to the birth of the Moosicology method, was based on this experience that songs made everything easier and more tolerable to learn. I used to loathe music theory above everything, and in this I was no different from most students.

With the birth of my son, I took on the challenge of making music theory exciting through specifically composed songs. It has been lovely to receive feedback from children all around the world who have become enthusiastic music students with the Moosicology Package.

The health benefits of listening to music

Science has shown that listening to music has health benefits from reducing pain in childbirth[1] to helping stroke victims to faster recovery.[2] It is also commonly used for mood regulation, helping us to unwind and relax in stressful circumstances and lifting our energy levels when we need to perk up, focus, and put in our best efforts.

For babies born prematurely, listening to music has especially significant health benefits. A study found that babies who are hear music in their neonatal intensive care units are able to leave approximately three days earlier than babies who do not get to hear music.[3] Staying at the intensive care units is highly stressful for newborn babies, and music is found to be a significant remedy for the emotional and developmental problems that premature babies are at risk for.[4]

As a mood regulator, listening to music occupies the top space in effectiveness alongside exercise – even above socializing and resting.[5] These effects are immediate, but they are dose-dependent. As music is highly enjoyable to listen to, this is hardly a task: it is emotionally worthwhile even if it doesn't increase IQ or test performance.

The most successful emotional benefits always come from listening to music we personally enjoy, as Schellenberg and his colleagues found when debunking the the Mozart Effect.[6] And research from the University of Oxford has recently revealed that making music produces much more endorphins than passive listening, except when one listens to their own favourite music.[7]

Music as a form of beneficial entertainment

We live in an era of fast-paced entertainment. Even though listening to music, as such, does not boost your child's intelligence, it is unique in that it does not decrease your child's brain activity either. In fact, studies have found that listening to music helps children self-regulate; it helps them calm down or energize depending on the chosen music, helps children become more focused and enhances their happiness and creative imagination.[1] Listening to music regularly at home in childhood is also linked to a better emotional understanding of music[2] and a better singing ability[3], contributing individually to the Music Miracle outside direct music training.

Compared to many other activities born out of today's technological advancements, listening to music does not produce an over-stimulation of the senses. Instead, it encourages concentrated listening. This is opposed to TV, video and computer games, the excessive use of which has been linked to attention-deficit disorders in children - a growing phenomenon in our times.[4]

Excessive video watching during the first years of life has been found to decrease the language development of babies and toddlers, especially when the videos have consisted of non-educational entertainment. A 2007 study from the University of Washington found that for babies up to 16 months old, each hour per day of viewing baby DVDs or videos corresponded to a significant additional language delay as measured by a standardized vocabulary test. The results showed that reading to a child once a day added an additional 7-point increase, but one hour of video watching produced a 17-point *decrease*: thus, the effects of video watching were two-and-a-half times as harmful to the baby's language development as the effects of daily reading were positive.[5] Another study from the University of Virginia (2011) has found that just nine minutes of watching a fast-paced cartoon – as opposed to the control groups in which children either watched an educational programme or did drawing for the same amount of time – caused the children to perform significantly worse afterwards on tests related to working memory and the all-important self-regulation.[6] Excessive TV-watching has also been found to cause behavioural problems and aggression in small children.[7]

In contrast to this, music consumption provides a safe form of entertainment. The University of Washington study on children's entertainment found no delay in language for babies or older children when they listened to music.[8] If parents want to have a much-deserved break from constantly attending to a small child, putting on music is a great way of entertaining the child in a way that doesn't intervene with the young brain's development.

Chapter 13

Musicality, the X Factor and the Biggest Myth of All

Possibly the biggest myth that hinders people of all ages from making music is the belief in a special kind of innate talent, a belief which claims that only *some* people are naturally musical. Popular talent shows such as the X Factor have made it easy for people to claim that the unsuccessful performers have no musical talent, are tone-deaf or have got no rhythm. It's even more tragic when you hear parents saying that they'd like their child to take up music but their child lacks musicality.

Nothing could be further from the truth. Just as our brains are wired to crave for music, they also possess the ability to create it. Musicality is something that is encoded deep into all of our brains. Most music educators have long held this opinion, but the recent findings of brain research should dispense the musicality myth once and for all.

Current brain research has shown that newborn babies' brains already differentiate between notes that are in tune or out of tune with each other – and that they, without exception, prefer the music that is in tune.[1] (The same preference for musical harmony has been found in baby chimpanzees[2] and even newly-hatched chickens.[3]) We are all born able to hear when we're out of tune, which is the prerequisite for learning to sing in tune.

Newborn humans also detect the beat in music, so rhythmic ability is not something that only some people can develop, but it is for everyone who chooses to use it.[4] Every human is born with the innate ability understand and create music.

Research has found that children only gradually gain the physical ability to sing in tune, due to the development of the coordination of vocal folds and breathing.[5] At age seven, roughly a third of children (30%) still sing out of tune.[6] But what is striking is that many children are deemed unmusical before they have even reached their fifth birthday and thus never get the chance to do the practice in the first place.

Contrast this with speech, where five-year-old children commonly mispronounce sounds and words. My son still calls yellow 'lellow' and useful 'looseful'. Pronunciation difficulties clearly run in the family, as I only learned to pronounce the Finnish 'r' sound (which sounds like blowing raspberries with your tongue instead of your lips) at the age of nine after a year of speech therapy. Regardless of language, speech deficits are common in small children, yet it would be unheard of to deem a child unable to speak if they haven't yet mastered all the sounds of their native tongue during the first five years – or even ten. The words 'musical' and 'unmusical' are commonly used, whereas there is not even an equivalent word for 'unmusical' when it comes to speech, indicating that we expect all children to eventually learn the correct sounds of their mother tongue.

Another sadly commonly used term is 'tone-deaf', which is commonly given to children who have not yet learned to sing in tune. 'Tone-deafness' is used to imply that the person is beyond remedy, whereas in the case of speech impediments the child is quickly guided into speech therapy.

Thus, we are all born musical, and an early exposure to music significantly increases this universal gift. A longitudinal study by Johannella Tafuri published in 2008 found a significant difference in the early development of musicality between babies and toddlers who were exposed to a weekly music class and the same-age control group who weren't.[7] Similar results were found in the 2012 study *Active music classes in infancy enhance musical, communicative and social development* by Canadian researchers Gerry, Unrau and Trainor who also found that the music training improved not only the musicality but also the communication and social abilities of the babies.[8]

As for the opposite cases, a group of leading music researchers from my home country Finland have studied a phenomenon called *musical restriction*. The research has found that people can become unable to enjoy or express music after early criticism by family members or teachers for their supposed lack of musicality.[9] The researchers note that 'the restrictedness seems to arise early in childhood. They write: 'It is especially traumatic because the experience does not necessarily have anything to do with real musical abilities; sometimes it is even evident that among this group there are also exceptionally talented and sensitive individuals who will carry this permanent emotional restriction all their life'. The researchers also point out that music instruction in itself can cause musical restriction if the teaching style has been overtly critical or humiliating.[10]

Another line of research in the 21st century concerns the condition called amusia, which is presented as a learning deficit for musicality. Amusia is estimated to occur in 3% or less of the adult population, but what is not clear is whether it is a genuine neurological deficit that some people are born with or whether it is a result of inadequate exposure to music. After all, none of the newborns that have been studied have exhibited amusia, and as we remember, they are even more capable of understanding complex rhythms than they will be at the age of eight months, unless they get regular exposure to them. What is clear is that the musicality myth is responsible for the less-than-optimal musical ability of many children and adults alike.

It is indeed a vicious circle and one that Graham Welch, Professor of Music Education from the University of London, describes with clarity in his concise book *The Misunderstanding of Music*. Welch points out that 'the limiting conception of humankind as either musical or non-musical is untenable. The neuropsychobiological research evidence indicates that everyone is musical, assuming normal anatomy and physiology. Moreover, everyone is likely to be uniquely musical. (...) Adults (and children) who have labelled themselves as "non-singers" and "tone-deaf" have been shown to improve and develop enhanced singing skills in an appropriate educational setting'. Welch ends his book in the statement: 'We are all musical; we just need the opportunity'.[11]

Another leading music educator, Edwin E. Gordon, who invented the music aptitude test commonly used by educators in American schools, states that most small children suffer from what he calls 'music abuse' – the lack of parental interest in developing their children's musicality which, in his view, harms the children's development in ways that can never be compensated for. Gordon contrasts the music abuse with the enthusiasm which most parents share when it comes to supporting their young child's language and speech development.[12]

Gordon, like the majority of music educators, states that children have a right to learn music for music's sake and he isn't too keen to bring up the benefits to the child's overall development outside the area of music. Whilst I also believe that every child has a right to learn music even if it didn't have any brain benefits, one could equally argue that all children deserve to develop their ballet or professional sports skills, which need to be started young in order to make the most of them. Tiger Woods started playing golf in his nappies because his father was a golf enthusiast. Are the rest of us suffering from golf abuse because we weren't given the chance to develop our golf potential?

In my view, music is special in its own right, but as much as I have devoted my life to music, I cannot see how musicality alone could, without any of its outside benefits, become something as widely encouraged as language development. No other subcategory of the human species is busier than the parent of a small child, so for parents to know that early music experience is a brain-boosting tool and not just a nice little extra-curricular and optional skill, could be what makes all the difference in whether our children get musical education at all. Most parents have their children's best interests at heart, and once they know about how they can transform their child's life with music, my guess is that fewer children would have to experience what Gordon calls music abuse and miss out on developing their potential.

It is also worth noting that although musical instruction is required for the brain benefits to occur, developing a musically healthy child as opposed to a musically restricted one requires no effort from the parent apart from the awareness that their child, like all children, is inherently musical. The lack of this awareness, although prevalent in our culture, is emotionally damaging. Studies on the musically restricted have found that they suffer anxiety and shame related to occasions where music or group singing is present.[13] This, in turn, has put them off musical activities for life.[14] As music is omnipresent in our society, this causes them unnecessary emotional and social harm.

One could argue that the brain upgrade effects of early music learning prove that children should be required to have music education even if they don't go on to become a professional musicians. (In fact, this is the philosophy behind the nationwide popularity of Musiikkileikkikoulu in Finland.) Music is obviously valuable in its own right – but so is ballet, street dance, graphic design, philosophy and anything else that could be included into the early years' curriculum. The options can be overwhelming, and it can be difficult to feel like we're giving our child the best without also feeling like we're forcing them in a specific direction. In the next part of the book, we will look more in detail at the wide-ranged brain-boosting results of early music learning. It becomes clear that if we truly want to unlock our children's hidden brain potential, there is one and only one activity that is capable of it all; the 'master key' to all talents.

Part Four

IQ or Multiple Intelligences? Music learning boosts them all

Music training for the young brain is like building motorways where dirt tracks would be. This allows information to travel faster back and forth between the brain cells.[1] As common sense would expect, this results in faster thinking ability.[2] It is thus not that surprising, after all, that early music training boosts the IQ – unlike any other activity. And this IQ boost alone is hugely significant.

As elusive as the quality of intelligence may sound, IQ (intelligence quotient) tests as a measure of intelligence are widely regarded as the most accurate and reliable tests that the field of psychology has ever produced.[3] Every additional IQ point is shown to significantly improve not only the school and career success of an individual, but also many other important life outcomes, leading to a statistically healthier and longer life, even when the effect of a higher income is accounted for. A systematic review on the links between IQ scores and the longevity of one's life from 2007 found that 'in all studies, higher IQ in the first two decades of life was related to lower rates of total mortality in middle to late adulthood. (...) Risk for death increased in the lower IQ scoring groups.'[4] Scientists have theorized that the better life and health outcomes related to higher IQs stem from the better capacity and motivation of higher-intelligence individuals to look after their health.[5]

IQ even affects financial wealth, as a 2007 study from the Ohio State University on over 7000 people of varying IQs points out: '(...) each point increase in IQ test scores raises income by between $234 and $616 per year after holding a variety of factors constant.' The researcher Jay L. Zagorsky writes: 'For example, two individuals with similar characteristics except for a 10-point IQ difference would have between $3500 and $6100 a year income difference. (...) This represents between a 9,7% and 17% difference.'[6] In the light of the IQ boost we're about to talk about, it looks like the financial investment into music training pays itself back every year with interest!

In this part of the book, we will look at how early music learning significantly increases your child's chances for happiness and health by substantially raising their IQ. We will also look at the groundbreaking work of Dr. Howard Gardner's Multiple Intelligences framework and see how music learning unlocks your child's true potential on every one of its eight domains of intelligence.

Chapter 14

IQ: Why it matters and how to raise it

Raising your child's IQ is no small feat. Every additional IQ point is shown to increase a person's life expectancy[1] and decrease the likelihood for health problems, from cancer to cardiovascular diseases.[2] In other words, it is the best way to increase your child's statistical likelihood of a longer and healthier life. An above-average IQ also predicts better performance on cognitively complex tasks, from banking to map reading and from interpreting news articles to career success.[3]

If raising the IQ is crucial, the bad news is that it is practically impossible to do. Longitudinal studies that measured people's IQ at different stages of life found that IQ, relative to age, does not change after the age of seven.[4] This means that if your child is of average intelligence at the age of seven, they will remain average intelligence for the rest of their lives. On the other hand, if you can boost your child's IQ and make them above average or even gifted, this intelligence increase will also last for the rest of their lives.

IQ points are not to be confused with percentage points. The difference between a person of normal intelligence (or, in the somewhat less flattering terms of IQ research, 'a person of average intelligence') and a person of exceptionally high, Mensa-level intellect is only 30 points, with the respective scores of 100 and 130 IQ points. The person of an IQ of 101 is statistically more likely to have better life outcomes than a person of an IQ of 100, who in turn have better outcomes than a person whose IQ is 99. Thus, when it comes to IQ, every point matters.

It is not known exactly how IQ is formed. The heritability of IQ is not straightforward as as there can be plenty of variation within family members. It is a curious combination of genetic and environmental factors, most of which yet elude scientific certainty. But some factors that affect IQ have been profoundly researched, and I have tried to bring them all together in this chapter to the best of my ability.

Most of the known IQ-affecting factors need to take place in the womb or shortly after. And most of them involve *not doing* something rather than *doing* it. These IQ-related risks are generally things that most parents avoid anyway simply based on common sense. For instance, by avoiding your fetus' exposure to alcohol, you're saving them up to an additional five IQ points.[5] By not beating up or sexually abusing your child, you are saving them from, along with the obvious psychological trauma, a decrease of eight IQ points.[6] Lead poisoning also affects the IQ by a decrease of 4.6 points per 10 micrograms of lead per deciliter in the blood.[7] Likewise, a factor that radically decreases a child's natural IQ is the kind of childhood malnutrition that is tragically commonplace in many developing countries.[8]

Breastfeeding during babyhood was previously shown to add up to three IQ points to a person's intelligence, an amount that the researchers considered alone to have remarkable effects for a person's life.[9] More recently, some studies have found no IQ effect from breastfeeding,[10] whereas others have found up to an incredible 7-point increase for children who have a particular gene that responds to the fatty acids in breastmilk.[11]

However, early music learning can boost any child's IQ by an incredible 7.5 points, when started young and continued for six years.[12] Less than a year of music training alone gives your child over three more IQ points than they would otherwise have.[13] This is significant not only for your child's intelligence, but for all the important life outcomes that each additional IQ point offers. As you may have noticed, the other IQ-boosting factors relate to nutrition and the avoidance of toxins and alcohol. Some of these factors cannot be helped – there are many mothers who would want to breastfeed but are not able to; and not all babies are born with the genes that, inconjunction with breastmilk, produce an IQ boost. But music training, started early on, is available for every child, and so is the IQ increase within it. In this sense, it is the most democratic of the brain nutrients.

Chapter 15

Building IQ

We know that the brain boost from music education strengthens neural connections in the entire brain, giving children multiple advantages throughout life. This musically-enhanced brain also processes information more efficiently. Indeed, when scientists have studied the relationship between music and neural processing of information, they have found that music learning makes the brain process information faster and more accurately.[1]

Alongside with general brain efficiency,[2] IQ is linked to both the brain's general volume[3] and the individual volume independent of the general brain volume of parts such as the corpus callosum[4] and the cerebellum.[5] The size differences between brains are an indication of the neural connections, and as we have seen, most of these are formed during the earliest years. Scientists have found that the brain volume does not change much after the age of five[6] and the IQ order does not change after the age of seven,[7] so in order to be effective, an IQ boost needs to take place before that.

As we remember from Gottfried Schlaug's study on the corpus callosum, musicians who had started playing an instrument before or during the age of seven had thicker corpus callosums, but the brain bridges of those who started playing after the age of 7 did not differ substantially from people who had never played an instrument in their lives.[8]

Indeed, a study from 2011 that measured the spatial-temporal IQ of children, some of whom were randomly selected to learn music at different early ages, found that those who started learning before seven increased their IQs and mathematical reasoning skills significantly, but those who started after 7 failed to get the IQ increase.[9] In other words, there is a critical age for children to gain the IQ benefits. We have discussed the biological and physiological reasons for this in the Chapters 5 and 6.

Here, parents may face a slight dilemma. It is much easier to find suitable music instruction for a child who is at least seven or older than it is for a younger one. Yet the younger you start, the bigger benefits you gain. Previous research has shown that children who studied music at three succeeded better in intelligence-related tasks than those who trained at 4, who in turn succeeded better than those who only started at 5, even when they all trained for the same amount of time (one year).[10]

Chapter 16

IQ Controversy: One or multiple intelligences? Music learning boosts them all

The tradition of IQ testing has its beginnings in the late 19th and early 20th century. Although there are several widely used IQ tests, some of which are based on spatial-visual intelligence, some on mathematical intelligence and some verbal, already in 1904 Charles Spearman observed that the results of the tests tended to correlate with each other. In other words, it was found that when one person scored well in one of the tests, they scored well in others, and vice versa. This gave rise to the concept of 'g', general intelligence, also known as 'Spearman's g'. To this day, a wide range of leading psychologists consider intelligence tests as the most reliable tests that the field of psychology has produced.[1]

Nevertheless, IQ testing has its critics. In 1985, Howard Gardner published his book Frames of Mind, which presented the theory of Multiple Intelligences to the world. This theory soon became famous amongst scholars and the wider public, and it even affected some school policies worldwide, although Gardner himself and other Multiple Intelligence followers have pointed out that many of these reforms have gone against not only common sense but the basic principles of the theory itself.[2] Thus, whilst Gardner's theory has been widely acclaimed by educators, the school system at large has not yet adapted to it in practice.

What are the basic principles of the Multiple Intelligences theory, then? In short, Gardner criticizes the general intelligence view of its narrow view of human abilities and achievement. Instead, he theorizes that there are at least eight or nine different intelligences which all require their own separate sets of abilities. He hypothesises that they depend on separate brain neural networks.[3]

Gardner emphasizes that he does not endorse any kind of test of Multiple Intelligences as this would go against his whole reason for formulating the theory in the first place. He says that the school system focuses too narrowly on only two types of intelligences – logical-mathematical and linguistic – ranking children according to those abilities alone, leaving the rest of the children feeling unsuccessful while they might have excellence in another type of intelligence, if given the chance to explore them.[4] As we have already seen with the discussion regarding the musicality myth, there is vast evidence that most children are simply not given the chances to develop to their potential with regards to their natural talents.

Howard Gardner's Multiple Intelligences

Linguistic intelligence: The ability to uncover the meanings of spoken and written language as well as to use it to express oneself effectively. This ability is the most highly valued skill within the school system, alongside logical-mathematical intelligence, and a high level of it is required for various professions that require writing or speaking, such as being a journalist, author, lawyer or speaker.[5]

Logical-mathematical intelligence: The ability to reason logically and solve mathematical and other problems. According to Gardner, this ability is highly valued in the school system, as reasoning and mathematics form the core of the school curriculum alongside with linguistic intelligence. A high level of logical-mathematical intelligence is required for various professions such as those related to science, mathematics, philosophical argumentation and computer programming.[6]

Musical intelligence: The ability to compose, perform and understand music. A high level of this ability is required for music-related professions.[7] Hence, it is regarded by many people as something rather specific that most children do not need to engage in developing unless their parents have high ambitions for them in that specific field. The central theme of this book, of course, is that far from being something that only a few selected children should benefit from, musical ability developed at an early age has crucial repercussions that unlock the incredible brain potential stored in every child.

Bodily-kinesthetic intelligence: The ability to coordinate the body or its parts in contexts such as sports, dance or performance. A high level of bodily-kinesthetic intelligence is seen, for instance, in athletes, dancers, choreographers and performing artists.[8]

Spatial-visual intelligence: The ability to understand space, for instance in contexts such as using maps, navigating by the position of stars, designing three-dimensional objects or playing chess. The professions that require a high level of spatial-visual intelligence include architects, interior designers, engineers and chess masters.[9]

Interpersonal intelligence. Interpersonal means 'between persons', and thus the interpersonal intelligence concept is practically indistinguishable from the concept of emotional intelligence that came into popularity in the early 1990s, no doubt partially influenced by Gardner's earlier detection of this type of intelligence. Both concepts (intrapersonal and emotional intelligence) deal with the ability to understand and interpret other people's emotions, as well as one's own, as shown in the intrapersonal intelligence below.[10]

Intrapersonal intelligence. Intrapersonal means 'within the person'. Gardner defines this type of intelligence as 'knowledge of the internal aspects of a person: access to one's own feeling life, one's range of emotions, the capacity to make discriminations among these emotions and eventually to label them and to draw on them as a means of understanding and guiding one's own behaviour'. As with interpersonal intelligence, the intrapersonal intelligence is largely included in the post-Gardner concept of emotional intelligence. Gardner writes: 'Since this (intrapersonal) intelligence is the most private, evidence from language, music, or some other more expressive form of intelligence is required if the observer is to detect it at work'.[11]

Naturalistic intelligence: An understanding of nature, its organisms and the relationships between them. A high level of this type of intelligence is seen, for example, in biologists, ornithologists, farmers and gardeners. Gardner mentions Charles Darwin as a prime example of this intelligence, as his keen understanding and observation of nature is what lead him to develop the theory of evolution.[12]

Along with these eight intelligences, Gardner has also hypothesised that there could be a ninth intelligence, an 'existential intelligence' which deals with higher-order thinking related to the existential concerns of humans or the cosmological questions related to the universe. A high level of the existential intelligence is often found in such professions as scientists and philosophers as well as novelists and others who deal with abstract and complex theories related to the existence of humans and the universe.[13]

The Multiple Intelligences theory has been criticized on the fact that it is not testable and doesn't have solid, provable facts behind it like the general intelligence tests do.[14] Gardner has explicitly announced that his theory doesn't depend on its empirical validity. He says that if intelligences would be tested, they should be tested intelligence-fairly, meaning that intelligences such as the bodily-kinesthetic or interpersonal should not be tested with pen and paper but instead in their natural environment such as on the dance floor (in the case of bodily-kinesthetic intelligence) or with a group of people (interpersonal intelligence).[15]

Mihalyi Csikszentmihalyi, one of the world's leading psychologists, says that 'if [Gardner's] manifesto were heeded, the future of our children would benefit immensely'.[16] As we have seen in the case of musical ability, it's all too easy to judge that some people just don't have talent for something, when they in fact have never been given the fair chance to develop it in the first place.

At the same time, it is important to add that while we may have multiple intelligences and separate neural networks, at the end of the day each of us has only one brain. And many higher forms of intelligence, as well as creativity, depend upon how well information can travel across different neural networks.

For instance, rhythm skills, a crucial component of Gardner's musical intelligence, correlate with the kind of logical-mathematical and visuospatial intelligences that IQ tests measure.[17] Motor skills correlate with rhythm skills,[18] so this connects the realm of bodily-kinesthetic intelligence to musical intelligence as well as general intelligence. As music and language share largely the same neural networks,[19] so do the musical and linguistic intelligences share an obvious connection. We will see in the Chapters 22–25 how the past ten years of research have made it apparent that language abilities and verbal IQ correlate with musical ability – and how the standard measurement for linguistic intelligence, verbal IQ, can significantly be raised with early musical learning.

From the scientific evidence, it becomes clear that the Music Miracle boosts all of the multiple intelligences that Gardner has identified:

The Music Boost for Multiple Intelligences

Linguistic intelligence. Gardner himself says that this type of intelligence is the basis of IQ tests along with mathematical-logical intelligence.[20] Music learning is shown to significantly boost the verbal IQ scores of small children.[21]

Logical-mathematical intelligence. Gardner himself admits that this intelligence is measured well by IQ tests.[22] As we have noted, music learning before or during the age of seven significantly boosts the performance in IQ tests.[23] As for mathematics, studies for several decades have consistently found that early music education boosts mathematical ability. We will look at this in more detail in Chapter 21.

Musical intelligence. Obviously, early music learning is the best way to boost a person's musical intelligence. Whilst anyone at any age can start learning music, it has recently been shown that musicians who started learning music after the age of seven could not catch up in their rhythmic skills when compared to those who started before the age of seven, even when they had since spent the same amount of hours practicing.[24] As Edwin E. Gordon famously said, 'lack of early musical learning cannot be compensated for'.[25]

Bodily-kinesthetic intelligence. Children and adolescents alike have been shown to improve their bodily-kinesthetic and motor skills, including the core athletic skills of jumping, skipping and overall fitness when they have trained those skills in connection with music. The children who had exactly the same instruction on these skills without music did not experience the benefits.[26] Even babies who learn music are more advanced at developing their motor skills than other children of their age.[27]

Spatial-visual intelligence. Over 2000 years ago, at the beginning of Western civilization, the Greeks thought of architecture as 'frozen sound', and it's only the scientific developments of the past decade and a half that have brought the links between these two abilities into light. Music learning has been shown to improve spatial intelligence (see Appendix: Spatial-visual Intelligence). It also improves visual memory and a better understanding of three-dimensional objects in space.[28]

An interesting scientific finding is that on a spatial test involving a complex maze, 100% of left-handed participants performed perfectly whereas only 50% of right-handed participants did so.[29] It is also found that although left-handed people comprise less than 10% of the population, their proportional presence is much more substantial amongst architects, the masters of spatial intelligence.[30] As the left hand is controlled by the right brain and vice versa, we can assume that as music training develops the use of both hands and thus influences the right brain in a way similar to writing with a left hand does, this could explain why music training promotes spatial-visual intelligence.

Another interesting finding is that girls, on average, tend to perform worse than boys on tests of spatial intelligence – but for the children who have trained in music, both girls and boys perform better on spatial tests compared to all children without music training, without gender differences.[31]

Interpersonal intelligence. As we will see in Chapters 30-34, early music learning has been shown to boost the recognition of emotion and expressive gestures in other people, as well as social skills, confidence and the ability to relate to others. Whereas for spatial intelligence boys tend to have a natural advantage, for emotional recognition girls are found to be ahead of boys. But boys who have engaged in music training have been found to perform just as well as girls in music training. Girls engaged in music training were ahead of other girls by one to three years in emotional skills, whereas the boy musicians were ahead of other boys by an astonishing three to six years, and at the same high level as the girl musicians.[32] These studies show that music training is even more powerful for your child's abilities than any inborn aptitudes.

Intrapersonal intelligence. As we will see in Chapter 32, music learning helps children value their inner emotional life, classify their feelings and interpret them better. Music has widely been called the language of emotions, and this could explain why a child who develops their musical abilities invariably simultaneously develops their sensitivity to their inner emotional cues. This heightening of intrapersonal intelligence could be one of the reasons behind the phenomenon widely observed in scientific studies: that music learning boosts self-esteem, confidence and emotional well-being.[33] (We will look at this crucial discovery in Chapter 35.)

Naturalistic intelligence. Howard Gardner writes of this intelligence: 'Persons with a high degree of naturalist intelligence are keenly aware of how to distinguish the diverse plants, animals, mountains, or cloud configurations in their ecological niche. These capacities are not exclusively visual; the recognition of birdsong or whale calls entails auditory perception. The Dutch naturalist Geermat Vermij, who is blind, depends on his sense of touch'.[34] As we may recall, music learning is a multisensory experience and involves the intense practice of all three modalities of learning – the auditory, the visual and the kinesthetic. People who have studied music are shown, in scientifically controlled tests, to process both visual and auditory information better, faster and more accurately than

those who haven't.[35] Even brain scans show that their brains process visual stimuli[36] and auditory stimuli[37] more effectively. Music learning also enhances the ability to name and categorize objects.[38] For this definition of naturalistic intelligence that Gardner gives, music learning is a rocket-speed boost indeed.
As for the ninth intelligence, or the intelligence number eight and a half as Gardner calls it because he is unsure whether to classify it as a separate intelligence in its own right,[39] it is easy to see that higher-order thinking related to existential, philosophical and cosmological questions requires significant cognitive ability. Not only is IQ a valid predictor of general cognitive ability, but it also indicates the ability for abstract thinking.[40]
Likewise, already in 1982, it was shown that music learning improves the abstract and conceptual thinking of children aged three to six, even without the effect of an IQ increase.[41] This only makes sense because musical concepts in themselves are highly abstract, yet unlike other abstract concepts, they are uniquely within the grasp of small children. Thus learning to understand and think with abstract musical concepts trains the brain to understand and think with other abstractions in general, such as those necessary for existential, philosophical and cosmological reasoning. Even the understanding of core social, political and moral concepts requires existential intelligence and thus the nourishing of abstract thinking ability should be regarded essential for an optimally functioning democracy.

In recent years, more experts have joined Gardner's thematic mission in their criticism of the school system.[42] All of them make the case that the current system does not take a wider range of abilities into account and children are ranked according to their narrow achievements in literacy and mathematics. (We will talk more about learning skills and the education system in Chapters 36 to 38.)

With this in mind, it would be hard not to support Gardner's view that children should be first and foremost allowed to learn and flourish with less emphasis on ranking them against one another in the classroom. But whilst the multiple intelligences worldview is valuable for celebrating our individual talents and differences, it would be a crime to entirely discard the power of IQ. If given the chance, what parent would not want to increase their child's likelihood to leading a longer, happier and healthier life? Every additional IQ point increases the statistical likelihood of this, and we know that early music learning has the most effective IQ-boosting effect of all.

The paradox is that if the IQ-raising power of musical learning has to take place as early as possible, and at the latest at the age of seven. Yet the earliest of ages are precisely where giving music tuition demands the most ability from the teacher: an ability what I could in Gardner's footsteps call 'pedagogical intelligence'. It is, of course, every teacher's right to choose whether they want to teach easily distracted little ones because instrument instruction requires a lot of patience and sustained interest. However, I wish that music teachers stopped telling enthusiastic children and their parents that they should wait until they are at least seven or eight. This common and utterly misguided myth discourages families from persisting in trying to find another teacher and their child misses out on the unique IQ-boosting activity of early music instruction.

But even when an instrument teacher is willing and able to teach a small child, early music instruction poses its own innate challenges. Parents must find ways to motivate their child to take the weekly lessons and practice every week. Thankfully, formal instrument instruction is just one way of learning music. When children cannot yet take up an instrument, they can be taught the key music skills such as rhythm and notation through other means. The traditions of

Kodaly, Suzuki and Musiikkileikkikoulu, as well as the Moosicology method which I formulated for my son when he was a toddler, help children to master the skills that not only form the basis of instrument playing, but provide the brain boost from as early on as possible. These programmes are effective even for babies and toddlers who would not be able to engage in formal instrument lessons even if their parents found a rare instrument teacher willing and able to teach them.

Chapter 17

The Surprise Link Between Music Skills and IQ

What is the one musical element necessary for the existence of music? What is the key factor that turns random noise, sound and vibration into the art form that we perceive as music? Please take a few seconds out to think of the answer.

If you have been brought up in a Western culture, let me guess that your answer was either melody, pitch, tune, tone or song. If you are classically trained, you might have even thought that the answer is 'notes'. These are excellent, educated answers, but they're still wrong.

The Western musical tradition is indeed centred around melodies, from the melodies of classical music to the catchy hooks of current-day chart pop. But what we easily forget is that melodies would not exist without rhythm. The underlying beat is what makes the individual pitch alterations into melodies and thus music. Without the element of rhythm – the component of the beat in particular - it would be impossible for us to even perceive the melody as melody in the first place.

Rhythm turns pitch alterations into a melody, tune or song. Without the beat, pitches would be just random noises, like the noises you hear when cars pass by or your cats voice their demands for food. There would be no melody without the element of rhythm, whereas there still would be a rhythm without melody. This is easy to perceive in the kind of percussive music which involves no melody but what we still perceive clearly as music. Melody alone cannot make music, but rhythm can.

What might be even more surprising is the new research into the links between timing skills and intelligence. It has long been known that the quicker a person's reaction time was in simple reaction tests, the higher their IQ was found to be in complex IQ tests. It was hypothesized that faster neural pathways were the common cause for quicker processing of information and faster thinking ability[1] (and, as we have seen in Chapter 15 and will look at further in Chapter 36, both of which are improved by music learning).

The link between rhythm skills and IQ seems less obvious to common sense. Because it may seem like an unlikely connection on the surface, it is little wonder that it is only over the past 10 years, with the new developments of brain research, that it has emerged that a person's general rhythmic abilities have a direct link with their IQ.[2]

In 2002, scientists Rammsayer and Brandler found that the brain mechanisms related to the discrimination of temporal intervals (which form the beat) are a good predictor of a person's general intelligence. They found that the more accurate a person was at performing temporal tasks, such as recognizing which one out of two sequences of sound lasts longer, and the ability to tap a solid beat, correlated significantly with a person's IQ.[3] Five years later, the same scientists found that rhythmic ability is not just as good, but an even better predictor of general intelligence than information processing speed and reaction time![4] It started to come to light that the skill of the beat is no small feat.

As early as 1976, scientist Douglas Phillips had noticed that there were close relationships between people's rhythmic ability and their intelligence.[5] 1988, Richard Lynn and his research group had published a study that had found a significant accuracy of simple musical tests to predict the famous Spearman's g, the very same general intelligence that IQ tests measure.[6]

In 2003, Lorna S. Jakobson who had previously found with her group of researchers that music learning improves working memory,[7] suggested that timing abilities could be 'the key to musicians' superior memory'.[8] Even though memory and IQ are different abilities, working memory ability is seen to contribute to IQ, and thus Jakobson's hypothesis of the cognitive benefits of what she called the 'time-tagging' ability predicted the interest that more and more scientists started to show towards the question of whether intelligence and the ability to hold a steady beat were intertwined.

However, it was only in 2008 that a group of brain researchers from the University of Stockholm discovered the reason behind this intriguing link. They found that tasks that demand high intelligence activate the same areas of the brain as a range of timing tasks, such as the ability to tap to a steady beat and the ability to discriminate rhythms.[9] The Telegraph famously reported their research in the tentatively titled article *Drummers are natural intellectuals*.[10]

There had been two possible explanations on the controversial finding that the more intelligent you were, the better you performed on simple timing tasks. One was a top-down explanation that more intelligent people were better at concentrating and thus they would be better focused on seemingly non-cognitive tasks such as steady tapping. The other explanation was called the bottom-up explanation. In this hypothesis, the correlation between rhythm ability and intelligence was beyond conscious control and instead a manifestation of more effective neural networks that in turn affected both abilities.

In 2012, Ullén and his research group indeed found that the link between intelligence and better rhythm skills did not depend on conscious effort. They tested various people with and without the promise of a reward that depended on how well they performed. The reward condition made all participants try to perform better, but the scientists found that the correlations between timing and intelligence remained the same whether or not the participants were more focused. In other words, the main link between timekeeping skills and IQ was not related to the superior attention skills–and intelligence, but instead to underlying neural connections between both abilities.[11]

Also in 2012, Holm, Ullén and Madison discovered that even though the brain's executive functions, the faculties involved in activities such as planning and other forms of higher-order thinking, were not directly involved in the simple timing tasks such as holding a steady beat, they were still indirectly involved in performing more complex rhythms.[12] Thus, there are two types of rhythm ability, and both of these contribute to intelligence in their own way. There's the learning of complex rhythms, which practices the conscious attention-holding abilities of the brain (top-down). And there's the bottom-up neural connections that build the basis for simple timekeeping ability and the ability to solve problems using one's intelligence.

What is of interest to parents is whether early music learning can improve these types of rhythm-related intelligence. In the case of top-down intelligence, early music activities are shown to boost the brain's executive functioning[13] as well as attention skills.[14] However, as the basic skill of holding a steady beat is not linked to the higher-order and executive abilities but basic neural properties, can it possible to boost a child's intelligence with simple clapping and tapping to a steady beat?

As deceptively easy as that solution sounds, that is exactly what happens. A study from the Aristotle University of Thessaloniki in Greece from 2008 found that the ability of children to copy rhythms by handclapping correlated significantly with all measurements of IQ, including total IQ, verbal IQ and vocabulary.[15] A 2010 study from China showed that just five months of rhythm training to four-year-old children significantly boosted their IQ.[16] In 2011, a study lead by Dr. Warren Brodsky from the Ben-Gurion University in Israel found that the better preschool children aged four and five were at handclapping songs, the higher their school grades were when they eventually started school throughout the first three grades when the research took place.[17] Conversely, since the very beginning of the new millennium, scientists have linked learning problems to diminished timing skills and the neural connections (or lack of) that underlie them both, again pointing to the importance of bottom-up connections that are built during the early years.[18]

As the IQ order does not change after the age of seven,[19] and the brain size which correlates with IQ does not significantly change after the age of five,[20] it looks like an IQ boost through rhythm needs to happen before the age of eight, and the sooner the better. The music and cognition researcher Rauscher has found that the children who start rhythm training before the age of seven have better mathematical reasoning skills, while those who start after the age of seven do not gain any of these benefits.[21] This matches the recent research that shows that those who start music instruction before or at the age of seven develop better rhythm abilities than those who start after the age of seven, even when the years and hours of musical practice are the same in both groups and even when the late-trained (after seven) group had intense additional practice time.[22]

In Rauscher's study, all music students, no matter what their instrument, gained significant benefits compared to the children who did not learn music. However, the children who studied rhythm instruments specifically exhibited an even bigger increase in IQ-related mathematical and logical reasoning than the children who studied other instruments such as the violin.[23] In other words, although all roads lead to Rome and all music instruction leads to the Music Miracle, systematic rhythm training whether by drums, percussion or handclapping gives a child an even bigger IQ advantage.

This is not to say that only rhythm matters. Training in singing or violin, in the same study, was linked to a bigger boost in language development.[24] As we will see in Chapters 26 to 29, melodic abilities are as essential to reading, verbal ability and foreign language learning as rhythm is to intelligence. In Chapter 40 we will talk more about differences between instruments. What seems to emerge from these studies is that to optimize their Music Miracle, a child needs to learn both rhythm and melodic abilities – at the latest at the age of seven, but the sooner the better.

Yet if your child is over the age of seven, there is no need to despair. Brodsky and Sulkin studied children who were already eight years old and found that those who were given rhythm training instead of regular school music lessons significantly improved their academic skills as a result.[25] Even 10- and 11-year old children have significantly improved their memory through music training.[26] Indeed, there are benefits in music training that you can access even as a pensioner and that you cannot get from any other activity.[27] It is never too late to start learning music and benefiting from it. Yet, according to all research evidence, to gain the unique IQ boost the training needs to start at age seven or before.[28]

Chapter 18

Rhythm at Birth, Skills Through Practice

The intriguing finding is that even babies can easily practice the beat-keeping skills that boost their intelligence.

Scientific evidence backs up the theory that rhythm skills and intelligence alike are best boosted as a baby, because this is the most important time of a person's brain development.[1] The Italian music educator Johannella Tafuri's study into children's musical development found that children who received musical training during their earliest of years came to develop crucial intelligence-related skills, such as keeping a steady beat, much sooner than had been expected. Tafuri concludes that if children have not learned the core rhythm skills before they start school, this is only because, as she puts it, 'they have been kept in a state of "musical deprivation".'[2]

Nature clearly wants us to learn these skills early on, as it is found that gaining music skills makes babies and toddlers happier. Zentner and Eerola found that rhythmic engagement with music in babyhood boosted the babies' happiness, measured by smiles. Babies who had better ability to coordinate their movements rhythmically to music smiled significantly more than when they were not able to follow the beat with their movements.[3]

Despite the common myth that only some people have rhythm, science shows that everyone is wired with the capability to develop rhythmic skills – even from birth. In 2009, scientists discovered with the help of advanced brain imaging that newborn babies' brains have the innate ability to detect the beat in music.[4]

But as the studies show, it takes practice. Just like a baby is born with the capacity for learning a mother tongue or three, this does not yet gave them the skill of knowing a language: the environment of a particular language(s) is essential for the skill to emerge. Neither do the rhythm skills develop on their own. For instance, the way parents and other caretakers bounce babies to rhythm significantly affects their rhythmic development.[5] And the way adults act around music significantly alters how a small baby pays attention to the tempo of music.[6] The potential for improving one's rhythm skills is in every newborn human, just like the potential for learning one's mother tongue – the ability is inborn, but the skill must be practiced.

Because your child's rhythm skills are not a given, you can significantly boost them (and hence their intelligence) surprisingly easily and quickly. For instance, a study from 2007 by Karin Nolan from the University of Arizona found that just a 6-week period of music training improved kindergarten students' ability to tap to a steady beat. All music participants increased the rhythmic tapping skills that are shown to correlate with IQ, whether they were taught with singing, movement or a combination of the two.[7] Another study showed that children learned rhythms more effectively when they learned through all three modalities – auditory, visual and kinesthetic – than when only one or two modalities were used. This means that listening, clapping and singing as well as seeing rhythms in visual forms helps small children master those crucial rhythm skills best.[8]

Scientists can measure timing abilities in a visual-kinesthetic or auditory-kinesthetic way, but it has been shown that learning rhythm skills happens best through the ear and not the eye – in other words, through music.[9] Learning rhythms through music produces better abilities linked to both rhythm and intelligence, and the end product, timing ability, can be measured either through auditory or visual means (tapping according to an auditory signal or a visual signal). As we will see in the next chapter, musical rhythm is meant to made us move, as listening to rhythms activates the motor regions of the brain.

Babies and toddlers who engage in early music instruction have also been shown to be more interested in listening to rhythms than little ones of the same age but without such learning.[10] Therefore learning rhythmic skills as a baby or toddler can start a lifelong positive spiral of IQ-related rhythmic skills as well as prepare the ground for instrument study. The flipside is that the children who miss out on developing rhythm skills fall short of their academic potential.[11] It is estimated that fewer than 10% of kindergarten children are able to feel and express the steady beat in music[12] – a great loss of potential in all ways, as lack of timing skills is one of the most consistent findings with all kinds of learning problems.[13]

As we have seen, intelligence and timing abilities share some of the neural networks.[14] This explains why better timing skills acquired at a young age could transfer to a higher IQ, which in turn leads to better school and career success, as well as a longer, healthier and wealthier life.[15] But as we will see in the following chapters, the benefits of the Music Miracle extend far beyond intelligence to other valuable domains such as language, reading, emotional wellbeing, social skills and even general creativity.

Chapter 19

Rhythm's Made to Make You Move

Have you ever caught yourself jigging along to a song that you hate? I'm not talking about the widespread phenomenon of guilty pleasures, secretly liking a song that's supposedly cheesy or uncool. I'm talking about that kind of song that you genuinely can't stand, yet one day you catch yourself dancing to it?

This happened to me during the Football World Cup 2010 when I had just spent two weeks in the company of my favourite singer-songwriter, Ken Stringfellow, whose music had always touched me as something so pure, fully emotional, yet intriguingly intellectual. We had started the process of recording my singer-songwriter songs to what would be my first album with Ken as my dream-come-true producer. Alongside my songs, we had been listening to the likes of Judee Sill, Radiohead and other types of sophisticated highbrow pop when talking about possible directions for the production.

But I could not stand the World Cup theme song that was being played whenever I ventured outside the studio, 'Waka Waka' by Shakira. I had been a massive fan of Shakira's older Spanish albums and thought her first English-language album had been a collection of catchy but original pop compositions, with a unique production hybrid of chart pop, alternative female rock and world music. But I genuinely could not stand 'Waka Waka', which to me didn't sound like it had any real musical ideas behind it.

I'll never forget the day when our musically sophisticated jazz drummer Julien, Ken and I went to the grocery store to grab lunch and suddenly, when we had been queuing by the till, I noticed that my body was creating some kind of dance choreography. It turned out the song was 'Waka Waka', which I absolutely hated, yet I had just caught myself passionately jigging along to it in the presence of two musically sophisticated geniuses. 'I hate this song', I said to them, 'so what is it about it that makes me want to dance?' Ken said that maybe the songwriters got the beat right.

In my head, I was immediately cursing manipulative commercial songwriters who knew the secret brainwashing tricks of making your body enjoy songs your mind disliked. Later, I discovered that the songwriters are just the tip of the iceberg. Beyond the waterline lies the invisible yet invincible power of biology.

A pioneering study lead by Joyce L. Chen from McGill University in 2008 measured the brain activity of humans when they are listening to music. A group of participants were told to listen to the music selection and to prepare to tap along with it later. Unsurprisingly, the scientists found that even when they were not tapping but simply preparing, the music activated the areas in their brain related to body movement. The real discovery appeared when the second group of participants was given no such instructions about tapping. They were simply told to sit back and listen to the music while their brain measurements were being taken – and when they did, the scientists found that this passive listening alone activated the same motor areas in the brain as listening with the conscious preparation of tapping.[1]

This shows that our brains, not the commercial songwriters, are the real manipulators of the phenomenon of dancing along to songs we consciously dislike. Despite what our conscious musical tastes decide, the unconscious brain is wired to activate in us the movement to synchronize our bodies to the musical beat we hear. In our brains, passive listening is linked to active movement. In 2012, it was even found that the motor system does not simply effect how we hear musical rhythms, it influences our ability to hear it in the first place. Thus, in a weird sci-fi twist, our auditory and kinesthetic abilities are in fact not separate, but the kinesthetic becomes auditory, and auditory becomes kinesthetic.[2]

Why then does rhythm activate our brains' motor regions? The brain wants us to synchronize our movements to the rhythms we hear. The tapping of the feet to music is a common phenomenon even in the most reserved of cultures (I'm looking at us Finns and Brits here). Perhaps it shouldn't surprise us that this, also, is wired into us at birth. In 2010, it was found that babies spontaneously try and match the beat they hear with their body movements.[3] Even more recently, a 2012 study lead by R. I. M. Dunbar from the University of Oxford found that singing, dancing and moving to music increases the release of happy chemicals, endorphins. The same study found that listening to music, in comparison, did not trigger endorphin release.[4]

It seems as if our biology really wants us to move to beats, starting straight out of the womb, or even in the womb. My Mum always tells the story of going to a rock concert when she was pregnant with me, and she had to leave after a few songs as I was bouncing so much inside her tummy that it was making her uncomfortable. As soon as she left the noise behind, I calmed down. We are still unsure whether this was because I loved the music or because I hated it. In the light of these studies, however, it seems that it could well have been the natural reaction of my motor system to the hearing of the rhythmic rock'-n-roll beat.

The obvious reason for this rhythm-movement connection to survive in the history of evolution would be to encourage little ones to build the intelligence-boosting neural connections that enhance intelligence and general learning ability. Moreover, Zentner and Eerola's study found that the better the babies managed to match the beat with their movement, the more they smiled.[5] In other words, their brains reward them for music learning.

Again, we observe the opportunity for an upward spiral. The more a baby has the chance to develop rhythm skills, the more rewarded they feel because of their abilities and are more likely to continue the rewarding behaviour of rhythmic movement. Thus they develop stronger rhythm skills and intelligence-related neural networks. Nature is rather intelligent indeed!

Chapter 20

The Music Miracle for Movement and Fitness

Because of the brain's inherent links between rhythm abilities and motor skills, it shouldn't come as a surprise that music boosts general motor and coordination abilities. This is why music learning is actually a crucial factor in boosting the bodily-kinesthetic intelligence that is one of Gardner's Multiple Intelligences. Listening to music whilst exercising makes a person feel less exertion than exercising without music, even when compared with other stimuli such as video.[1] This is likely to explain why back in 1960s and 1970s it was found that people exercise harder and longer with music than without music, from sit-ups[2] and push-ups[3] to walking further and with less effort.[4] Suddenly it becomes obvious why the Body Pump class blasts louder dance music than your average nightclub.

In the recent years, a growing number of scientists have been concerned with the increasing inactivity in children and adolescents. The question has been, with knowledge on the damage to physical and mental heath that a lack of exercise causes, how can we make the children keep up a healthy lifestyle in a world dominated by sitting in front of various types of screens?

In 2008, a longitudinal research from the University of Sydney was published and it found an important cause for a future healthy lifestyle. The scientists had measured various motor skills of five hundred children back in 2000 – skills related to object control, such as throwing and kicking, and locomotor skills such as hopping and galloping. Six and seven years later, these children had grown to adolescence, and the scientists found that those who had had better motor skills in their childhood were significantly more likely to exercise actively. They concluded by stating: 'Motor skill development should be a key strategy in childhood interventions aiming to promote long-term physical activity.'[5]

Already in 1967, a large study of over 600 children in elementary school found that the children who were taught these skills through music mastered them significantly better than those who were taught without music. 'The experimental and control groups were both given the same skills practice with identical number of repetitions. Every effort was made to have the rhythmic accompaniment as the single variable in the study.' In this study, the rhythmic accompaniment was provided mostly by playing music records, but also through piano, drum, clapping and singing. Thus, even though the study uses the word 'rhythmic accompaniment', we can see that what is meant by it comes down to a more familiar word: music.[6]

What is striking is that the whole study period lasted only for 10 weeks, and that this alone was enough to boost all the various motor skills of the children in the music group – from throwing and catching to climbing, balancing and leaping. As the control group did not experience significant improvement,[7] here we see that physical education classes in schools should jump on board the Music Miracle. It is only with music that the optimum motor skills can flourish in children. This is especially poignant in the light of how childhood motor skills promote a healthy lifestyle for the years to come.

Similar findings have been made in our new millennium. A study from 2004 by Evridiki Zachopoulou and her research group compared two types of physical education activity for 4- to 5-year-olds. The other group continued with standard PE classes without music whereas the other group took part in a music and movement programme instead. After just two months, the researchers measured the motor abilities of both groups of children and found that the music and movement group had improved their motor skills and balance whilst the standard PE group had experienced no such improvement.[8] If schools find it hard to find the time for those all-important music lessons, here would be an opportunity to bring musical activity into PE lessons.

Whereas these studies measured only motor and physical skills, not rhythmic ones, another Greek study from the following year did. Dr Pollatou's research group in Athens found that high school students who were involved in physical activities accompanied by music, such as dance, had significantly better rhythm skills than students who were involved in non-musical sport activities such as basketball or other team sports.[9] As early learning of rhythm skills directly boosts academic achievement,[10] the music and movement-combining PE lesson would be one of the ways that schools would improve their pupils' all-round capabilities, which would make it easier for the students to learn and teachers to teach.

Chapter 21

Mastering Mathematics with Music Training

"Music is the pleasure the human soul experiences from counting, without being aware that it's counting."
Leibniz, 18th Century Philosopher and Discoverer of Calculus[1]

Music and academic performance has been studied from almost every angle, and the connection between music and mathematics has been a favourite topic of many researchers.

Music education has long been shown to give children a significant advantage in learning maths.[2] Nowhere is this more pertinent than in studies on children who do worse in maths than other children and who, after less than a year of music study, have surpassed their previously high-achieving peers in their mathematics scores.[3]

There are several explanations to why music learning boosts mathematical skills. One is that both music and maths involve numbers and patterns, fractions and divisions.[4] Learning how the basic musical concepts of beats, bars and note values function thus helps children to understand the core concepts of math in a more concrete way. This is particularly crucial for small children, as it is widely acknowledged that individuals do not develop abstract thinking before they hit puberty. Mathematics is a highly abstract science, and nowhere can it be made more concrete than in music - without compromising the development of a mathematical understanding.

Many studies have observed that reading music is crucial for gaining the music boost for math. Some studies have found that when children have been taught other music skills but not that of reading music, the children have experienced other brain boosts, but not the one related to maths.[5] What could explain this particular result?

It could be suggested that learning musical notation and singing, clapping and playing from it helps children grasp the mathematical concepts of note value in a concrete and in-depth way. Another scientific finding that may explain the transfer from music skills to mathematatcis is that the level of visual-motor coordination a child has predicts their success in math.[6] Music instruction, in turn, has been shown to boost visual-motor coordination[7], which, in itself, is hardly surprising: we would be hard-pressed to find a better way to train visual-motor coordination than making music (a motor activity) from notes (a visual stimulus). A study that compared two groups of children aged four to six, one of which studied music for 24 sessions, and the other studied movement and coordination instead, found that only the children who undertook music training improved their visual-motor integration. Learning movement alone was not enough to boost this crucial link to the mathematical mind – music training was essential.[8]

Yet another possible explanation for the mathematical boost has emerged from the field of brain research. Brain scans on expert mathematicians have shown that their years of mathematical training have increased the neural connections in their inferior parietal lobule, a region in the neocortex. The same area is identified as one of the many regions of the brain that is boosted by music training.[9]

Studies on expert mathematicians have also found, however, that mathematical ability does not boost musical ability.[10] It seems that while exercising the neural networks through music training produces a transfer effect for mathematics, exercising the same networks through mathematicss does not transfer to musical abilities.

The reasons for this can be hypothesized. Crucially, music involves the auditory realm, so it is little wonder that a pen-and-paper training in math does not produce auditory benefits. And as we remember from the auditory scaffolding hypothesis from Chapter 5, the realm of the ear is suggested to be the building block for all reasoning, whether auditory or not.[11]

What is of particular relevance to your child's success in mathematics is that according to the leading theories on childhood development, such as the classic Piagetian theory, children do not grasp abstract concepts until at the threshold of adolescence. Musical concepts may be the concrete scaffolding onto which an abstract mathematical understanding is built years down the line. Understanding basic relationships between numbers in kindergarten predicts success in later mathematics achievement years down the line, so grasping numeral relations through music, sound and notation can be of crucial help.[12]

When it comes to fractions, understanding them is of more than fractional importance. Your child's level of understanding fractions predicts their total mathematical achievement years down the line, in adolescence.[13] Research has established that children who learn fractions through musical notation learn 50-100% better than children who are taught fractions the traditional way[14] or through innovative computer games.[15] These comparisons show that evolution has built our brains for learning through making music rather than through pen and paper, let alone a computer. After all, making music precedes the written word and the invention of mathematics by hundreds of thousands of years. Ever since the human race was born, music was a part of it, whereas writing and mathematics only developed a couple of thousand years ago. Our brains have not changed much since the caveman years, and a wise educator adapts their education methods to the factual features of the developing brain rather than wishful thinking of how it would be convenient to teach it.

Many children struggle with an understanding of mathematics or the motivation for it. Music interventions have shown to be successful in motivating pupils for mathematics.[16] It is hard to think of two subjects that could be more easily integrated into one than music and mathematics. From the counting of beats to the fractions of note value and the times tables for different notes in various time signatures, music offers a unique opportunity to help the children grasp core mathematical concepts in a way that does not take away their joy for mathematical discovery.

Part Five

Linguistic Intelligence and the Music Boost for Language(s)

As Edwyn E. Gordon notes, whilst parents are eager to support their offspring's language development, most of them consider musical development as optional.1 There is an obvious reason for this. Our culture places a high value on language skills, even more so than the mathematical-logical skills. Language is not only the basis for communication between humans, but within a human – through thinking. A person's level of command of their mother tongue directly influences their ability to reason for themselves, understand the world around them and be understood in it.

Howard Gardner specifically points out, when writing about the topic of intelligence-fair tests, that individuals with a superior linguistic intelligence can easily appear to succeed within any other domains of intelligences better than a person who has more ability within the other intelligence(s), but who is less skilled with language. In other words, linguistic intelligence gives an 'unfair' advantage in tests to those who have more of it, often at the expense of those who cannot express their skills quite as eloquently through language. 2

Nevertheless, Gardner's point also successfully illustrates how – despite all the multimedia frenzy – linguistic competence is still a core skill that every one of our children would benefit from increasing. In the following sections, we will look at how music training at an early age boosts language skills for life - and why.

Chapter 22

The Astonishing Secret of Language Skills

In 2009, Joseph M. Piro and Camilo Ortiz from Long Island University in the US found that children who had taken regular piano lessons had significantly higher levels of vocabulary and verbal ability than children who had not studied music.[1] But again, it is far from necessary to wait until a child matures enough to engage in instrument tuition. Simply teaching music concepts and skills to children is shown to remarkably boost their linguistic competence.

Already in 1975, it was found that young children who learned music concepts such as rhythm, melody and music theory – without even learning an instrument – gained significantly better language skills than the children who missed out on this learning.[2] Recently, this line of research has greatly increased. An American study from 2004 tested the language skills of 3- to 6-year-old developmentally disabled children before and after a music intervention and found that their total language scores improved over the course of just six weeks of two 25-minute music classes per week.[3]

But it was only in 2011 when scientists discovered that music learning boosts the verbal IQ of developmentally healthy children. The study conducted by Dr. Sylvain Moreno at York University consisted of measuring the verbal intelligence of children aged four and five before and after a music learning programme that consisted of teaching them musical concepts related to rhythm, melody and notation – and without any instrument tuition. Within just twenty days of music intervention lessons that lasted one to two hours at a time, the children significantly improved their verbal intelligence.

The control group was engaged into learning concepts related to visual arts and did not experience any benefits.[4] But why is there a transfer from music to language skills?

Studies have shown that in the brains of babies, children and grown-ups alike, language and music abilities rely largely on the same overlapping neural networks.[5] During the early years, a child's musical and linguistic development are indistinguishable from one another.[6] What's more, children develop musical abilities before linguistic abilities, which is why scientists recommend music as a tool for boosting the language development of the early years.[7]

Scientists used to think of music as a type of language. Like any spoken and written language, music has its roots in the auditory, yet it is translatable to written symbols – those of musical notation. Learning a language and learning music both involve learning a set of symbols and the inherent rules that govern them. In recent research, it has emerged that language is a type of music. Melodic communication, with tones and utterances, developed 500 000 years ago in the course of human evolution, whereas speech with words appeared much later, only 200 000 years ago.[8] Human speech started off as music and wordless singing; and this is the order in which the babies of today still develop their language skills.[9]

In this part of the book, we will look at how the gaining of the understanding of musical structures and meanings results in better linguistic abilities within the brain. The benefits of music learning to language have been observed in babies, toddlers and even children up to eight or nine years old who take up music study, so the critical age for language is slightly later than the age for the overall intelligence boost.

Alongside reading, music training is the best way to gain a bigger linguistic competence and all its associated benefits in a communication-obsessed society such as ours. For children who do not yet read, it is the best way to build their brain connections for the gift of language. The young brain learns fast. All the children in the groundbreaking 2011 study significantly improved their verbal intelligence with just four weeks of music instruction. Whilst the children's training in this research, at two hours a day, was more intense than that in other studies on the music boost (which have used an hour or less of music training a week for a longer period of time to achieve the Music Miracle), it still took less time than what many children spend watching television on a daily basis.[10]

Chapter 23

Melody: The basis for communication and vocabulary

A melody consists essentially of the pitch differences between sounds. Without rhythm, there would be no music, but without pitch, there would be no melodies. Pitch is also essential for verbal communication. In the domain of speech, the variance of pitch is called intonation. For instance, in English and most other languages, there is commonly a rising intonation towards the end of a phrase that constitutes a question.

Intonation, along with other non-verbal properties of speech (rhythm and stress) is what constitutes prosody. Prosody is the non-verbal component of speech and it is crucial for understanding vocal expression. The significance of prosody for babies is shown in the universal cross-cultural phenomenon of 'mother-ese' or 'parent-ese'. It is a biological, instinctive phenomenon of all human parents to speak to their babies with an exceptionally expressive voice where the intonation rises and falls widely, much more so than in regular, adult-to-adult speech. Better prosodic abilities, in turn, are crucial for helping babies and toddlers distinguish words from speech and thus build the basis of their own speech and vocabulary as well as language competence.[1]

As music learning helps even babies to gain better prosodic abilities, it is thus little wonder that babies and children who engage in early music learning are shown to have better communication skills and a more developed vocabulary than their peers.[2] Simply singing to a baby may benefit their linguistic development significantly: babies whose mothers use more melodic variations in their speech develop better and faster than babies who are exposed to a lesser amount of prosodic variation – they even gain more weight faster, which is a hallmark of optimal health in babyhood.[3]

However, it is shown that for children older than babies, engaging in songs, rhymes and musical games does not, as such, produce benefits for prosody or vocabulary. Only the specific teaching of musical concepts and skills does. Researchers from the National Autonomous University of Mexico, one of Latin America's leading universities, conducted a comparative study between two programmes for five-year-olds – one a standard school musical sing-a-long programme and the other a specifically developed method of teaching music using auditory and visual components – found that the educational music programme produced significant vocabulary gains, whereas the musical games activity did not. The researchers concluded that 'the activities must be primarily musical in nature and music have the specific objectives of discriminating sounds and forming auditory-visual associations. They must also involve sequences of auditory and visual stimuli.'[4] As usual, a mere game does not produce a gain.

It was already found in 1996 that the better a child is at recognizing and remembering sounds, the higher their level of vocabulary.[5] Again, this ability is not inborn, but trained: new research by cognitive scientist Manuela M. Marin from the University of Vienna (2009) has found that musical training helps babies and small children to remember new words easier as well as to understand the structures of language better.[6] This is crucial information for new parents keen to develop the vocabulary of their little ones.

Other recent studies show that music instruction trains the brain to balance the activity in speech perception more evenly between the right and left sides of the brain, whereas those without musical training maintain a left-brain dominance for speech and language.[7]

It's notable that the more evenly your brain activity is spread between your brain hemispheres, the better you are at detecting pitch changes in both speech and music.[8] This would explain some of the brain mechanics behind the language-related side of the Music Miracle. Music instruction balances the sides of the brain by building the brain bridge (corpus callosum) and helping the right side of the brain develop to its fullest.

Although language is processed on the left side of the brain, the left side alone is not enough to detect what is happening when it comes to spoken language. Some intriguing brain research shows that even 'non-emotional' speech perception has its underpinning in the speaker's emotions and thus, interestingly, on the right side of the brain.[9] This means that whenever we listen to someone speak, we hear their words only through our filter of emotion. Music training makes for a better filter, as it trains the right side of the brain to detect the emotional undertones of spoken language, whilst teaching both brain parts to co-operate in interpreting the message. In this sense, boosting the 'non-logical' side of the brain results in an overall more logical brain.

A short amount of music training has been shown to alter the brains of even eight-year-old children to detect pitch better. When a group of children without a previous background in music was randomly assigned into a music learning group and a painting group, the scientists found that just eight weeks of musical training boosted the children's ability to detect pitches better.[10] For those who cast this study as one in which scientists waste research money on proving that ice is cold, it may be worth bearing in mind that if indeed the pitch-boosting abilities of music learning are so obvious when the multiple benefits of pitch detection are equally obvious, the question maybe should be: why is only a small minority of children to this day gaining access to real musical training?

Better pitch detection skills do not just boost the vocabulary.

They are the key to developing core components of emotional intelligence, as we will see in Chapter 31. Perhaps more surprisingly, pitch detection also forms the foundation for learning to read without learning disabilities. Scientist Mireille Besson found in 2007 that dyslexics have trouble detecting the kind of pitch changes that normal readers and the majority of people easily distinguish.[11]

It has been found that training, not inborn differences, are a significant cause of the pitch detection advantages or disadvantages.[12] In 2011, a group of reputable neuroscientists including Gottfried Schlaug from Harvard Medical University found that tone-deafness and dyslexia share common neural resources. The implications of these findings are, like we discovered in Chapter 13, that both are curable, or at least strongly remediable, by musical training – at least when started early enough in line with the brain development.[13]

If your child is dyslexic, there is a vast chance for improvement by music training. Studies have found that dyslexic children aged up to 12 can significantly improve their literacy with pitch training in a relatively short time.[14] We will look at dyslexia and the development of reading skills in the Part Six of the book. In the meantime, let's explore how your child learns language - and how you can unleash their full linguistic competence.

Chapter 24

What Explains the Music Boost for Language?

What is particularly curious is that the music boost does not end at speech. It boosts the your child's all-round language skills. How is this possible?

In linguistic terms, language consists of two components: the syntax and the semantics. Syntax is the form of language and deals with the structural and grammatical aspects of language use. Semantics refers to the meaning of language, which is the content that the words and structure can convey.

A good command of both syntax and semantics is crucial to a good command of language. Bad syntax does not simply mean that a person makes more grammatical mistakes; it is much more impairing than that. Just as there is no melody without rhythm, there is no language without structure. It is ever-present in any use of language, whether we're thinking to ourselves, reading, writing or engaging in any form of speaking, whether publicly or in private.

Yet it is equally inconceivable to have a human language based purely on structure and not on semantics at all. There are complex linguistic systems that operate fully on syntax and not semantics at all – just like there is percussive music without tone or pitch alterations – but these are computer languages. The computer does not know the meanings, it simply follows the structure of the programming language. In human communication, however, words are always laid with meanings, references to the objects and phenomena outside the mere linguistic symbols. Now let's look at how music learning affects both of these abilities.

Structures of language, information and understanding

As the learning of music – just like the learning of one's mother tongue or a second language – involves learning the inherent structure(s) of a symbolic system, this could explain why music learning directly translates to a better grammatical and structural understanding of languages.

Manuela M. Marin (2009) studied the language abilities of 4- to 5-year-old children and found that those who had musical training had better language skills, especially for structural (syntactic) skills and memory for words (a bigger vocabulary and the ability to learn new words more easily). Marin suggests that in early childhood, the mechanisms for learning the structure for both music and language may be developed supporting one another.[1] A study by the acclaimed scientists Jentschke and Koelsch from the University of Berlin found in that early music learners develop syntactic abilities sooner and more strongly than other children because syntax processing in both music and language rely on overlapping neural resources.[2]

Recent brain research from 2011 by French neuroscientists Francois and Schön shows that music students' brains are more efficient at learning the structure of any language than those participants without music training.[3] Interestingly, another study by Francois and Schön from 2008 found that our brains – babies and grown-ups alike – learn the structures of a spoken language better when they are taught through songs than through speech. This could explain why simply singing to a baby somewhat boosts their language abilities: it helps them familiarize themselves with the inner rules of their mother tongue.[4]

Just like with mathematics, pupils often consider the learning of grammar both difficult and tedious. These recent developments in brain imaging clearly show a more effective alternative to boost grammar abilities – one that gets better results because it works with, and not against, the brain's tendencies. Both music training and songs as methods of teaching grammar open up new avenues to ensure your child's brain is optimized for grammar genius.

Brain science has found that one part of the brain in particular, called Broca's Area, is responsible for understanding of the learning of grammar and structure of language.[5] People with damage to the Broca's Area are unable to make coherent sentences and use language properly, even when their other intellectual abilities are intact. Conversely, the denser your Broca's Area, the better your syntactic abilities.[6]

In 2001, scientists from the Max Planck Institute of Cognitive Neuroscience made the discovery that Broca's Area does not only process the structure of language, it also processes the structure of music.[7] Indeed, music students have been shown to have denser neural networks in their Broca's Areas than people who have not studied music.[8]

We already know that babies' linguistic skills are built on their musical skills. But Francois' research group also notes that the structural understanding of sound and speech affects general abilities to spot patterns and structures in all modalities – not just the auditory.[9] In this sense, a part of the general IQ increase from music study could come from the improvement of this ability, as intelligence constitutes partially from an ability to recognize similarities and differences between stimuli. This would be in line with the evidence in line with the Auditory Scaffolding Hypothesis: the ear may be our first tool to access pattern recognition and thus, all higher levels of intelligence alike.[10]

'What do you mean?' Semantics: The meaning of words and phrases

Interestingly, music training improves semantics as well as syntax. In the recent years, it has been found in brain imaging studies that both syntax and semantics are basic aspects of music, just like language. When the brain processes music, both of its syntactic and semantic areas are activated.[1]

When researching this topic, I found it easy to grasp that music has a structure in a way that parallels language. After all, from a musicological point of view, music is essentially highly structured sound. This is different from the term 'structure' when applied to composition, which means simply that compositions have different parts, such as the verse and chorus in practically every song in popular music (which is equivalent to the classical composition structures with their alternating A and B parts). The syntax is omnipresent at every level: notes, beats, rhythms and melodic phrases are an essential part of what we perceive as music. Thus, it becomes clear that music consists of patterns alike to the grammar in language.

But what I found surprising is that the brain processes meaning in music in the same way as it processes meaning in language.[2] The meaning in language is obvious. Almost every word, whether adjective, noun or verb, refers directly to something that we could see with our own eyes (if the objects of reference were present). Take any sentence, like, 'The pink pig is running.' We can find the pinkness, the animal and the movement in the real world. As opposed to this concreteness, the meaning in music is highly abstract as well as emotional. So how is it possible that music training boosts one's semantic abilities in the realm of language?

It turns out that this boost links to what the scientists call semantic memory. The semantic memory is the memory capacity of our brains in processing meanings in anything we experience in everyday life, whether through our senses, emotions or thoughts. In 2000, it was found that the semantic memory is directly responsible for our understanding of words and the subtle meanings of differently formulated sentences.[3] A surprising finding was made in 2011 by Sharpley Hsieh and her research group at the Macquarie Centre for Cognitive Science in Australia. They found evidence that the brain regions that process musical emotions overlap with neural networks that process semantic memory.[4] In other words, by studying music, we engage our semantic memory. This could explain the many links we can observe between skills of language and music, such as children's ability to increase their verbal IQ and great singer-songwriters' gifts for writing high-quality poetry as lyrics.

And let us not forget that hundreds of thousands of years before mankind invented words, the meaning of verbal utterances was expressed through musical elements alone.[5]

Chapter 25

Music as the Key to Foreign Languages

As music training boosts all the language-related networks in the brain, we would expect that it creates benefits for learning foreign languages. And as research from recent years has established, it does.

A study conducted in Finland in 2008 found that when a child has a good level of music skills, their language production skills in a foreign language are advanced, and that when a child lacks in music skills, they also lack in foreign languages.[1] Music students also display an advantage in hearing subtle differences in a foreign language, which results in better pronunciation skills.[2]

I recently listened to a speech given by my ancient ex-boyfriend, who a few years ago relocated to Oxford for a postgraduate degree. When I knew him, we were living in Finland and his English pronunciation skills were as rough as those of the famous Finnish formula racers. (No offence intended - you should hear the pronunciation skills of our standard English teachers.) Now, some years later, he speaks in proper Eton-educated Queen's English – I could hardly tell his voice from that of David Cameron. I was shocked, because I had been taught that people cannot easily change their pronunciation skills. Then I remembered that he had played piano as a child. Lesson learned: even if you spend your childhood and adolescence in the industrial town of Lahti and your 20s in Helsinki, with the music boost, it is never too late to become an English aristocrat in your 30s!

Indeed, music learning gives your child an advantage with regards to even taking up a whole new foreign language later in adulthood. In 2007, it was found that adults who have a background in early music learning detect pronunciation differences in a foreign language that they had not heard before faster and more accurately than those adults who do not have a background in music training.[3] Cutting-edge research from 2013, on the other hand, has identified that music training makes it much easier for a person to pick up any new language, in its grammar, colloquialisms and vocabulary.[4]

Likewise, the increased abilities in syntax and semantics that we tackled in the previous chapters extend to all languages, from one's mother tongue to foreign languages. For those of us who have not gained English as a mother tongue, the benefits of this are essential. But even for native English speakers, there is a growing interest in the advantages that come with learning foreign languages. There are many beneficial languages to learn in the world - Chinese, Russian, Arabic, French and Spanish to name but a few - and what a better way to ensure your child can pick up all these languages if needed, than by teaching them the master language that transcends all others: music.

My contention as an average Finn who speaks four languages (Finns speak an average of three to five languages, presumably because nobody understands our obscure tongue) is that knowing languages is fun. It allows you to engage with different cultures with a more of an insider's point of view. And you never know when you may need the ability to learn a new language quickly. Ken Stringfellow famously married a French woman, Dominique, and moved to Paris in his mid-30s, and has since picked up the whole language from scratch. At first I was amazed at how he had learned it without any background, compared to my 12 years spent studying French at school. But the research explains it. As a musician who has made music from toddlerhood, he would have significantly boosted his brain's capacity for the syntax, semantics and pronunciation of learning any new language in adulthood.

Part Six

Don't Believe the Rhyme: Music skills as the route to literacy

We instinctively think of reading as a visual activity. But surprisingly, when we first learn to read, it is not our visual but auditory abilities that determine how easily we grasp the black and white symbols on the page into words. It is the skill of the ear, not the eye, that determines how easily your child learns to write and spell.[1]

Specifically, it is the fine-tuned discrimination of individual sounds that makes it possible for children to make the leap into reading. There are two proven ways to boost your child's ability in this regard: training in phonics and training in music. Phonics is more and more commonly used at schools but music training is a vastly underused method with heaps of potential for beginnin readers. Latest research has established that training in music is just as effective, or even more effective, than training in phonics when it comes to reading success.[2]

When you hear about how to facilitate your child's reading skills, teachers often emphasize reading them rhymes. Yet the notion that rhymes contribute to reading success has been debunked in scientific studies since the 1990s,[3] most recently in yet another comprehensive study from 2012.[4] Somehow this information has not travelled from the scientific world to the real-life world of teaching.

It is auditory training, not language training, that boosts reading skills.[5] It is evenfound that the music skills of children correlate one-to-one with their reading skills. Several studies from the end of 1960s to the early 1970s found that musical instruction boosted the reading scores of preschoolers and first graders.[6] In 1989, Julia Barwick and her research group from the University of London found a significant relationship between tonal memory (the ability to remember pitches) and reading age, even when the effect of IQ was partialled out.[7] In 1993, Lamb and Gregory found that pitch discrimination skills correlated with reading performance.[8]

Lamb and Gregory also found that unlike the all-important pitch, timbre discrimination does not boost reading skills.[9] The ability to distinguish timbre is the ability to recognize the sounds of different instruments when they are playing the same pitch. This result shows that it is the 'abstract' aspects of music theory and melody discrimination that boost reading. The ability to know what individual instruments sound like does not provide this boost, yet most early music instruction focuses largely on learning to recognize different instruments, due to the general lack of teachers' musical expertise.

In 2000, a large study by Ron Butzlaff from the University of Illinois comprising of samples of over 500 000 pupils found that there was a strong and reliable association between the reading test scores of children and the amount and quality of music instruction they had had.[10] Two years later, Jovanka Ciares and Paul Borgese found that there was a 'direct one-for-one positive correlation between number of years spent in musical training and increases in reading grade levels'.[11]In 2009, Sylvain Moreno and his research group studied 8-year-old children who were randomly placed either into a 6-month music training group or a 6-month painting group and found that the music training significantly improved the reading skills and pitch processing of these children. The children also had their brain patterns measured, and after a period of music training, the results showed measurable improvements in the neural networks relating to the processing of both pitch and speech.[12]

Chapter 26

Phonological Awareness and Speech Segmentation: From hearing to reading and writing

A good level of reading ability is crucial for success at school, because most learning material still exists in the form of text. And for reading success, the critical component is phonological awareness.

Phonological awareness is the ability to focus on units of sound in spoken language rather than their meaning. This is yet separate from syntax. Whereas syntax deals with structures within symbols (such as structures within words in language or within sounds in music), phonological awareness is the ability to recognize the individual sounds on their own, whether in music or language. Because music education is the best way to train a child to focus on sounds, it is not such a surprise that it is the best way to boost a child's reading skills. Children with music training acquire the reading skills with ease compared to their peers, and they remain more efficient readers.[1]

The significance of music learning to reading acquisition became famous in the academic world with a 2002 study that examined the music and reading skills of a hundred preschoolers. The study found that the musical skills of the children correlated significantly with both phonological awareness and reading development.[2] Likewise, it is found that dyslexic children and adults have a substantially inferior level of phonological awareness, to the point where 17-year-old dyslexics perform worse than 8-year-old average children on tests of phonological awareness even when they had a substantially higher IQ.[3]

An ability that already in the 1990s was found to be crucial for reading skills is that of speech segmentation, the ability to identify the boundaries between words and syllables in spoken language. It is closely linked with phonological awareness. A recent 2012 study by Clément Francois and his research group at the Neuroscience Institute in France reported on the their two-year period of testing the speech segmentation skills of children. In this research, groups of children aged eight were randomly assigned to either music or painting classes. After two years of involvement in either music or painting, the speech segmentation skills of the children were tested, and it was found that the music learners had experienced a direct boost and were way ahead of their painting peers.[4] Again, for those who wonder why such obvious studies are made, it may be more interesting to ask why early literacy so often focuses on not only rhyme but the repeated recognition drill of letters, which, in itself, is just a visual activity.

Chapter 27

Music Training: the Foundation for Reading

The lack of sufficient phonological awareness poses a severe and unexpected risk outside the realm of reading. What is interesting (or rather, shocking) for parents to note is that children who lack phonological awareness feel more lonely, less confident and less accepted by their schoolmates.[1] Lack of sufficient phonological awareness is also is one of the leading signs that the child may be developing a learning disability.[2]

As the studies have shown, these risks can easily be avoided or counteracted with early music learning. Most children acquire their phonological awareness by chance, for better or worse. There are only two ways to deliberately boost a child's phonological awareness: phoneme awareness training and music training. The first one is integrated into phonics as the teaching method. But groundbreaking studies from the past ten years show that music skills are even more effective in predicting a person's later phonetic ability than a standard phonetics test.[3] The very latest controlled studies have brought into light the astonishing fact that training in music skills is just as effective - if not more effective - in boosting a child's reading skills than phonics training.[4] As many children struggle with learning to read, this scientific discovery opens up whole new opportunities for families who want their children to grasp reading without a demoralizing uphill battle.

The integrated teaching of music and reading has also been shown to engage the attention of children much more so than other forms of training, such as traditional teaching[5] and multimedia training[6]. This should be of interest to teachers who often complain that their pupils do not listen. Rightly, it is challenging to engage a group of small children into learning: this gives ever more the reason to teach the reading awareness skills through music. Not only do children learn the real skills that boost the brain's ability to learn to read, such as phoneme awareness, but they will also be more attentive and motivated to learn them.

A bold teaching experiment that had become legendary through the academic world is a Swiss study where the teachers replaced five hours of general weekly reading and math instruction with music training. It turned out that the children in this experiment significantly overtook traditional Swiss classes in their reading scores and remained as proficient in math as the students who were taught more math but no music.[7] Studying music at the expense of the core subjects turned out to be no expense at all. On the contrary, the fact that most children are not given adequate music instruction is an ongoing expense that could be redirected to effective methods. No amount of pushing can help our children improve their reading levels if they are not given the right tools to do so.

Chapter 28

What Are Little Words Made of? The Three Components of Phonological Awareness

How is it possible that the teaching music improves a child's reading scores more than teaching to read?

There are three subdomains that make up phonological awareness: awareness of syllables, awareness of onset-rhyme and phonemic awareness. The awareness of syllables means the ability to recognize and divide words into individual syllables according to the context of the grammar. In 2011, a study lead by Julie Chobert of the Mediterranean Cognitive Institute of Neuroscience compared the syllable processing of children who learned music to children who didn't, and found that the musician children recognized and processed individual syllables better. Not only were they more conscious of the syllables, but their brains also processed them better even when they weren't making conscious effort.[1] The brain evidence came a year later. Parbery-Clark and her research group found in 2012 that music instruction boosts the processing of speech syllables at the neural level, therefore giving music learners a brain advantage in the syllable area of phonological awareness.[2]

Another part of phonological awareness is called the onset-rhyme (also spelled 'onset-rime') awareness. This is the ability to recognize which part of words rhyme and which part is different. Recently, when I spoke to some primary school teachers about early reading instruction, they said that the best way to boost a child's reading readiness is by reading them rhymes. Unfortunately, as we've already discussed, this claim does not hold up to scientific scrutiny. A child's levels of onset-rhyme awareness are irrelevant to their reading success.[3]

In contrast, the third part of phonological awareness, phoneme awareness, is what makes all the difference to reading skills. A phoneme is the smallest unit of sound, such as the sounds 'c', 'a' and 't' in 'cat' or the sounds 'ch', 'u', 'r' and 'ch' in 'church'. Phoneme awareness has been shown to be the most important contributor to reading skills. The onset-rhyme awareness is shown to develop only as a byproduct of phoneme awareness. Studies have found that when children are taught onset-rhyme awareness, they do not develop their reading skills, whereas when children are trained in phoneme awareness, both their reading skills and onset-rhyme awareness have improved.[4]

Please do not get me wrong, I am personally crazy about rhymes (hence I normally write songs and not books). I believe rhymes are fun and important in their own right. It's just that we cannot teach a child to read through them, no matter how much we want to. All the evidence shows that it does not work. So why does the "rhyme hype" persist?

The obvious answer is that it is infinitely easier for teachers to read rhymes than to teach music skills, as only a small majority of school teachers have had any proper training in teaching music, yet they, like every reading-able parent, are obviously fully equipped to read poems and rhyming stories. Teaching rhymes instead of music may be convenient for the schooling system in the short term, but it isn't helping the students, because rhyme instruction does not boost phoneme awareness. It is only phoneme awareness that boosts both reading and, as a sideline, the onset-rhyme awareness.

I also used to believe the rhyme hype. As a child, my mum would constantly read Finnish children's poems to me, especially the classic poetry by Kirsi Kunnas who is recognized nationwide as a children's wordsmith second to none. (Her poetry is indeed linguistically incredible. It's a shame that it is not possible to translate such high-level wordplay onto other languages in all its genius.)When I started to make up my own spoken poetry and eventually, at around age five, to write my own books, my mum reasoned that this was due to the rhymes. The assumption seems logical, as one would think that training in words results in words, and training in music results in music. Thus it's ironic that according to science, it was likely to be the music training that gave me the early academic skills that my parents were in awe of – and that it was the rhymes that instilled in me the love of poetry and the need to pursue art over academics. Rhyme-reading parents beware. Your children may grow up to be rhyme writers themselves!

But why is it that training in music rather than rhymes results in a boost for reading? This links to the fact that phonemes are the smallest possible units of sound. Thus, if a child didn't have any phonemic awareness, it would be impossible for them to link spoken information with letters that symbolize sounds. We are all born with the ability for phonemic awareness, and all children eventually acquire a sufficient level of phonemic awareness – even alongside traditional reading instruction – in order to read.

Phonemic awareness involves highly developed capabilities of distinguishing different types of auditory stimuli. This is one of the auditory abilities that is developed by music training. Music training, by definition, consists of developing a higher awareness of sounds, and this translates to sounds in speech as well as in music. Rhymes, in contrast, do not develop the detailed awareness of sounds that is required for linking speech with letter symbols.

The importance of phoneme awareness is well illustrated by the peculiarity of the Finnish language. An Ofsted publication, 'Getting

Them Reading Early' from 2011, points out that 'one reason why children in Finland learn to decode [text] very quickly is that the sound-spelling system of Finnish is extremely regular. (Finnish grammar is rather more complex.)'. [5] Finnish children learn to read, on average, in half the time it takes of an English child. All of the Finnish sounds correspond one-to-one with the letters of the Finnish alphabet. Even though there are 29 letters in the Finnish alphabet as opposed to the 26 in the English one, seven of these letters (b, c, q, w, x, z and the Swedish letter å) do not feature in Finnish words and thus Finnish children only need to learn the correspondences of 24 phonemes to their equivalent letters in order to read fluently. As opposed to this, not only do the phonemes of the English language have irregular spellings, but there are a whopping 44 phonemes in the English language, nearly twice as many as in Finnish!

This comparison illustrates just how crucial phonemes are to reading. Learning to read in Finnish does not require such a high level of phonemic awareness as it does in other languages. Because all Finnish phonemes are regular, there is no teaching of phonics for the children – there is even no word for it; the word 'spelling' (tavata) in Finnish translates as 'spelling by syllables'. Despite the difficult grammar, Finland boasts 100% literacy.[6] (I have heard it suggested that Finland's universal school success in the PISA tests would be down to the phonetic regularity of Finnish. This is not the case, as proven by the relative unsuccessfulness of other countries with a regular written language, such as Italy.)

But the ease of linking sounds to symbols is available to everyone with a high level of phonemic awareness, no matter what their language of reading is. The price us Finns pay for the ease of reading is, evidently, that our spoken language sounds monotonous and lacks the 'musical' variance that is inherent to practically all other languages, from English, Swedish, Chinese and Arabic to the obvious French and Spanish. (I do wonder how Italian manages to sound so pleasant despite being phonetically regular.) My contention is that the common reputation of spoken ugliness has only been ascribed to the German language because the world population is unaware that Finnish even exists. Perhaps this is the reason why early musical learning is so highly valued in Finland. It allows the children to discover the beauty of sounds that they're otherwise not exposed to!

Nevertheless, early music education would be even more crucial for the countries whose languages are harder for children to read. In languages such as English, a child's level of phonemic awareness has a direct effect on their reading success. In Finland, most children learn to read with ease. In English, children commonly struggle with the irregularities and multitude of sounds, and this problem is precisely targeted with early music education.

Already in 1980, it was found that reading and spelling skills during the first school years could be predicted with high accuracy from the level of phoneme awareness skills that the child has years before starting school, in kindergarten.[7] This shows how crucial it is for children to gain music skills before going to school. In fact, it is the make-or-break factor for early success at reading. Reading in turn could arguably be the single most important area to master during the first school years with regards to school success, which makes this result even more significant. It has been shown that school success in the first grade predicts academic success all throughout to the adult years, and lack of early school success, in turn, predicts academic struggle throughout the later years right up until university.[8]

Studies have found that if early phoneme awareness deficits are not addressed, they will not be outgrown, but persist and cause a lifelong struggle in reading.[9] Just like normally able children, children who are at risk of reading failure are shown to benefit crucially from phoneme awareness training (with phonics or music training) as opposed to training with rhymes or by general reading instruction.[10]

How many fewer reading deficits would children have if

their phoneme awareness was trained? It has been shown that for kindergarteners, just four months of music instruction (of a modest amount of 30 minutes a week) significantly improves phonemic awareness.[11] Any parent who wants their child to have a smooth start at school and avoid the frustration of encouraging a child struggling with reading could give their child a whole different schooling experience by simply engaging them in music learning 30 minutes a week before they reach school age.

Yet even 8-year-old children have been shown to significantly improve their reading skills through music. In 1994, Scottish academics Sheila Douglas and Peter Willatts placed 8-year-old schoolchildren randomly into groups of either music instruction or groups that trained their verbal skills in discussion. After just 6 months, they found that the music group participants had boosted their reading abilities, but the discussion group hadn't.[12] This is yet another warning example for parents whose children are likely to encounter a lot of verbal instruction at school yet a deficient amount of training in music skills.

Chapter 29

The Curious Case of Dyslexia

Dyslexia is a painful deficit for those who have it. This learning disability is defined as persisting reading deficits in people of average and above-average intelligence. My husband, who did not have the benefit of early music learning, is dyslexic, and by his own account, struggles on a daily basis because of it. He is very intelligent, and his favourite reading topic is science, but because of his dyslexia, he faces the kind of frustrations and delays that normal readers do not have to think about.

The possibilities of music training to help dyslexic children has been studied with interesting results. It is found that reading-disabled children can discriminate rhythm patterns as well as other children, but their rhythm performance and memory for note relationships are worse.[1]

One scientist who has intensely studied the effect of rhythmic training on dyslexics, Katie Overy from the University of Edinburgh, had found that dyslexics have difficulties with timing but not with pitch.[2] In contrast, some other scientists have found that both rhythm and phonological awareness correlate significantly with reading skills but out of these, phonological skills are more important[3] and these are best boosted with general music instruction that largely involve melody and pitch discrimination as well as tonal ability. Whatever the underlying reason, Overy has found that music lessons focused on rhythm improve the phonological skills and spelling skills of dyslexic children but not their reading skills.

Recent developments in conquering dyslexia have turned the

focus from rhythm to pitch. It is shown that dyslexics do not acquire appropriate levels of phoneme awareness,[4] which is likely to be linked to the fact that dyslexics cannot discriminate between musical pitches that normal readers distinguish easily.[5]

Recent research from Harvard Medical School in 2011 states that 'phonemic awareness skills are positively correlated with pitch perception–production skills in children. Children between the ages of seven and nine were tested on pitch perception and production, phonemic awareness, and IQ. Results showed a significant positive correlation between pitch perception–production and phonemic awareness, suggesting that the relationship between musical and linguistic sound processing is intimately linked to awareness at the level of pitch and phonemes. Since tone-deafness is a pitch-related impairment and dyslexia is a deficit of phonemic awareness, we suggest that dyslexia and tone-deafness may have a shared and/or common neural basis.'[6]

As the neurologists conclude that 'the present results suggest that dyslexia and tone-deafness are related and may share a common basis',[7] we can draw parallels between what we learned from the 'false' tone-deafness described in Chapter 13: Musicality, the X-factor and the Biggest Myth of All. In the vast majority of cases, children are not born tone-deaf, but become that way due to lack of exposure to music. Indeed, science has not yet identified babies whose brains would not be automatically encoding pitches at birth. My husband here is a case in point: he did not have much exposure to music in childhood. His mother was an extremely artistic hands-on mother, but her focus was on arts and crafts.

But some caution must be exercised here. Dyslexia clearly has a neurological basis, as most children end up acquiring a sufficient level of phonemic awareness even without music training (although much more slowly). It has not yet been shown that anything can cure dyslexia completely. But the results of Overy and Harvard Medical

School look very promising. If something can cure or ease dyslexia, it is likely to be linked to music, whether rhythm, pitch or both. It may be that dyslexia cannot ever be completely cured, but the evidence shows that its harmful effects can be effectively minimized through music training.

Part Seven

The Sense of Sensibility: Emotional Intelligence, Social Skills, Well-being and Confidence

In 2009, Professor Graham Welch from the University of London and his research group studied the music skills of over 1200 children in the UK and asked them questions about their personal experience of school life. The study found that the better the children's music skills were, the more likely they were to have friendships of better quality and the higher were their levels of wellbeing.[1] What could explain this astonishing link? Why do music skills boost your child's friendships, wellbeing and quality of social life?

A part of this could be explained with the link between music skills and phonological awareness. As discussed in Chapters 26 and 27, children who had the lowest levels of phonological awareness felt more lonely and more rejected by their peers.[2] As music skills directly affect a child's level of phonological awareness, it would stand to reason that they also boost the children's social well-being.

But music instruction has been shown to boost emotional intelligence and social skills in its own right. This could be because music largely involves the emotional domain, possibly more so than any other activity.

Music activates most of our emotional brain structures: the limbic brain which we share with other mammals as well as animals such as birds, and even the paralimbic brain which we can trace in the course of evolution back to the most primitive forms of animals.[3] Along with other parts of the limbic brain, music activates the amygdala, the managing of which scientist Daniel Goleman in his best-selling book Emotional Intelligence has deemed essential for happiness and success.[4]

In the past few years, science has taken big leaps in discovering the emotional miracles of music making. In 2012, it was discovered that when people make music together, the activity of their brain waves synchronize.[5] This sci-fi sounding finding may explain why music making is such a powerful tool to promote group well-being and cut down bullying and violence, as we will see in Chapters 33 and 34. And I had always wondered why making music as a duet or in a band seemed to contain a strong element of mind reading and an uncanny feeling of spiritual connectedness, even when playing with complete strangers!

Neuroscientists Istvan Molnar-Szakacs and Katie Overy have brought forward a theory based on the recent scientific discovery of 'mirror neurons'. Mirror neurons are the parts of the brain that activate whether you are doing a particular action or watching someone else perform it. We may recall from previous studies that listening to music activates the movement-related networks in the brain. Developing these findings further, Molnar-Szakacs and Overy propose that the mirror neuron system is what connects music not only to movement, but to the whole range of human emotions and understanding them in one another. They write: 'Emotion, especially as communicated by the face, the body and the voice is an active motor process. Emotion and action are intertwined on several levels, and this motor-affective coupling may provide the neural basis of empathy - especially the aspect of empathy that requires no intermediary cognitive process, but rather, is our automatic and immediate "motor identification" or inner imitation of the actions of others.'[6]

In this part of the book, we will discover the fascinating facts behind music and emotion – and more importantly, how your child can, through them, receive direct benefits in all areas of their emotional and social life. As the acclaimed neuroscientist Stefan Koelsch from the University of Berlin put it, 'Making music is an activity that involves several social functions: (1) when we make music, we make contact with other individuals (preventing social isolation); (2) music automatically engages social cognition; (3) it engages co-pathy in the sense that interindividual emotional states become more homogenous (e.g. reducing anger in one individual and depression or anxiety in another), thus promoting interindividual understanding and decreasing conflicts.'[7]

In short, whether it is love, friendship or emotional well-being that we most wish for our children, music training at a young age is an optimal tool we cannot afford to ignore.

Chapter 30

Learning Music, Learning Emotion

Music may have often been called the language of emotion, but the question that puzzled scientists for a long time was whether music evoked the same emotions as real-life situations or whether it evoked different aesthetic emotions that were not linked to the real emotions we feel when we are happy, upset, angry, content or so forth. Some music researchers had previously theorized that music does not engage genuine emotions. This theory undoubtedly would sound suspicious to anyone who has ever cried when listening to a sad piece of music. Once again, the improvements of brain imaging technology came to the rescue, and in 2010 it was found that music indeed evokes the same emotions in us as the real events in our lives.[1]

As music engages our authentic emotions, this could explain why learning to understand and create music helps a child learn to better understand both their own emotions and those of others. As music evokes real-life emotions, learning to manage musical information involves learning to manage emotional information. Managing emotional information, in turn, is the essence of the concept of emotional intelligence.

It has been found that when children train in music, they are learning to self-regulate, which is a crucial component of child development as well as emotional intelligence. Even babies and toddlers who study music are shown to have a better level of self-regulation than their non-music peers.[2] Self-regulation is about managing your emotions and it is, alongside phonological awareness and handclapping skills, a key factor for success at school.[3] More importantly, some reputable scientists such as Daniel Goleman claim that it is the key to success in practically every area of life.[4]

Howard Gardner's ideas from the early 1980s relating to interpersonal intelligence and intrapersonal intelligence can be seen as precursors to the concept of emotional intelligence that took off in the early 1990s, an era where scientists evoked their interest in the domain of emotion. In 1990, Peter Salovey and John D. Mayer formulated the theory of emotional intelligence as a testable ability separate from IQ. This was brought to the attention of the general public with scientist Daniel Goleman's best-selling book Emotional Intelligence (1995), which applied a wider concept of emotional intelligence than that of Salovey and Mayer, mixing in wellbeing, psychological health and plain old happiness.

Around the same time, another instant bestseller, Descartes' Error: Emotion, Reason and the Human Brain by neurologist Antonio Damasio was published. Damasio had found in brain studies that humans cannot actually separate the emotional and cognitive (information-based) domains from one another. What's more, the cognitive domain is based on emotions. One may sometimes play with the idea that having a computer-like mind detached from emotion might be beneficial for making unbiased decisions in life. But when Damasio investigated studies on brain-damaged subjects who had lost the ability to feel (psychologically and emotionally), he found that despite having their cognitive abilities intact, they were unable to make decisions of any kind. It turns out that emotions are necessary for using any kind of information in the first place.[5]

Damasio's discovery is significant as it demolishes the age-old myth of the separation of emotion and intellect. Cold intellect simply does not exist, or it does in computers, but certainly not in the human brain. The constant and unavoidable undercurrent of emotion in every human activity could explain why Goleman and many other scientists claim that emotional management skills are even more crucial to success in life than IQ.

As music evokes the emotional domain, musical concepts could be seen as a kind of emotional symbol system. The reason to better self-regulation could be that music skills involve learning to consciously use emotional-musical symbols such as rhythm and melody, both of which evoke highly emotional states depending on the precise properties of however a rhythm or melody sounds like. Creating music involves creating emotion. Therefore music training is, among other things, training in emotion.

Interestingly, cross-cultural studies have found that emotion recognition in music is universal and not dependent on culture. It has long been known that we have universal human emotions and that we can recognize displays of basic emotions such as happiness, love, anger and sadness in the facial expressions any human being, even if they come from a culture completely different to our own. But the discovery that the same applies to music has been rather more recent. In 1999, Laura-Lee Balkwill and William Forde Thompson from York University, Toronto found that Westerners who had never previously heard a type of North Indian music (Hindustani raga) were able to identify the emotions it represented as accurately as those born in that culture and surrounded by that music.[6] In 2009, a study by a group of leading researchers from the Max Planck Institute for Human Cognitive and Brain Sciences found that a native African (Mafa) population who had previously not even heard the radio before were able to recognize the basic emotions in our Western music, and vice versa for the Westerners who for the first time listened to the Mafa music.[7]

The emotional benefits of music are possible to observe even in babies and toddlers. For instance, distressed and crying babies calm down 94.5% of the time when someone sings to them, much more often than through other means such as cradling and cuddling.[8]

Furthermore, babies who engage in music training develop their emotional, social and communicative skills faster than other babies, even when all babies were previously on the same level of development.[9]

The importance of developing core music skills was illustrated by the 2012 study lead by neuroscientist David Gerry, in which the control groups also took part in music classes, but these classes did not teach music skills. They focused on listening and playing alongside classical music pieces playing in the background. The babies in the groups that listened to music but did not receive musical training did not gain any more benefits than babies who do not take part in music classes at all, whereas the babies who received the weekly training reaped huge benefits with regards to their emotional intelligence and communication skills.[10] (This is yet another reason to destroy the Mozart Effect myth – see Chapter 11 - as only music instruction offers real results.)

This study expanded earlier findings from 2010 that showed that toddlers who had taken part in music training classes had more advanced skills related to emotional intelligence, such as self-regulation, the ability to self-soothe, calm oneself down, and be more patient and persistent.[11] These are the skills that are found to predict positive life outcomes - from health to career success - for life.[12]

Chapter 31

Do You Hear What I Feel? Music training and Emotion Recognition

The basic component of emotional intelligence is the ability to identify emotion in oneself and others. Recent years of research have found that music education makes a significant difference with regards to recognizing emotion. Music learning boosts children's brain connections that relate to recognizing emotion in sound, whether the source of the sound is music or speech.[1] And just one year of instrument training helps young schoolchildren to recognize and correctly label which kind of emotion a person is expressing in speech.[2] Again, we see that emotion recognition is an ability that can be developed and not something that either is or isn't given to us at birth.

Interestingly, a group of Yale University researchers found in 2004 that the mere ability to recognize emotion in music correlates with general measures of emotional intelligence: the better you are at recognizing emotion in music, the higher your emotional intelligence test score tends to be, and vice versa.[3] Although every human is wired to respond emotionally to music, it is shown that music training significantly boosts the ability to recognize emotion in music.[4]

The earlier the children start, the more effective neural connections are formed in their brain in those areas that process emotion in both music and speech. The leading neural research in this area has found that children need to start at the age of seven at the very latest to develop their pitch- and emotion-processing capacities to the full.[5] This links in with the other findings on the benefits of music education. It's never too late to gain brain benefits from music learning, but all the research shows that to unlock all of your child's inherent gifts to their fullest, it is best to start as early as possible. As we know, many children are not training in music, and those who are often start too late at the recommendation of teachers who are oblivious to its developmental benefits.

Whilst nothing beats music training, some studies have found that even having adequate exposure to music boosts the emotion recognition to a degree. Children who do not get adequate exposure to music at their environments (such as home and nursery) do not necessarily develop their emotional intelligence to its full potential. It has been found that home music environment – not the age of the children – boosts the ability of children to recognize moods in music.[6] This means that emotion recognition does not develop with age but with exposure to music. So while listening to music at home does not increase intelligence like the Mozart myth claims, it may have some emotional benefits. But the fact that just one music training lesson a week for four months is found to have a substantially bigger effect than 15 to 20 hours of weekly music listening at home and in class shows the power of music training.[7] Still, mere exposure to music also contributes to the skill of emotion recognition.

An array of brain imaging studies by Patrik Jusslin and Petri Laukka from Stockholm University has found that understanding and interpreting emotion in speech and music share the same brain resources.[8] It's perhaps no wonder that music learners have an advantage in both, as has been found in several studies such as those conducted by Daniele Schön's research group at the Mediterranean Cognitive Neuroscience Institute.[9]

A comprehensive study lead by Russian neurologist E.S. Dmitrieva that was published in 2006 had especially enlightening results for parents. It found that children who trained in music skills had a significant mental age advantage at recognizing emotion. Girls who received music training were more developed than their female classmates by one to three years and the boys studying music were ahead of other boys their age by an astonishing *four to six years.*[10]

It seems that music training is an important vehicle for the life success of all children, but especially to boys with regards to developing their emotional intelligence. As we remember from the list of Multiple Intelligences and the Music Miracle in Chapter 16, girls have a slight advantage at emotional skills, just as boys have a slight advantage at spatial intelligence. What is remarkable is that in both cases, the children who train in music become, regardless of their own gender's tendencies, better at both of these domains than those who have a natural advantage for it but do not learn music.

Curiously, the emotional recognition abilities that music study boosts are not restricted to the auditory domain. Music training has been linked to a better ability to recognize visual forms of emotional expression, such as tests of facial expressions on screen.[11] Scientists found in 2012 that labeling of emotions, whether in the auditory (such as speech) or visual (such as facial expressions and gestures) domain, share the same neural networks in the brain.[12] Musicians are even shown to imitate gestures better than non-musicians,[13] which shows that they not only recognize the visual communication better, but are also better equipped to reproduce those gestures themselves.

This shows a music learner's advantage for not just emotion recognition in physical gestures but also a better ability to execute what scientists call nonconscious behavioural mimicry. Scientists have found that when we engage with someone, we unconsciously mimic their gestures. Furthermore, 'the chameleon effect', the ability to subtly mirror the non-verbal communication of someone you're socializing with, has shown to be beneficial for social interaction.

This could be one of the reasons why music learning boosts social skills.

The ability to recognize emotion in gestures and facial expression should not be undervalued. Social scientists have long been puzzled by the research findings that every new person we meet (even for just a few minutes) can potentially convey a striking amount of accurate information. It has been found that strangers can evaluate the personality of a test subject after a brief interaction potentially just as accurately as the test subject themselves. There is, therefore, great potential in a person who can master the recognition of emotion and nonverbal communication - the so-called 'body language'. These skills are useful in all areas of life – from career skills to satisfying social relationships.

Chapter 32

Taming the Wild Horses: Managing and appreciating emotion

Emotional intelligence involves the ability to generate appropriate emotion and modulate emotions in oneself and others. Children who study music are better able to calm themselves down in stressful or ambiguous situations. They are also more able to control their emotions and focus on tasks.[1] These skills show significant gains in the emotion-generating and modulating parts of emotional intelligence. Perhaps this explains why early music learners are shown to be able to focus better on tasks and have a significantly higher mental age than their same-age peers who have not learned music.[2]

Another component that makes up emotional intelligence, according to its founding researchers John D. Mayer and Peter Salovey, is the ability to appreciate emotional meanings. Western society is generally noted for its focus on pure reason at the expense of emotion and emotional meanings. The ideology that pure reason could (and should) be separated from emotion has its origins in the birth of philosophy in Ancient Greece 2500 years ago. The title of the book Descartes' Error makes reference to a somewhat more recent classical philosopher René Descartes, who in the 17th century placed emphasis on pure reason, separate from emotion and experiences, in formulating his philosophical theories.

Nevertheless, as reported in Antonio Damasio's Descartes' Error, brain science has found that our cognitive domains cannot function without the emotional faculties – and indeed our cognitive judgments are based on our underlying emotional reactions, mostly without us even noticing. Paradoxically, we cannot *know* without the ability to *feel*. As for communication, research on how our brains interpret speech has established that even speech that would traditionally be labeled non-emotional has its roots in the emotional faculties of the brain, found on the right side of the brain.[3]

In the light of these findings, it wouldn't be surprising if a part of the intellectual advantages that early music learning gives would actually stem from the better understanding of emotion. The ability to appreciate emotional meanings is not something that is in the standard school curriculum, yet it is a crucial benefit of training in music.

Not only is music the language of emotions, but music training boosts the capabilities to attune oneself to musical meanings, which, as we have seen, are inherently tied to emotional meanings in the brain. Emotion is central to all music making, all the way from the 'music babble' of babies. Even a virtuoso level of playing technique alone is not considered to produce impressive music. The most technical conservatoire-style instrument training still depends on the interpretation of emotion through music, as studies on computer-performed virtuoso pieces where emotion has been neutralized have shown.[4]

Thus, an essential part of the value that our culture places on music is tied to its ability to evoke feelings in us. Research shows that when music does not evoke emotion in its listeners, they consider it worthless.[5]

The benefits for your child's emotional intelligence are obvious. By helping your children appreciate music you are effectively helping them appreciate emotions – their own and those of others. In the next chapters we will look at the remarkable effects music training has for harmonious social relationships.

Chapter 33

Music Brings Harmony to Schools

"In elementary schools, the prevalence of bullying ranges from 11.3% in Finland to 49.8% in Ireland. The only United States study of elementary students found that 19% were bullied. (...) School bullying is associated with numerous physical, mental, and social detriments. A relationship also exists between student bullying behavior and school issues such as academic achievement, school bonding, and absenteeism. Prevention of school bullying should become a priority issue for schools. The most effective methods of bullying reduction involve a whole school approach."

Joseph A. Dake, James H. Price, Susan K. Telljohann, The Nature and Extent of Bullying at School (2003)[1]

It becomes obvious when studying the curriculum and lesson timetable of any school that the time spent on developing literacy and mathematical reasoning is vast, yet the guidance for social development is practically nonexistent.

It is implicitly assumed that children develop social skills automatically and without formal training, yet as we have seen in this chapter, this is not the case at all. Boys who learn music are four to six years ahead of other boys with their emotional skills and even girls a full one to three years ahead of other girls.[2] As social skills and wellbeing are the basic prerequisite for mastering the academic subjects[3], it is clear that a larger inclusion of music education in the school curriculum would kill two birds with one stone by benefiting both the heads and the hearts of the pupils.

During my short period of studies there, I was surprised to find that in the leading teacher training university (University of Helsinki) in the world's leading country of education (according to OECD's PISA tests), Finland, the focus is to this day on the academic domain only. As I was aware that bullying is a major problem in Finland – on average a minimum of two or three pupils per class suffer from ongoing bullying[4] – and yet there are effective policies to stop bullying altogether, I was keen to learn about these bullying prevention techniques that teachers could put in place in class and ensure that no child should have to go through what I and others did in our school days. I asked one of the professors about this, and she remarked, 'Oh yes, bullying. We will have a bullying-themed lesson at some point during the fifth year.'

Considering how the teachers are trained every single day over their 5-year degree to teach numeracy and literacy in the most effective way, and that bullying has famous life- and brain-damaging consequences, I found this lack of focus on the student wellbeing surprising, if not downright shocking. This could be taken as a sign of our reason-based Western culture in which intellectual abilities are trained at the expense of emotional and social skills.

When teachers are not taught how to deal with bullying and how to prevent it, it is little wonder that so many children continue to suffer from it. Having been a victim of bullying as a child has its effects even in adulthood: problems from disturbed behaviour to suicide proneness.[5] As many as 27 percent of UK schoolchildren in primary are bullied 'sometimes' or more often.[6] New research from 2009 shows that abuse by name-calling by peers alone, even without any physical violence, significantly reduces the all-important corpus callosum thickness of a child or teenager, even when the child has good relationships with their family.[7] Many people to this day believe that bullying cannot be stopped, whereas scientific studies have clearly shown that it can,[8] but only if the teachers and their supervisors make deliberate effort. To learn to do this, they need help. Bullying is not going to disappear unless an intentional change is made, both at the level of awareness and the curriculum.

As an example of an anti-bullying approach, Yovanka B. Lobo and Adam Winsler from George Mason University found in 2006 that just 12 weeks of music and movement training significantly boosted the social skills and behaviour amongst preschoolers. The behaviour and social competence were independently rated by teachers and parents so they also experienced the direct benefits. Children who instead went to a class of free play and movement, engaging in exactly the same content but without the music, in comparison did not get the boost in social skills and behaviour.[9]

Additionally, a pilot study from 2010 on a music intervention on highly aggressive children found that the music training significantly reduced the aggression of these 'problem children' in just 15 weeks, as rated independently by parents, teachers and a psychological test.[10] These results show that ending bullying need not be a pipe dream.In the next chapter we turn to look at the mechanics through which music training brings harmony to schools, as well as all other forms of social life: empathy, the skill of relating to what other people are feeling.

Chapter 34

Empathy: The Missing Link between Emotional Intelligence and Real Life

Tests of emotional intelligence measure only ability, not empathy. But in real life, empathy is the fuel without which even the best of social skills will amount to nothing but self-serving manipulation.

It would be easy to assume that people with high emotional intelligence are good people who are nicer to be around. However, emotional intelligence is only an ability, and just like high IQ, a high 'EQ' (or 'EI' as it is also called) can be used for good or bad. Howard Gardner, the father of emotional intelligence with his ideas of interpersonal and intrapersonal intelligence, emphasizes that all of his multiple intelligences are morally neutral. It is easy to see that many of the leading dictators of world history have not only had an above-average IQ but, perhaps even more importantly, a high level of emotional intelligence. Without an extremely good eye for manipulating other people's emotions (by understanding those emotions and being able to generate them), someone like Hitler would not have left his tragic mark onto the history of humankind.

A most striking example of emotional intelligence being inherently separate from good intentions is that of sociopaths. Psychologists have found that sociopaths often have brilliant social skills, yet underlying it is their inability to relate to other people's emotions. They are skilled at perceiving emotion in others and manipulating the feelings of others to their advantage. Yet within, they lack the ability to relate to others – even in the worst cases of human suffering (although they are famous for feigning sympathy that often seems more authentic than the real sympathy of normal non-sociopathic humans). Dr. Martha Stout states that when a sociopath is exposed, usually by getting caught (whether at lying to committing a terrible act of violence), the people who knew him or her are usually openly shocked as to them, the sociopath had seem like 'the nicest person in the world'.[1]

In the case of bullying, the widespread myth is that bullies lack self-esteem. What studies have found, however, is that they have too much of it. Victims of bullying suffer from low self-esteem, but the bullies themselves hold as high a view of themselves, their attractiveness, attributes and popularity as the lucky children who are neither bullied nor bullies.[2] What bullies lack is not esteem but empathy – the ability to put themselves in their victims' shoes.

Moreover, children who have high self-esteem but low empathy are risk for developing narcissism.[3] Narcissism often leads to general life problems in both relationships and career.[4] Narcissistic individuals have excessively high levels of aggression and antisocial behaviour[5] as well as an increased risk for violence[6] and rape[7]. Therefore, developing the empathy of children is crucial for not just the functioning of the human society but also for the future of the bullies themselves.

Music training is empathy training

Empathy, interestingly, can be measured. It is measured completely separately from the ability-based tests of emotional intelligence. To make a crude distinction, one's level of emotional intelligence determines their theoretical level of social ability, and empathy directs how much they're putting the ability they have into practice. Just as emotional intelligence can be developed, so can empathy. It turns out that music training is a proven way to do both.

As with the other abilities, the sooner children start developing them, the higher levels they can reach. A 2008 study by Dr. Eva Brand and Ora Bar-Gil from Bar-Ilan University in Israel studied children aged four to six and found that the more active a child was in music education activities, the greater their improvements were in all areas of social skills and emotional intelligence, such as self-awareness, listening to others and collaboration.[1]

A study from 2010 by Kirschner and Tomasello from the Max Planck Institute in Germany found that cooperative music making increased the amount of spontaneous helpful and cooperative behaviour of the 4-year-old participants. The control group of 4-year-olds did exactly the same activities without music and did not experience these benefits. The researchers write: 'Our results show that (...) joint music making enhances prosocial behaviour in 4-year-old children. The children in the non-music condition interacted with one another in the same way as those in the musical condition – shared the same goals, coordinated their actions in time, even imitated each other's movements and verbal comments, only without music and dance – our study isolates the special effect of music over and above social and linguistic interaction in general.'[2]

In other words, their carefully controlled study found that it was music, not the other means of communicating, that produced the empathy increase. Most recently, a 2012 study by Rabinowitch, Cross and Burnard from the University of Cambridge found that music and empathy share underlying cognitive resources. The scientists researched children aged eight to ten and found that the music group, as opposed to several control groups that did other activities instead, significantly boosted their empathy according to videotaped samples of social interaction.[3]

When I started researching this topic, I found that the groundwork studies on the effects of music on the empathy of small children were already made in the late 1980s and early 1990s, and in my birthplace of Finland. Researchers Mirja Kalliopuska and Inkeri Ruokonen from the University of Helsinki found in 1986 that just three months of music activities once a week significantly boosted the empathy of 6-year-old children by all leading measurements of empathy. The control groups achieved no increases in empathy.[4] Again in 1993, a study by Kalliopuska found that music instruction increased empathy, respect and appreciation of others.[5]

The most recent studies from Max Planck Institute and University of Cambridge have focused on group music making as an empathy booster. But do children who learn music skills alone reap equal social benefits? There has only been one study so far on the empathy measurements of children who study an instrument with private tuition and not within a group, and the results have shown that it is music training that boosts empathy, regardless of whether it is done in a group or individually. In this study, the researchers Kalliopuska and Hietolahti-Ansten compared primary school aged instrument players to same-age children who did not play an instrument and found that the musically skilled children (who had played for an average of six years) had significantly higher levels of both empathy and self-esteem.[6] (We will talk about self-esteem more in the following chapter.) The non-musician children, in turn, had lesser scores in both empathy and self-esteem.[7] Far from being opposite forces, respect for others and respect for oneself seem intriguingly intertwined.

There is no doubt that parents and educators can boost future generations' ability to relate to others by music training. As the older generations can sometimes blame the younger ones for being so selfish and self-centered, there is no excuse to believe that 'it is what it is'. As we have seen, just three months of music learning significantly boosts the empathy of preschoolers, and keeping up the hobby of music further develops this capacity. Thus, by engaging your child in regular music training, you are not just helping you child but making the whole society a better, more harmonious place.

Chapter 35

Self-esteem, Confidence and the Musical Key to Happiness

As we have seen with the cases of narcissism and sociopathy, without empathy, a high level of self-esteem can be harmful.[1] Yet when combined with empathy, self-esteem is possibly the most important ingredient on the path to happiness.[2] A wealth of research has established that high self-esteem leads to greater happiness. It has even been found that self-esteem is a better predictor of young people's subjective happiness than parenting style or personality traits[3] - this is sure to have come as a surprise to us the readers of parenting books! Conversely, low self-esteem has been found to lead easily to depression.[4]

Even before scientists knew that music boosts the brain, it had become apparent that it boosts self-esteem. Over the past twenty years studies have consistently found that music training boosts the self-esteem of children.[5]

Studies find that a high self-esteem comes partially from achievements, such as academic achievement.[6] Throughout this book, we have seen that music training is what gives an edge to the academic success of children. But this is just one part of the equation of why music training boosts confidence.

When Eugenia Costa-Giomi from the University of Texas in Austin set out to examine whether children aged nine or older benefited academically from music training, she found that they didn't. They were past the critical age for the Music Miracle, so even three years of piano instruction did not boost their academic, mathematical or language achievement.[7] Despite this, she found that the music training had significantly increased their confidence.[8] Therefore, even when a child is past the age to maximize their brain boost from music, it is not too late to gain significant emotional benefits from music training. It has been found that adults[9] and pensioners[10] alike can boost their self-esteem and confidence by music training.

Conversely, music training offers a great opportunity to build up your child's self-esteem right from birth. The 2012 study lead by David Gerry found that babies who study music learn not only to communicate better, but also to express their needs and wants better. And this was no tantrum-like 'free expression': these babies also exhibited more awareness of other people's needs than other babies their age.[11]

This indicates the same increase of self-esteem and empathy in babies that can be observed in older children. A 2012 study from Monash University in Australia assigned over 350 children (from pre-school age to third grade) to either music classes or control groups who continued with their usual curriculum. As a result, the musician children had much higher levels of self-esteem than the non-musicians in the study.[12] Another study from the University of Helsinki on the self-esteem of children who had played music for six years since the age of six found that these children, who were now 12 years old, had statistically a high self-esteem, compared to their non-musician peers who only had moderate self-esteem.[13]

But is it only music that boosts self-esteem? The 2012 Monash University study found that as a comparative activity, juggling may have had beneficial effects on the self-esteem of the third- grade children but not on the self-esteem of the preschoolers and first graders.[14] How about activities that happen *to* music, such as dancing? A study by dance and movement researchers Jan Burkhardt and Cathy Brennan, also from 2012, examined the benefits of dancing as a hobby and found only limited evidence that dancing would improve the self-esteem and psychological and social well-being of children and adolescents.[15] A general review on the benefits of hobbies on children has found no self-esteem boost from extracurricular activities as such.[16] This is not to say that they do not have benefits, as another study found that extracurricular activities tend to reduce school dropout.[17] But a controversial result has also been found: that strangely enough, involvement in team sports may increase the risk for adolescent alcohol use.[18]

In short, the evidence for the self-esteem boost from hobbies in general remains inconclusive. In the light of these studies, it seems that music is a special activity not only when it comes to brain training and emotional skills, but also confidence and self-esteem.

One could think that a person with low self-esteem is prone to feel more stress. This may be true, but studies have shown that stress and stressful events are also a direct cause, not just the result, of low self-esteem. Persons who experience stressful events are more prone to have their self-esteem lowered and damaged.[19] This can create a vicious circle which at its very worst can lead to suicidality. [20]

But how do we break the cycle, when sooner or later, life throws stressful challenges at each of us? A comparative study from 2011 measured the stress hormone (cortisol) levels of young adults participating in different creative art activities. One group participated in piano playing, another in clay molding and a third in calligraphy. The control group did no activity. After the session, the stress levels of the participants were measured in a blood test. All participants in the creative art groups had reduced stress compared to the no-activity group, but the positive effect of piano playing was found to be significantly greater than of the other activities.[21]

This indicates that music making taps into a core need of humans, having a much more beneficial effect on our self-esteem and wellbeing than other activities. Our Western culture is quite unique in its sense of making music something that only the ‘specialists’ can achieve, as opposed to a natural activity that anyone can participate in from an active standpoint. From an evolutionary angle, we could infer that all humans are made to make music, just like they are meant to learn to talk. Both are essential forms of self-expression that millions of years of evolution have wired our brains to do.

As music making also promotes empathy and social skills, it can be concluded that the more we engage people of all ages into making music, the more well-adjusted our society can become. As self-esteem is the leading cause of wellbeing, music training turns out to be the optimal activity choice for a parent wanting to promote their child’s happiness not just in the future, but also right here, right now.

Part Eight

Creativity and New Learning: Remedies in the face of the challenges of today and tomorrow

Education experts in the new millennium have woken up to the realization that the traditional methods of school instruction are not the final word in our ever-changing world. Focusing exclusively on literacy and numeracy (or the linguistic and logical-mathematical intelligences, in Gardner's terms) will not prepare the future generations for the changing demands of tomorrow's workplace. Because of the wide-ranging changes in technology, economy, environment and culture, whole new domains of jobs are being created and traditional ones are vanishing. The kind of jobs that used to occupy the majority of workforce just a few generations back are now being replaced with technology, machines and outsourcing to countries where it is deemed economically advantageous for the big corporations. Whether we like it or not, this is the reality that we must prepare our children for.

Because of these changes, the school system is slowly changing course like an ocean liner from rote learning to the philosophy of 'learning to learn'. In previous generations, a basic level of literacy and mathematical reasoning was enough to sustain most people's working capabilities throughout their adult lives. These days, as manual jobs are disappearing from the way of information-based professions, the concept of 'life-long learning' is becoming recognized as more important than a basic level of narrow skills and information regurgitation.

Already in the late 1980s, it was acknowledged that the weekday edition of New York Times contained more information than the average person in 17-century England was likely to come across in his lifetime.[1] In 2000, scientists Peter Lyman and Hal R. Varian from Berkeley University took on the task of measuring the information currently produced and found that the information explosion was indeed exponential, concluding: 'It is clear that we are all drowning in a sea of information. The challenge is to learn to swim in that sea, rather than drown in it. Better understanding and better tools are desperately needed if we are to take full advantage of the ever-increasing supply of information.'[2]

What would these tools be? Simply getting by in this new world of information overload requires a capacity to constantly take in new information and use it in a productive, resourceful way. Creativity, in turn, is recognized as the key factor not only in a person's ability to innovate, but for simply adapting to unexpected changes in a resourceful manner.

In this section, we will talk about how the Music Miracle is the key to developing these two new core skills of school success: creativity and learning to learn. The fact that music learning boosts your child's capacity to upload information faster and remember it better could just be the key 'tool' that Lyman and Varian call out for. After all, one's brain is one's primary tool.

It is interesting to note that despite all this information, little is put in place in the existing school system. Any kind of system that involves millions of people and thousands of bureaucrats (and massive investments of taxpayers' money) is understandably slow at changing its course – just think of the ocean liner. However, what parents can do is to put these changes in place immediately within our own offspring and thus ensure that at least our own children – the ones whose fate we're directly able to affect - get into the lifeboat in time.

Chapter 36

The Brain Upgrade: How Music Training Increases Memory and Brainpower

Nowadays, computer skills (ICT) are gaining a more prominent status in the UK. Changing the way ICT is taught is one major focal point of Education Secretary Michael Gove's ongoing project of the school reform. As Gove notes, this is a reflection on the changing environment: suddenly, without ICT skills, you are, in most jobs, as unemployable as those who cannot read or write.

This may be true at the very moment, although it depends on the profession. The problem with making ICT a core subject is that the pupils of today are taught the computer skills of today, which, by the time they are at the employment market in fifteen to twenty years time, may well have become yesteryear's skills and about as useless and nostalgic as learning Latin.

Now, I am not condemning ICT or Latin. As a teenager, I studied my stint of Latin and found it fascinating. I am just saying that when it comes to realistic employability, one may well become as much of a dead language as the other. I personally love learning bygone skills as a hobby. However, it is ironic that ICT is lifted up to a core subject status when what we need is not today's hip skills that will be out of time in two years, let alone fifteen to twenty when today's children enter the workplace. Learning to code, in turn, might be genuinely beneficial for children, but the ICT lessons seldom extend to this level of practicality.

What we need is a way to teach the children to adapt to new

situations and new information, including new, yet unimaginable technologies. Just ten years ago in the early 2000s, there was no social media, not even Myspace, let alone Facebook, Twitter or LinkedIn. Google and blogging barely existed. The inventions of the iPad, touch screen and smart phones have only appeared over the past few years. Provided that we avoid the climate catastrophe, the technological changes will undoubtedly keep happening faster and faster. In short, we do not need to focus on this year's form of ICT, we need to teach our children to adapt to new teachings. This is the real key to future employability – not teaching whiteboards to five-year-olds.

Information technology changes every year. What your child gets to keep for life is the upgrades of their brain.

Swimming in the sea of information technology

The current importance of ICT should instead be taken as a sign that our children need to be taught how to learn, rather than the specifics of what to learn. The Lyman and Varian study is now, at the time of writing this, twelve years old, and it doesn't take a superbly upgraded brain to see that their predictions of drowning in a sea of information have become more prominent than ever. Indeed, when the scientists revisited Lyman and Varian's findings in 2003, they found that each one of the three years had produced 30% of more information than the previous year.[1]

The Music Miracle is ideal for managing the influx of data. Music learning boosts the brain's working memory, developing the brains of children to process and hold a larger amount of information simultaneously and to perform multiple operations at the same time.[2] A good level of working memory is essential for any task that requires complex information, whether learning something new, piecing together information from separate sources or just holding several pieces of information in mind at once. For example, any type of writing requires working memory, as one has to hold information in mind whilst formulating how to best express it in written language.

School theorists famously talk about the importance of active learning. As opposed to passive learning (also titled rote learning) where students mechanically memorize the learning content and then regurgitate it in the classroom or an exam, active learning is applauded as the key to real learning. With active learning, a person not only learns something more efficiently but retains the learning material much better in long-term memory, so that they can use the information in the future.

The catch-22 is that in order to learn actively, one needs to have a good level of working memory to begin with. A good working memory is essential for the brain to process new information and to use it in a productive way. This foundation makes active learning easier and more enjoyable, which in turn leads to more ease and pleasure in learning. Without higher-functioning memory levels, a pupil just feels confused and frustrated when asked to put their own personal spin on the learning material. Rather than enjoying the freedom of active learning, they just wish that the teachers would continue to tell them exactly what to memorize and how. Thus, trying new and trendy methods of active learning is not going to help students who lack in working memory efficiency.

What we need instead is a system to boost the working memory of all children. Scientists Elyse M. George and Donna Coch from the Ivy League University Dartmouth College know how. Their 2011 study shows that those people who have music as a hobby have a much more effective working memory. They outperform non-music hobbyists on all tests of auditory, visual, and executive memory and their brains' neural networks have been found to be more effective, working faster and more accurately.[3]

Music training is also found to improve long-term memory, which may be another explanatory factor for the school success of music students.[4] This means that children who study music not only process new information better, they also retain it in the brain for longer periods of time. As practically all study subjects are 'scaffolded', meaning that new material is built on previously taught material, this gives an additional advantage for pupils who have better long-term memory. Instead of teaching children to separately memorize individual learning contents, a school system would do better with focusing on upgrading the children's underlying brainpower, because only this will ensure that the children have a chance of mastering any core subject in the first place.

Just like you cannot browse the internet with a 1980s computer no matter how much your teacher tries to push you, you cannot expect children to master a multitude of topics if they haven't even been given the chance to optimize their brain's learning capacity.

Chapter 37

The Boss of the Brain: Executive functioning

Our son has a book on the human body which taught him that the brain is the boss. Now, whenever he says or does something innovative and I ask him how he came up with it, he says, 'Because my brain told me to.'

The ancient Egyptians thought that humans were governed by their hearts, which is why they sucked the dead body's brain through their nose in the mummification process and left the sacred heart intact. Now we know what my son does: the brain is the boss. But what, in turn, governs the brain? According to brain science, our brain is not a singular governing entity but more like a committee of network-workers, communicating with and against one another, often with conflicting interests. In this sense, the brain of a human is like the European Parliament.

Yet the brain also has a boss. The boss of the brain is called the executive functioning, and it only works when we choose to use it. This is the conscious, non-automatic part of the brain that enables us to deliberately take control of the chaos, decide what to do or not to do, and then put it to action – to execute it. The executive functioning is crucial for succeeding in tasks that are novel – anything that requires abilities such as concentration, planning, problem-solving, resourcefulness or creativity.1 Just like working memory, a good level of executive functioning is necessary for a person – child or adult – to participate in active learning, as it crucially requires independent planning and problem solving. Even for rote learning, the executive function enables a person to focus on a task better, longer and more efficiently and override the impulses of boredom or distraction (or, in the case of make-or-break exams, despair!).

As executive functioning is crucial for succeeding in situations that we don't have a routine solution for, improving a child's brain capacity for executive functioning is one of the best ways to equip them for the fast-changing world. As old jobs are disappearing, a resourceful person with a better capacity to learn is much more likely to succeed in spite of what happens in the economic climate.

Distinguished scientist Dr. Ellen Bialystok has established over the past decade that bilingualism gives a child an advantage in executive functioning.[2] Surprisingly, in 2009, a study lead by Bialystok found that music learners have an even better level of executive functioning than all other people, including the bilinguals.[3] Considering that to become bilingual you either have to have parents with separate mother tongues or put your child to a full language-immersion nursery at a young age, it is interesting that just an hour of weekly music training gains the same – and indeed, better – results.

Perhaps surprisingly, IQ does not correlate with executive functioning; it is possible for a child to have a high IQ yet low executive functioning, and vice versa.[4] Therefore it is especially interesting that music learning boosts both abilities, making for a higher IQ and better executive functioning. In 2011, it was found that just a short-term music training of 20 days, two hours a day, boosted the children's executive functioning and intelligence compared to the children who did not undergo the training. The children who were tested were only 4 to 5 years of age and their music training did not include learning to play an instrument – instead, it consisted of training in music theory concepts such as rhythm, melody and notation.[5]

Along with standardized tests, the brains of the children were also scanned and found to be more effective in the structures related to executive functioning – all this within the course of just twenty days. These results have promising indications of how we can unlock the learning capacity of our children and help them thrive in the world of information overload. However, is should be reasonably assumed that to keep up the brain upgrade, a child needs to engage in a regular, ongoing amount of music training (of roughly 60 minutes a week) in order to not lose their new neural networks to the pruning process. The good news is that even a year or two of music training, when done young enough, boosts the brain in a lasting way.[6]

Chapter 38

The Creativity Crisis of Children

Our fast-paced, constantly changing world rewards not just learning at warp speed, but resourcefulness. In the new world, creativity is not an airy-fairy luxury that only children and starving artists can indulge in, but a necessity even for the most cutting-edge of businessmen. This came to light in 2010, when research on no less than 1500 leading global CEOs revealed that out of all qualities, creativity was considered to be the best predictor of business success.[1]

Sir Ken Robinson's TED talk, currently the most watched presentation to date in the respected TED series with over 13 million individual views since its online broadcast started in 2006,[2] brought creativity into wide public attention. More specifically, educationalist Robinson argued for the unique need for creativity in the new world and how the traditional school system discourages it.

Shocking research results seem to back up Robinson's claim that creativity is educated out of children. In 1968, scientist George Land measured the creativity of 1300 American schoolchildren aged 3 to 5 with the same creativity test that NASA uses to measure creative thinking in scientists and engineers. An astonishing 98% of the children scored at the highest 'genius' level of the test.[3]

The children were retested at the ages of eight to ten and it was found that only a third of the children, 32 percent, were still capable of genius creativity. Retested once again at the ages of 13 to 15, only 10% of the children were at this high level of creativity. Land then tested adults aged 25 and found an even further decline. Only 2% tested at genius-level creativity.[4]

Human creativity has become an endangered species. Land's longitudinal study was made several decades ago, but the situation has only worsened. For the first time in recorded history, the creativity of Western children has dropped significantly, predicting an even steeper decline in people's creative abilities.[5] Considering how creativity is the driving force behind all of society's innovations and technological improvements that are so highly valued in the world today, this creativity crisis is something that we should take very seriously.

Can creativity be taught?

Fortunately, not all formal learning poses a threat to the inherent genius creativity of our children.

The idea that creativity can be taught formally seems counterintuitive. Isn't the whole point of creativity that it reaches outside the box, so how can it be taught within a system?

Nevertheless, it is possible to boost a person's creativity through selected activities. Children nurture their own creativity and resourcefulness naturally through free play – a simple, informal self-directed activity. But what is extremely surprising is that the best way to increase the creativity of children within a formal and guided activity is – you may have guessed it – the learning of music. That music training boosts musical creativity could be expected. But how is it possible that music learning boosts the all-round creativity with regards to all its various domains?

Chapter 39

How to preserve your child's creative genius

The standard definition of creativity is the ability to come up with something both new and useful. We can see that Einstein's theory of relativity was both new (nobody had thought of it before) and useful (it has, ever since, formed the basis of technological inventions as well as modern science), and therefore, he exhibited a genius level of creativity.

Curiously, science has shown that creativity and IQ are separate abilities.[1] For instance, a person of average intelligence is as likely to be extremely creative than a person of superior intelligence, and a person of a higher IQ is no more likely to be creative than his lower-IQ peers. Therefore, the fact that music learning boosts both IQ and creativity is a testament to the importance of the Music Miracle itself.

A high IQ is not required for creativity, just like creativity is not required for high IQ. Unlike IQ, which can be largely out of our control and remains stable throughout life after the early years, we know that 98% of children aged four and five exhibit a genius level of creativity. We can thus assume that at birth, 100% of children are born with a creative genius mind, and 98% of them manage to retain it until they start school. It is worth noting that the earliest years in the children's lives is where they are most encouraged and allowed to engage in free play - something that changes drastically once the children enter formal schooling.

Some researchers speculate that the creativity crisis is not just the fault of schools but that it is also linked to the invention of widespread entertainment technologies. Leading creativity researcher Kuyng Hee Kim states: 'Video games constitute an ever increasing part of a child's day. (...) Programming or designing these games may sometimes be creative, but I do not believe playing them generally fosters creativity. (...) Here's a creative solution: figure out how to hack into the software, and change its properties, or even better, turn off the machine and learn something useful. The chromatic musical scale has only 12 pitches, but they can be manipulated in ways that give us unlimited music. Playing an instrument can create something useful: playing a video game may teach us how to control a drone aircraft, but it cannot create something novel.'[2]

Twenty years ago, children would be coming up with their own arts and crafts, but these days they draw on the iPad painting app instead. While this is a less messy option for the busy parent, a pre-designed app does not give the child the option to create something from scratch and experiment with materials. The iPad is - both literally and visually - already the "box" within which a child is pursues even those creative activities that traditionally would have given them the opportunity to think outside of.

But how is it possible that formal music learning – a box in its own right – increases the creativity of children? Let's first turn our eye to the studies that show that this surprising transfer does indeed take place.

A 1996 study on adults who were not professional musicians but had music as a hobby showed that the more advanced their musical skills are, the more creative they were as a result.[3] Traditionally, creativity has been linked to the right hemisphere of the brain, but it has been noted in advanced brain research that this myth does not hold true. Creativity does not exist in one part of the brain, but rather involves networks on both sides of the brain. Yet the place of the right hemisphere remains crucial. In 2011, it was found that the faster a person's reaction time is in the right hemisphere of their brain (even in standard non-creative tasks), the higher their degree of creativity in real life. Conversely, the slower the reaction time was in the right hemisphere, the less creative ability that the person had.[4]

What the brain imaging studies show is that both the right and left hemisphere hold an important place in creativity. Creative thinking is commonly divided into divergent and convergent thinking. Divergent thinking is the ability to come up with many alternative solutions, which could be seen as a feature of the holistic right brain. Convergent thinking is the opposite, as it involves evaluating several answers and choosing the best one of them. The standard school tests generally only involve convergent thinking, but for creativity it is necessary to be able to come up with alternatives before trying to narrow down the best or 'correct' answer.

Creativity and innovation, in its divergent phase, has been linked to right-brain dominance within the creative task.[5] But convergent thinking is needed to choose between the multitude of options that divergent creativity produces. Convergent thinking is well measured by tests in which there is always one right answer – such as the IQ test.

Consistent with this finding, the first brain imaging study into the creativity of musicians and non-musicians from 2008 showed that musicians were more creative than non-musicians, and they were more creative precisely because they had acquired better connections between the left and right side of the brain.[6]

Thus, in creativity, both sides of the brain matter. A 2011 brain imaging study lead by neuroscientist Simone G. Shamay-Tsoory from the University of Haifa in Israel found that 'a balance between the two hemispheres affects a major aspect of creative cognition, namely, originality'.[7] This verifies that the right side of the brain is crucial for new ideas, but a balance of both brain hemispheres is needed for developing them into something truly unique and useful. For information on how to do this, we can recall the studies by Harvard neuroscientist Schlaug and his colleagues: music training builds up the connections between the two sides of the brain -- the corpus callosum, the brain bridge,[8] yet this only happens when music training is started at the age of seven or before.[9]

The standard school curricula focus on developing convergent thinking, as school success is measured by exams each question of which there is always only one right answer. This may also explain some of the general findings of the creativity crisis, and indeed, both Ken Robinson and George Land hold the school system responsible for stifling creativity.

As for children, a groundbreaking study by Elena Chronopoulou and Vassiliki Riga from 2012 measured the creativity of five-year-old children before and after a music training programme. They found that just a three-month programme of 45 to 60 minutes of music training (again without instrument tuition) twice a week significantly boosted the creativity of the children in all measures. The control group, which did not take part in this three-month programme, did not experience this increase in creativity.[10]

Perhaps unsurprisingly, seeing how language and music share the same neural networks, scientists have also found that there is also a direct correlation within a person's verbal and musical creativity, both in the brain and in real-life measures.[11] In our culture, musical creativity may be viewed as something rather fluffy and unnecessary, but the science would indisputably warrant it a higher importance because it directly corresponds to all those verbal innovation skills that are crucial for writing anything creative, from novels and journalistic articles, screenplays and political speeches to witty Twittering and other forms of language-dominated social media.

What is especially interesting about the 2012 study by Chronopoulou and Riga is the finding that simply the formal learning of musical concepts boosts the creativity of children. They were not taught instrument playing or even musical improvisation. Instead, simply the learning of the language of music – its theory concepts as well as learning to clap and move along to them – was alone enough to significantly boost the children's creativity on all measures.[12] Thus, for those teachers and parents who fear that anarchy would result if the schools encouraged more creativity, the fact that formal music learning boosts creativity in itself is intriguing.

Ken Robinson claims that schools discourage creativity, but how? Scientific research has consistently found that the more creativity a child has, the less likely their own teachers are to like them.[13] Researchers Westby and Dawson from New York's Union College state in their research that 'judgments for the (teachers') favourite student were negatively correlated with creativity; judgments for the least favourite student were positively correlated with creativity. (...) This in turn suggests that schools may provide an inhospitable environment for creative students (...) It has also been clearly demonstrated in previous research that children's performance is affected by teachers' attitudes towards them. (...) Potentially creative students might learn to conform so as to improve the teacher-student relationship.' [14]

The researchers suspect that the characteristics necessary for creativity, such as individuality, emotionality and being progressive, pose a challenge for class management in the eyes of the teachers. 'Research has indicated that even teachers who appear to be interested in promoting creativity have a negative view of characteristics traditionally associated with creativity.'[15]

These days, formal education makes claims to encourage creativity, yet the real-life measured creativity of children is going downhill and fast. For parents to preserve our children's natural creative genius, music training is an important activity to put in place while waiting for an educational revolution that has music as its foundation. We have already seen that far from producing a class disturbance, music training promotes not only creativity but the all-important empathy and consideration of others, as well as the mastering of the traditional subjects at school. Sounds like a good deal for the future of the teachers and humankind alike.

Part Nine

What next? Music education and its opportunities and obstacles

We have seen that a great deal of myths surround musical education. This part of the book is intended as a general yet practical overview on the different ways to educate your child musically. Most parents who want their child to take up music learning spend some time in anxiety wondering about where to start -- what instrument, what genre and what teacher is right for their child.

The littlest ones, the ones who are not yet capable of handling an instrument, are the ones who stand to gain the most from music training. The downside is that more often than not, the music groups intended for babies and toddlers center around musical games as opposed to music training. Musical games, fun as they may be, do not produce the Music Miracle. Yet the formal, regimented way of teaching feels alien to the vast majority of toddlers and preschoolers. Standard formal teaching, as it currently stands, is better suited for the child who can already read and who already has been in the classroom for a couple of years. The catch-22 here is that it is only the child who starts training under the age of eight who gains the full Music Miracle. And the sooner they embark on their musical journey, the easier their formal learning becomes once they reach that point.

The optimal way for a parent of a small child is thus to find an age-appropriate way to train their child for music. Literacy is built on awareness of sounds, and music training gives the best possible boost for this. Likewise, handling musical concepts is crucial training for future success in mathematics and science. Not to mention the social benefits of a better self-regulatory ability -- here we may recall the classic marshmallow study and how early self-regulation paves the way for immense success in later life. And this is also the only point in your child's life when you can take direct action to boost their IQ in a remarkable way, with lasting consequences to their future learning skills and career success.

Awareness is power. Once you know what characterizes good music education, you are free to choose the best fit for your family -- and for the future of your child.

Chapter 40

Navigating the maze to the Music Miracle: the three elements of music training

As we have seen in the comparative studies throughout this book, not everything related to music produces the Music Miracle. Neither listening to music nor musical games creates the brain upgrade.[1] Learning about music does not produce brain benefits - learning music is the only way.

Edwyn E. Gordon says that with parents and schools, there is a great deal of confusion about what constitutes music learning. He notes that both often mistakenly think that a music 'lesson' where children simply listen or play to music is competent for music education.[2]

This is equally the case with many small children's music groups where parents simply sing songs to them without actual music learning content integrated into the enjoyment. Whilst this can be enjoyable, real musical learning is what provides the most enjoyment. Not only is it at least as fun to learn music, but children are shown to prefer music learning to non-music learning,[3] even over organized play activities.[4] As we will see in the final chapter, it also gives them the overall tools for the real joy of life lived to one's fullest potential and used in a productive way to benefit others as well as oneself.

As for schools, it is no wonder that music education becomes misdirected. As Gordon himself notes, a significant proportion of primary teachers do not have musical knowledge and experience themselves, and thus are unable to pass it on.[5] Research on music education programmes at schools has found that teachers indeed do not feel confident in their abilities to teach music, and they feel they haven't gained enough guidance from their teaching degree to do so.[6]

With this in mind, it is little wonder that most primary music education consists mainly of recognizing different instruments: 'Here's a clarinet; this one's a violin, here's a tambourine.' This is something that anyone can teach without a background in music training. Sadly, this skill (in technical terms, the ability to recognize timbres) does not produce any of the benefits of the Music Miracle.[7] Learning *about* music does not produce the brain boost, just like learning *about* exercise does not make you fitter.

Recognizing genres of music and learning about the eras of classical composition are a part of cultural history rather than musical training. When a music class is not teaching *music* but *knowledge about music*, the Music Miracle cannot occur. As an analogy, imagine a PE class where instead of engaging in physical activity, the pupils were expected to get healthier by reading about how exercise works. Instead, the research into the benefits of music – such as the research featured in this book – points a clear way forward for what produces the Music Miracle.

Rhythm: Clap your hands for a higher IQ

You often hear people claiming that they 'haven't got any rhythm' or 'cannot keep a beat'. Even if this was the case, they were not born that way. In 2009, Istvan Winkler, Professor and head of the Institute for Psychology of the Hungarian Academy of Sciences, and his research group discovered that the brains of newborn babies detect the beat in music.[1] This shows that your child is indeed born with an innate ability to master rhythms.

Rhythmic inability, where it is perceived, is simply a lack of practice. And as we remember from Chapter 17, rhythmic ability is not just for those aspiring to follow in Michael Jackson's dancing footsteps: rhythmic skills are, perhaps rather counterintuitively, essential for a child's academic and intellectual success.

Handclapping is a case in point. Research shows that the better children are at handclapping songs in kindergarten, the better they do at school in the years to come.[2] The children who had the highest levels of handclapping skills in preschool had, years later, the biggest academic success in first grade. During the second grade, the benefits extended to various abilities such as verbal memory and handwriting as well as mathematical skills.[3]

The study also found that the standard music classes given at school did not help children boost their rhythm skills nor their school success. What children needed was training in handclapping – and when they received this training, their academic scores shot up. The researchers note that children spontaneously engage in handclapping, but that to maximize a child's rhythm development and thus their school success, they need to be encouraged to do so and allowed to practice their skills.[4]

Passive listening to music, thus, does not help - just like watching the London Olympics did not make this mummy any less of a couch potato.

There is one exception. Simply listening to rhythmic music does have an impact on the very youngest ones: babies and toddlers. Just as we're all born with the understanding of rhythm, we're also given the gift for moving to the beat at birth. Because listening to music with a rhythmic beat (such as popular music where drums are commonly used) activates the movement-related regions in the brain, music is made to make us move.[5] Babies are, in the scientists' words, 'born to dance', as even the smallest of babies naturally try and match their movements with the beat of the music they hear.[6] And the better the babies are at matching the beat of the music, the more they smile.[7] Your baby is waiting to become a rhythm master.

Thus, Mother Nature has programmed us to move to the beat. It is only with external restrictions that many of us grow out of this natural tendency - or more accurately, learn to suppress it. Jigging along to music is something that babies do naturally, yet it does not take many years until children often get told off for the same behaviour and to sit still instead. This is why rhythm training is almost essential to keep the beat alive in a world dominated by passive multimedia consumption.

Most astonishingly, the better a person does at keeping the beat, the higher their IQ.[8] And the lesser a child's rhythm skills are, the lower their IQ tends to be as a result.[9] Thus, by allowing your child to train simple handclapping skills and teaching them to move accurately to the beat of a song, you are boosting your child's full-scale intelligence and future school success.[10]

Equally, you are making life easier for your child and yourself, as not many things are quite as stressful for a parent than learning difficulties and failure at school. Inadequate rhythmic skills lead not only to lesser academic achievement, but also increase the risk for learning disabilities such as dyslexia and dyscalculia.[11]

A simple way is to start by clapping along to songs you listen to, and encouraging your child to do the same. Choose a song and try and clap on every beat, and recognize the pattern in them. For instance, most songs are in 4/4, also called common time, and the pattern is the repetition of four beats. Each unit of 1-2-3-4 is called a bar. Another common time signature is 3/4, where the bar consists of a repetition of three crotchets instead of four.

In practice, consulting specialist methods like Kodaly, Suzuki or Moosicology can be immensely helpful to the busy parent who does not have time to become an instant rhythm expert, yet wants to ensure their child gets a minimum of 40 to 60 minutes of rhythm training a week. No more than 60 minutes a week is necessary for the brain benefits (as evidenced by the studies that this book is based on), but no less than that and the benefits are unlikely to take place.

Melody: Tune your way to success

Just like with rhythm, it has been discovered that newborn babies recognize whether a sample of notes is in tune or out of tune.[1] It is found that mothers instinctively sing to their babies when they are little, and that babies prefer listening to singing rather than speech.[2]

New research shows that this could be nature's way of ensuring optimal language development. It used to be thought that singing was just a by-product of speech. Now it turns out that babies develop speech based on their musical ear, and that it is speech that has developed as a by-product of singing.[3]

Thus, nobody is born tone-deaf, except in the very rare case of a developmental disability called amusia. A more common phenomenon is what is called 'musical restriction', which comes from being belittled as a child for performing musically.[4] If a child gets to hear that they 'cannot sing in tune', they can commonly take on board this belief - and the shame attached to it. Extensive studies made on musically restricted adults have found that not only did they lack a musically supportive environment in their childhood years but they, even as adults, continue to suffer from the shame of 'not being musical', suffering more anxiety and withdrawal than persons with a healthy musical upbringing.[5] Of course, they *were* musical; everyone is, except those with the rare case of severe amusia. Just like all developmentally normal children learn to talk, they can all learn to sing. As Professor Graham Welch from the University of London says: "We're all musical – we just need the opportunity."[6]

Most children only learn to sing in tune after the age of five.[7] Sadly, it is not uncommon that parents label their children 'tone-deaf' as early as a toddler or the age of two or three, way before it is even physiologically possible for them to produce correct pitches.[8] This way the child stops singing before they even can, and never get to develop what would have been a perfectly healthy singing voice.

And just like with rhythm, melodic abilities are beneficial for all children, not just for the future Whitney Houstons and Mariah Careys. The better a child is at recognizing pitches, the easier they develop reading skills, and the better their reading skills remain.[9] The musical abilities directly correlate with their reading and writing abilities.[10] This is because the ability to hear phonemes, the smallest units of speech, correctly is what makes for reading skills.[11] The best way to train in phonemes is an intensive ear training for small distinctions between sounds.

One could hardly imagine a better way to train the ear to distinguish between sounds than music training. Over the past four years, studies on the effects of music training on the ear and the auditory cortex have caused scientists to label music training as auditory fitness. Neuroscientists Nina Kraus and Bharath Chandrasekaran from Northwestern University, USA state that "akin to physical exercise and its impact on body fitness, music is a resource that tones the brain for auditory fitness."[12] This is what the melodic component of music training, specifically, is about.

This explains why studies have found that the melodic abilities of children directly predict their reading success.[13] Music training is as effective or even more effective than phonics training in teaching children to master reading.[14] And a test in musical ability is an even better predictor of a person's future phonetic ability than a direct phonetics test![15] Problems in recognizing musical pitches, on the other hand, increase the risk for dyslexia.[16]

But the importance of melodic abilities extends even further, to the social and emotional domain. The ability to recognize pitches and melodies increases many components of emotional intelligence, such as the ability to correctly identify different emotions in other people's verbal expression.[16]

Thus, rhythm alone is not enough: to produce the full Music Miracle, training in melody and harmony is necessary. You can teach your child to distinguish between pitches and chords just by teaching them the core music skills that relate to melody and harmony, such as whether a scale or melody goes up or down, which pitch is higher than the other, how to recognize different intervals by ear, how to produce them by singing or playing an instrument such as the glockenspiel or piano and whether a chord is a major or minor chord. This kind of training is exactly what is done in Suzuki, Kodaly, Musiikkileikkikoulu and Moosicology: these are the precise skills that increase the reading and emotional recognition abilities of small children.

Notation: Reading music, counting maths

Learning musical notation has, in many studies, shown to produce crucial benefits in areas such as spatial-temporal IQ and mathematics, to the point where these benefits would not have occurred without music reading, despite the other components of music training staying the same.[1] Notation is also an excellent tool for teaching fractions: children who learn them through music reading are, astonishingly, from 50 percent to a full 100 percent better than their peers who were taught through traditional mathematics instruction.[2]

Children who receive musical training are, unsurprisingly, better at reading musical notation; as with the other musical skills, some children are not magically born with it but all learn by doing.[3] But this does not mean that you have to grill your two-year old in reading small black-and-white notation that even many musicians-in-training struggle with. For instance, coloured notation is found to be slightly more successful for children than the standard black and white.[4] The children also find it more fun and motivating, which is essential in engaging the little ones.[5] The Moosicology method represents notes as trains of different lengths, so that children get an engaging visual cue that prepares them for real-life note reading. Giving different shapes to different pitches has also been found helpful – this is known as the 'shape note' method.[6]

Furthermore, teaching music reading by melodic shapes (such as whether a melody goes up or down) is found beneficial for beginning music readers.[7] Surprisingly, the Kodaly hand sign method (where all notes of the major scale have different hand signs) is found to not prepare children for reading notation.[8] This could be because the hand sign method, unlike the other methods here described, forfeits the rhythm element and focuses only on melody. In music notation, the rhythm element is described by horizontal movement (as opposed to the vertical which describes pitch variation). Grasping this seems to be key for successful music reading. Donald A. Hodges from the University of Texas points out that emphasizing the vertical (melodic) elements alone has not helped children grasp music notation[9] - this would also explain why the Kodaly hand signs do not help children read music (as they focus exclusively on the melodic element).

Thus, the horizontal, rhythmic aspect of notation emerges as the core skill to master for reading music. But this does not necessarily mean that the vertical representation of melody should be forfeited. Hodges' research overview points out that 'placing song texts higher or lower in conjunction with higher and lower melodic pitches was found to facilitate music reading' in several studies.[10] That said, this requires that the child already knows how to read text. Yet, as we have seen, it would be most beneficial for children to train in music in preparation for future reading skills, as opposed to wait until formal reading emerges, as by then it may be too late for the full Music Miracle, obviously depending on the age of the child.

Already in 1978, educator Mavis J. Lloyd remarked: "Learning music and learning to read closely parallel each other. (...) It is not common for children to read music in kindergarten and grade one; but actually, reading music notation, as long as it is not on a stave, is much easier than reading the alphabet." [11] Professor Susan Hallam from the University of London also points out in her recent overview of studies the evidence that reading notation helps children gain reading skills.[12]

My contention is, when examining the studies that this book is based on, that the three skills of rhythm, melody and notation must all be in place for the full Music Miracle to emerge. But there does seem to be an order of importance, where the rhythm and melodic skills have the most wide-ranging benefits. Notation should be taught not as the main focus, but as a supporting element, as it is required especially for the mathematical benefits, and it helps with reading and pre-reading skills.

Most formal instrument tuition, in contrasts, focuses on playing from notation. Research by Diane Cummings Persellin from Trinity University has found that children aged seven or under perform worse in rhythm skills when they are taught mainly through visual cues, as opposed to auditory, kinesthetic or multisensory ways. The visual way of teaching was successful only when combined with the auditory and kinesthetic elements in the multimodal approach.[13] This is why the child-centred Musiikkileikkikoulu is widely used in Finland to initiate younger children into music training, often for years until the children have mastered the 'pre-instrumental skills' of rhythm, melody and notation. These pre-instrumental skills are, of course, those that alone are enough to produce the Music Miracle. As long as a child starts as early as possible, and at the latest at the age of seven, they will, according to all evidence, gain the full brain benefits, even without formal instrument tuition.

An educational music programme with an emphasis on rhythm, melody, notation and music making through singing, clapping and moving can thus be expected to produce these benefits, even before a child is old enough to handle an instrument – as long as they begin at a young age and engage in training approximately one hour a week. Even though the emphasis between the different pedagogical methods may vary, they all differ from the entertainment-focused music classes by the degree of musical knowledge possessed by the teachers. Unlike so often in the mummy-and–baby singalong groups, the teachers are professional musicians and music educators who each have decades of musical experience to offer. Furthermore, these methods are developed precisely for small children, so that they may learn according to their natural musicality rather than being forced to learn in adult ways.

Many leading music educators have expressed concern regarding the suitability of formal, notation-based instrument tuition on children who are aged seven and under (and therefore in the prime age for the Music Miracle). Edwin E. Gordon notes that it may be futile or even counterproductive to force formal instrument instruction upon a child who has not yet developed the basic musical ear, 'audiation', required for real musicality.[14] Another legendary music researcher and Professor of Psychology John Sloboda similarly advocates emphasizing the aural musicality for beginning learners and points out that "no-one would consider teaching a normal child to read while he was at a very early stage of learning spoken language. Yet it seems the norm to start children off on reading at the very first instrumental lesson without establishing the level of musical awareness already present."[15]

This is, indeed, why in the music academies and conservatories of Finland the phrase 'pre-instrumental classes' is used interchangeably with 'Musiikkileikkikoulu': even the future Sibeliuses are expected to develop the core musical skills before they take on formal instrument lessons. We can draw parallels to the requirement of phonological awareness to reading. Just like sound discrimination is crucial for a child to learn to read (as discussed in Chapters 26-29), it cannot be any less important when it comes to the formal practice and reading of music, the whole art of which is based ultimately on sound. As the legendary music psychologist David J. Hargreaves, author of this book's foreword, wrote back in 1986 in his book The Developmental Psychology of Music: "The intuitive experience and enjoyment of music should come first, such that the latter acquisition of musical skills occurs inductively, that is, as an integral growth of the child's experience. A good deal of traditional music education has worked deductively: the formal rules have been taught in the abstract, for example, through verbal description or written notation, rather than in the practical context of making the sounds themselves."[16]

Focusing on notation and formality at the expense of the direct, practical, intuitive and aural experiences of learning music is therefore akin to throwing the baby out with the bathwater. In summary, we can see that the optimal way for children to take up music training –and gain the Music Miracle - is by learning the various skills of listening, singing, playing and recognizing rhythmic and melodic concepts. Learning notation plays a crucial supporting role, but it should not overtake the music itself.

Chapter 41

All instruments and genres lead to the Music Miracle

When children do take up formal tuition on an instrument, the options are wide and varied – and not always the ones you would expect.

The 'Tiger Mother' Amy Chua writes that her daughters were never allowed to play any other instrument than the piano and violin. She famously claimed, 'playing drums leads to drugs'.[1] Contrary to Chua's parenting beliefs, research has found that if anything, drum-loving children have a slight advantage in the IQ-related temporal discrimination when compared to other instrumentalists[2] - even the piano and violin which Chua has, unlike sleepovers or school plays, mercifully chosen to accept.[3]

As the Music Miracle can be produced –and often has – even without instrument tuition (see the previous chapter), it should come as no surprise that any instrument is a good instrument for the Music Miracle. All instruments require the coordination between the multitude of brain parts that are involved in music making, and they all involve the auditory, visual and kinesthetic senses. Thus it is safe to say that the best brain-boosting instrument for your child is one they themselves are motivated to learn. Drummers may have a small advantage when it comes to the IQ enhancement compared to instruments like the violin, but any instrument that is practiced regularly produces the best brain boost.

Meanwhile, training in violin produces a slightly greater

advantage at recognizing pitches than other instruments,[4] which is hardly surprising considering that with the violin – as opposed to most other instruments – the pitches haven't been marked out, so the player has to carefully listen to the differences between notes in order to find them.

The same principle applies to singing. Indeed, it is found that singing tuition for children, when combined with music theory, also produces the additional pitch advantage that violin instruction does.[5] (Here it is important to note that simply singing songs does not result in these brain benefits, but singing must be taught in conjunction with musical concepts by a professional music tutor.[6]) In contrast, most other instruments, from flute to piano and the guitar, have the basic pitches readily on display, so the player doesn't have to fine-tune their pitch recognition ability to the highest possible degree.

According to studies, the piano is a real middle-ground instrument. It involves recognizing pitches and thus produces benefits for reading and emotional intelligence that the drums may not necessarily boost to such a high degree, since drums barely centre around pitch. Yet the piano also involves rhythm, and was the test instrument in Schellenberg's groundbreaking study to produce the incredible IQ gain. (That said, Schellenberg's results can be generalized to all instruments, as professional singing lessons including music theory also boosted the IQ in the same way.)[7]

When your child is ready and willing to take up formal instrument tuition, what is most important is that you find lessons that suit your child and your family and that you find a suitable teacher to teach it. The brain boost that comes from music training is what makes the real difference; the specifics of playing a particular instrument are just tiny details.

The reason my mum wanted to learn the piano and why she put me to piano lessons was that the piano is arguably the most versatile of instruments. With it, you can play melodies, harmonies and bass lines at the same time, and you still have your mouth free for singing along. For a long time in my teens, I was upset that I had not learned to play the guitar instead. We had had an introduction to rhythm guitar playing at school when I was 11, and I had been motivated to learn more. Unfortunately, my parents were against me getting such an instrument, as in an Amy Chua-type of fashion my mother believed that it would lead to sex, drugs and rock-'n-roll, so I persisted with the piano and made up a way of playing rock music on it instead. Years down the line, my parents' misguidedness seems like a blessing, because it is only with the piano that I have been able to form my own one-woman band rather than having to always find new musicians to play with, especially as we have moved around so much! However, no studies have found increased drug use related to guitar or drums. On the contrary – taking up drums has been a successful form of therapy for drug addicts.[8]

Playing the guitar, in turn, is shown to produce benefits almost exactly alike to that of the piano. Violin and the drums are extreme instruments in some ways. One is focused on pitch at the slight expense of rhythm, and the other focuses on rhythm at a slight expense to the pitch. Most instruments reside somewhere in the middle. But it cannot be emphasized enough that the differences between little drummers and little violinists barely count as differences when compared to children who are non-instrumentalists. What counts is not what instrument your child plays (or sings). What counts is that they keep playing.

Informal and formal learning, classical and popular music

Professor Lucy Green from the University of London has researched alternatives for the standard ways of music teaching that are dominated by a classical approach. She has written about her experiments conducted in sixteen UK secondary schools in her 2008 book Music, Informal Learning and the School: A new classroom pedagogy. In the experiments, standard music tuition was replaced by popular music type of self-initiated learning: students worked in small groups forming bands, choosing the popular music pieces they wanted to learn and figuring out how to learn the pieces by ear. The experiments were shown to be a success. All of the music teachers commented that it had changed their views on music education for the better. Even louder praises were sang by the pupils themselves, whose excitement in these self-directed lessons shines all throughout the book's reports.[9]

The genius of Green's experimental music programme was the bridging of three worlds often kept artificially separate: the formal learning at school, the real-life self-initiated training of popular musicians and the real musical interests of adolescents. Adolescents are mad about music in their spare time, and the experiment brought their enthusiasm into the classroom where they could use it to propel their musical skills. They also learned some classical pieces in this informal way, and although they were much less excited about the classical genre (some were even downright hostile), as one would expect with the early enculturation phenomenon discussed in Chapter 12, the consensus was that many pupils started to appreciate classical music more than they had before.

At the ages of 14 and 15, I was lucky to have a teacher at school whose teaching methods were uncannily similar to those reported in Lucy Green's research. We were able to choose our own pieces of music (from that era's pop hits via Blur to Finnish punk), learn to play as bands, swap between instruments and even perform at school occasions. During those two years, I learnt to play the drums fluently enough to be able to play them on my first demo years later at age 19, despite not having had access to drums for the years in between. All of the pupils helped each other to play. It was not the teacher, but one of the boys in the class who had previously been a bit too 'cool' to associate with me who gave me the drumming tips I needed to get started.

The teacher's genius was to stand back and let us help one another, like the teaching practices in Green's experimental programme. The whole experience of my music class could pass as a textbook example of the empathy benefits of joint music making (as discussed in Chapter 34), as even the bullies seemed to be able to cooperate with me and others in the class in a friendly manner.

Lucy Green states that 'there is something almost natural about informal music learning practices, our society had for decades or even centuries, alienated us from them by removing them from the realm of everyday life, as well as from that of formal music education, so that we are now in a position of having to teach them back to ourselves!' By 'teaching them back to ourselves', Green refers to her research on asking pupils before the experiment how they think popular musicians gain their skills, and none of the pupils in the sixteen schools seemed aware of the informal ways of learning music.[10]

Music training has become so overtly formalized that the natural, everyday ways of music making are forgotten about. Studies have shown that self-taught musicians are fluent at a task that involves playing by ear, whereas classically trained musicians have often lost this ability already in adolescence and tend to focus on the technical aspects in a manner that actually diminishes their musical capabilities.[11] Overtly formal can be harmful! But with the results of the visual-motor and mathematical boosts in mind, it seems as if a middle ground would be suitable to incorporate both aspects. Music is not notes, music is sound – but music reading can be highly enjoyable if taught correctly. Reading notation is also the crucial visual component that is needed as well as the auditory and kinesthetic to unlock all of your child's inherent gifts.

But even with formal tuition, genre alone can make a difference. In my case, I was fed up with piano lessons when I approached the age of twelve and none of my mum's bribing attempts would change my mind about quitting. My continuing of piano lessons was only saved when my wise teacher swapped the musical scores from classical notation to the piano score of Blur's album 'The Great Escape'. She even taught me to transcript music by ear into notation, which launched my ability to play by ear simply by showing that it was possible in the first place.

Many of those lucky children, whose parents organize early music lessons for them, sadly start to lose interest in their music making when it becomes the time to learn the highly abstract music theory. The first years of learning an instrument formally can feel uninspiring due to the learning curve, but afterwards, when music theory knowledge is needed to proceed further, children and adolescents of all ages feel most negatively about music theory.[12]

Indeed, for songwriting, formal knowledge of music theory is not necessary – an intuitive understanding is enough. The muses of music creation are unpredictable, and they certainly do not reside in the logical mind. A knowledge of music theory and, indeed, formal instrumental training, is largely irrelevant to the musical success of composers (at least in a vernacular or popular genre). Neuroscientist and musician Daniel Levitin points out in his best-selling 2006 book This Is Your Brain On Music that this is the case with performing songwriters such as Eric Clapton, Joni Mitchell and Stevie Wonder.[13] (I'd like to add that this applies to the Beatles too.) Likewise, Ken Stringfellow toured with REM for ten years without reading a single note, thanks to his exceptional abilities to learn by ear and improvise, as well as his intuitive musicality.

But for the academic skills of small children, the benefits are unquestionable, as demonstrated throughout this book. Learning the musical concepts related to rhythm, melody and notation are crucial for the brain upgrade. When children get the opportunity to first learn music through child-centred methods which are based on the experiential realm of music rather than the conceptual, they get the best of both worlds: musical intuition and the benefits of formal learning. It is only when jumping straight into an exclusively formal musical training that the inherent musicality can be harmed with the counterproductive result that the person ends up, paradoxically, less musical despite having a higher technical ability.[14]

We may conclude, perhaps quite counterintuitively, that whilst music reading and theory are far from necessary for music making, they are essential for the Music Miracle; but the experiential ways of teaching should always take prominence.

Chapter 42

The Personal Touch and Feeling the Invisible: the 'sixth sense' of music education

> "Cheri, a successful career woman, when speaking of her elementary school encounters with singing describes them as humiliating and dreadful experiences. Sydney, a retired health care professional, has not sung in 65 years based on an incident involving an elementary teacher. Marjorie, an urban planner, described her elementary music teacher as the wicked witch of the west. Maria, a young instrumentalist, has refrained from singing in the last ten years because of a comment made about her singing ability by a secondary teacher. Cheri, Sydney, Marjorie, and Maria now regard themselves, because of these negative encounters in the education system, as adult non-singers."
> - The Injustice of Singer/Non-Singer Labels by Music Educators by Dr. Colleen Widden, University of Calgary (2008)[1]

Throughout this book, I have reported on the benefits of multisensory music training. But there is one sensory realm that is as crucial to music making as the three modalities of the auditory, visual and kinesthetic: the realm of feeling. Because of the way that music biologically connects to our most crucial emotion centres, music training could never be a purely intellectual exercise.

Studies have verified that the main reason people listen to music is the emotion it creates in them.[2] Likewise, having early positive experiences in music is shown to be crucial for later successful music practice.[3]

It is possible to learn to read and count without an emotional connection, but even in these cases, emotions make all the difference. Positive emotion facilitates learning and intellectual performance – after all, that is what the whole Mozart Myth started from! The connection between music and emotion, however, goes even deeper than this. Music can express sadness, anger, joy, love, despair, longing, nostalgia and all other conceivable human emotions. This is why the music educator is faced with the challenge of being aware of this and what it means – essentially, that a music pupil is not simply learning a technical skill but is also learning to express and experience deep feelings.

In Chapter 13, 'The Musicality Myth', we discussed the research on the phenomenon of musical restriction. The researchers write: 'the fear to sing and perform music is caused by the wrong kind of music education. (...) This kind of singing -fear is learned, because it doesn't occur among small children: they sing spontaneously even to strangers with no restraints. (...) In music, the separation between good and bad, talented and not talented, tasty and vulgarity, high standard and usual etc. is easy, because music has a sophisticated assessment system and it is tightly connected to power relationships'.[4]

Another study points out that 'the significance of music in the early stages of childhood and the close relation to the total personality and feeling of self esteem is proved, showing a considerable correlation between the individual's musical expertise and early experiences of music in life'. Thus, because of the evaluation and exposure of their innermost selves, children are even more vulnerable to self-esteem setbacks in music experiences than in other activities.[5]

Here we can observe that not even all formally correct music teaching is made equal. Indeed, scientists note than one of the most important factors in a child's early musical development, alongside positive experiences of listening to music, is the emotional warmth of the teacher.[6] The young pupil needs to feel supported, not critically analyzed, on their musical journey.

If we remember the vastness of talents in all children, even in newborn babies, we can see that even though they need instruction to bring out their musicality, the music is already in them. This inner musicality is what the music educator needs to keep in mind. As the Finnish researchers note, hardly anything is easier than to destroy a child's confidence in their musicality, and thus affect their whole self-esteem and self-expression negatively. Thus, not all music education is beneficial. With the wrong kind of teacher, music training is counter-productive, and at its worst destructive. They write: 'The fear to sing and perform music is caused by the wrong kind of music education. This kind of music education did not notice that music and emotions related to it belong to the most vulnerable part of the human mind. An incompetent music teacher is like an elephant in a china shop, when his/her every turn breaks something and pupils' negative attitudes towards music and music education are getting stronger all the time.'[7]

Because music is inherently connected to feelings, music education cannot overlook the importance of nurturing the child emotionally as well as musically. A teacher must be encouraging and approach the child from the assumption that the child has an inner musicality that needs to be nurtured. As we have seen, this is what the studies confirm.[8] If, as opposed to this, a teacher focuses on hostile evaluation of the child, the psychological damage that results cannot be understated. We do not live in an ideal world where every music teacher is a naturally nurturing and encouraging personality.

Most music teachers may well be emotionally suited to their profession, but in talking with parents, and also from my personal experience, I have seen that one needs to look out for the warning signs. I have heard a music teacher refuse to teach a child because they 'did not have any musicality' and a few years later, beg for the child's mother to enroll him in her training because he was 'so musical'. It was clear that the teacher had no concept of how their belittling and confusing remarks might have affected a small child's self-esteem and motivation to make music.

There are many more examples that one hears when talking to people who have practiced music in childhood: stories of humiliation that more often than not lead to giving up music practice for life. We must beware of the teachers who attempt to inspire through shame and make sure that our children receive instruction from someone who can lead with the observable five senses, but also the invisible sense of emotion as well.

Epilogue

Training for Happiness

> 'Genuinely happy individuals are few and far between. How many people do you know who enjoy what they are doing, who are reasonably satisfied with their lot, who do not regret the past and look to the future with genuine confidence? If Diogenes with his lantern twenty-three centuries ago had difficulty finding an honest man, today he would have perhaps an even more troublesome time finding a happy one.'
> *Mihaly Csikzentmihalyi*[1]

Emotional stability is undervalued in our society. In most school curricula, there is no active effort to boost the emotional and social ability and wellbeing of children. Children are expected to pick up these essential skills automatically, whereas the academic subjects are drilled into them on a daily basis. Perhaps here we can ask the question: what is possible when we offer our children support for their whole selves through music?

When people are pressed to come up with an answer to what they most want from life, the answer they come up with is almost always related to happiness. Yet, as Mihaly Csikzentmihalyi notes, happiness is not something that we can take for granted, but we must actively navigate our way towards it.

The philosophers in Ancient Greece made an important discovery concerning happiness. They contended that there was two contrasting types of happiness that a person could pursue: hedonic and eudaimonic.

Hedonic happiness is the pursuit of immediate happiness; in today's world, an example of hedonic happiness in childhood would be a child who spends their days eating marshmallows and playing video games while ignoring their inherent talents, whether academic, artistic, social or otherwise. Eudaimonic happiness, instead, takes the view that it is important to keep an eye on the longer-term benefits of our actions. The child who builds up their mental, physical, social and emotional resources is following the eudaimonic path to life-long happiness.

One of the most renowned researchers in contemporary psychology, the aforementioned Mihaly Csikszentmihalyi, has written about the hedonic view of happiness – the pursuit of pleasure – in a way updated for our times: 'Pleasure is an important component of the quality of life, but by itself it does not bring happiness. Sleep, rest, food, and sex provide restorative homeostatic experiences that return consciousness to order after the needs of the body intrude and cause psychic entropy to occur. But they do not produce psychological growth. They do not add complexity to the self. Pleasure helps to maintain order, but by itself cannot create new order in consciousness.'[2]

In contrast, Csikszentmihalyi writes of eudaimonic happiness, which he calls enjoyment: 'Without enjoyment, life can be endured, and it can even be pleasant. But it can be so only precariously, depending on luck and the cooperation of the external environment. To gain personal control over the quality of experience, however, one needs to learn how to build enjoyment into what happens day in, day out.'[3]

Csikszentmihalyi is most renowned for his research concerning the state of flow. Flow is when we are so immersed in a constructive activity that we 'lose ourselves' into it. In Csikszentmihalyi's words, people in flow 'stop being aware of themselves as separate from the actions they are performing'.[4]

Csikszentmihalyi calls flow the optimal psychological state and the key to personal growth and authentic happiness. The basic guidelines for achieving flow are that the activity must be just demanding enough for the person to have to stretch their capabilities, but not too demanding as to demotivate the person. 'Enjoyment appears at the boundary between boredom and anxiety, when the challenges are just balanced with the person's capacity to act.' [7] He also notes that 'the reason it is possible to achieve such complete involvement in a flow experience is that goals are usually clear, and feedback immediate'.[5]

The fact that music training seems to be made for these descriptions of flow and its requirements have not gone unnoticed from Csikszentmihalyi himself. Music making offers instantaneous feedback – you make a sound, by singing or playing, and hear the result immediately, and there's always something new to learn, right between boredom and anxiety where the blissful, constructive flow lies. Throughout his research into flow, Csikszentmihalyi keeps referring to the activity of musicians, whether professional or amateur.

Indeed, research finds that children who engage in music making, from infancy to school age, experience a natural state of flow during their activities.[6] Music making fits all the criteria for flow-inducing activity: the musician can lose themselves in their singing, playing or composing whilst developing themselves in a meaningful way, striving for a higher level of development. No matter where you are in music, whether a beginner or a full-fledged professional, with the right kind of training (including being self-taught, as is the case with many popular musicians), you are never short of things to practice, make and learn that stretch your abilities to help you grow.

Csikszentmihalyi remarks based on research that "happiness is not something that happens. It is not the result of good fortune or random chance. It is not something that money can buy or power command. It does not depend on outside events, but, rather, on how we interpret them. Happiness, in fact, is a condition that must be prepared for, cultivated and defended privately by each person.'"[7]

At the same time, Csikszentmihalyi emphasizes the need for guidance when it comes to children. He remarks that small children have no problem being in a state of flow for a substantial proportion of the hours they spend awake. Yet this intrinsic curiosity declines, generally after the children have spent a few years at school.[8]

We can draw parallels to the study by George Land that found that 98% of kindergarteners exhibit creativity at the genius level as measured by the NASA test, yet only 2% of adults reach the same heights.[9] Csikszentmihalyi's research indeed notes the similarities between the states of flow and creativity. He remarks: 'When people are asked to choose from a list the best description of how they feel when doing whatever they enjoy doing most – reading, climbing mountains, playing chess, whatever – the answer most frequently chosen is 'designing or discovering something new'.'[10]

In Csikszentmihalyi's words, we are 'programmed for creativity.'[11] If creativity is essential for flow and thus, happiness, we can see how significant it is to actively encourage our children to build up on their natural creativity. Otherwise, with a 98% statistical likelihood, they will lose this key path to natural happiness by the time they reach adulthood - perhaps the greatest gift given to them at birth.

As we have seen throughout this book, training in music significantly promotes your child's emotional resilience, wellbeing and mental and physical health. We started this book by examining the wealth of research on how music training makes your child more intelligent and more skillful in all areas of the academic and non-academic subjects. But achieving external success does not necessarily lead to happiness.

Likewise, throughout this book we have observed evidence that we are programmed for making music (see, for instance, Chapters 10 and 35). We have seen studies that find that children who engage in making music have a higher self-esteem than non-musician children, and that self-esteem is the most reliable indicator of happiness. We have seen this even in babies. Infants who practice music exhibit greater signs of happiness, by smiling more[12] and having more positive interactions with their parents.[13] We have also seen that happiness spreads: the music training that a baby and toddler engages in improves the parents' mental health and reduces their stress.[14] Likewise, music training improves the self-esteem and empathy of kindergarteners[15] and school-aged children[16] alike. A happier child means a happier family.

It is well known that despite the material wealth of today's western world, the levels of happiness have not increased. Most parents are focused on meeting the immediate needs of their children, but how many of us make consistent effort to build up their emotional well-being and mental health? At the end of the day, the story of the unhappy over-achiever has become prototypical of our culture. Thus, although music training gives your child the ability to live up to their potential, the most important manifestation of success may be in the form of a peace of mind and a contented relationship with oneself and others. Indeed, it can be said that it is only then that your child's full potential is actualized.

It is said that one does not appreciate health before it is lost. This saying can be applied to mental health just as strongly as to the physical. It may be that happiness, even the eudaimonic and constructive happiness, is not the ultimate meaning of life. But it is certain that without a level of happiness, a human being is not even capable of pondering such deep questions, let alone resolving them. A human mind living in anxiety or depression is a human mind that is as far from its natural capabilities as a bird whose wings have been clipped.

Hundreds of studies now conclude that music training, especially when started early on, produces benefits such as academic ability, enhanced intelligence, improved memory and a better learning capacity. But of what use are these benefits, if not for happiness? My contention is that no matter what your child decides to do with their life, music training at a young age is the all-in-one brain-booster than will have given them better skills to succeed in whatever it is they decide to do. More abilities equal more options to engage in meaningful activity, at work, in hobbies, and in personal relationships. In Csikszentmihalyi's terms, this equals more opportunities for flow, which in turn equals greater happiness.

Now that science has shown the way, there is no reason to deny our children this opportunity to build their brains and a better life as a result. Because what could possibly be more important than ensuring a good life for our offspring, a life full of happiness, meaningful relationships and purposeful activities? Your child is born with incredible potential right within them - and unlocking it is the way forward for the whole humankind.

Acknowledgements

Thank you to everybody who contributed to making this book happen. Aside from the most essential two - the All-That-Is and the 'Delete Your Profile' button on Facebook - there are many others that I wish to thank for. Writing is a solitary process, but thanks to you all, it wasn't a lonely one.

First and foremost, I want to thank my husband Travis, who was immensely encouraging from the start, and supportive throughout the research and writing. Thank you for seeing my potential before anybody else did, and thank you for pointing it out to me ad infinitum until my low self-esteem got bored and bu★★ered off (good riddance). Thank you for tolerating me in writing mode and thank you for also kindly pointing out when I was overdue to have a bath.

Thank you to our son Toivo, without whom I would never have even thought about these parenting things in the first place. Thank you for being a genuine and kind person with endlessly interesting and original thoughts, questions and observations. Most of all, thank you for being you.

Thank you to my birth family - Mum and Dad for always doing the best they could - sorry that my book wasn't available at the time, but well done, you managed to get many things right anyway, most importantly the love and music bits. Not to mention the writing bits -- thanks for always rushing to buy more notebooks and papers when I had used up the existing ones. Thanks to grandparents, deceased and existing, for being kind and being present - Terttu Suoninen and Toivo Henriksson - shoutout to Mummu Terttu Henriksson who does not understand English but can spot her name here. Thanks to Markku and Ritva for much valued feedback and encouragement. Thanks to Putti and Erja for the rock'n roll spirit!

Thanks to Viivi for being such a well-adjusted person, showing a great example to me, although you are much younger! Good luck with the future and your studies in Psychology.

Thanks to the nice members of the English family I married into: Martin and Angie, Olly and James, Kianna and Jake, Mac and Monica, Terry and Jenny, Steve and Maria, Tracey and 'The Budgie Steve', Ian, Wendy, Lydia, Callum and Liam, and everyone else; thanks for welcoming me in, and I hope that somehow this acknowledgement in my book would make up for some of the birthday cards I never remember to send. We don't do stuff like that in Finland!

Thank you to Jussi K. Niemela - it is impossible to say if I'd ever thought about being able to write an academic non-fiction book in the first place, if it wasn't for your initial encouragement years ago! Thank you for being a true intellectual and for not having hang-ups about encouraging others in the same path.

Thank you to Asko Keranen who made all the difference in my musical path when I needed it the most.

Thank you to Ken Stringfellow - my first proper mentor, and an unintentional one at that! I came to you to have my music produced in the best possible way and ended up having that and so much more, due to you sharing the light of your immense wisdom and vast life experience. Thank you to Dom Stringfellow for your kindness, caring and intelligent points of view regarding this and that. The genuine, unpretentious, wise way of life you both embody is a true inspiration.

Thank you to all the people who supported Moosicology in the first place, all the way from its first prototype: Paula, Steve and Maya Hearsum, Lucy Green, Dr. Maria Varvarigou, Kristin Harris Walsh, Jennifer Milioto Matsue, Dr. Evangeline Cheng, David-Emil

Wickstrom, Carina Serrano, Paul Harkins, Patricia Collingbourne and Dr. Steve Jones. Thank you Olivia Doyle, Lindsey Kerr, Tuija Wasko, Jane and Adam Lynch, Maggi Garfield, Christian Savill, Beth Winslet and Henry Steedman and all your kids for keeping me motivated on this topic due to your immensely encouraging feedback. There is nothing like getting an answer phone recording of a 3-year old singing about crotchets and quavers, when it comes to staying motivated!

Thank you to George Swift for being so much more than a life coach - that title would not do you any justice. Thank you for helping me push through the barriers of my initially low self-esteem and for making me make this book happen. Thank you to Tracey Miller for all your encouragement and support along the long way, and thank you to the whole Success Group at Bigger Brighter Bolder - writing this book has sure been a huge personal milestone and it was crucial to have the mental and emotional support of an encouraging tribe!

Thank you to Cherilyn DeVries for being the most amazing editor - I couldn't have wished for a better one! Thank you for your sensitive and encouraging attitude as well as all the tough love where needed - all the spot-on remarks on what needed to be improved. Working with you has been truly amazing -- you are able to give constructive feedback at its best.

Thank you to Giles Taylor for the typesetting - thanks for your patience and attention to detail. Thank you to Vikki from Vie Photography for helping me relax at the photo shoot and for taking such amazing pictures that look nothing like my scrubby self in writing mode.

Thank you to Dorothy Farr for having been the first reader of my book - your encouragement has meant a lot to me along the way. Thanks to Sirje Niitepold for always being there. Thanks to Laura Reivinen and the family for great energy-fuelling diet advice, and great discussions on writing. Thanks to Melinda Messenger for your interest, encouragement and understanding of this project!

Thank you to all the people whose studies I have quoted in this book - without you this book would have literally not been possible! Thank you for researching such important topics and dedicating your careers to finding out this new information and bringing it out for the world to benefit from.

I want to express an immense thank you to David J. Hargreaves. Thank you for taking interest in my work and giving constructive feedback and a much-needed boost for my self-esteem. Thank you for a great foreword. Thank you for being an inspiration on so many levels.

Thank you to all three legends of the field of music education: David J. Hargreaves, Lucy Green and Graham Welch - thank you for taking the time amidst your busy lives to read my book and review it - the encouragement from all of you has been invaluable, and it is an inspiration to see people who are so genuinely interested in their very important fields of study.

Thank you to Neil Finn, whose great music (both solo and in Crowded House) kept me company for all those years that were otherwise so dark. Thank you for the deep wisdom in your music. 'Truth cannot be denied'.

Thank you to our cats Sox, Tinkerbell and Herman B.B.B. Scruffy, all of whom couldn't care less about this acknowledgement or anything except sleeping and eating, thus providing a much welcome balance into my life. You natural yogis - existing in the 'now' and stretching into unimaginably supple positions. Thank you for keeping company throughout my writing-phase isolation, and sorry for having pushed you away all the times you wanted to perch on the laptop.

Liisa

Citations

Introduction

1. See, for instance, Wetter, O. E., Koerner, F., & Schwaninger, A. (2009). Does musical training improve school performance? Instructional Science, 37(4), 365-374.
   And
   Fitzpatrick, K. R. (2006). The effect of instrumental music participation and socioeconomic status on Ohio fourth-, sixth-, and ninth-grade proficiency test performance. Journal of Research in Music Education, 54(1), 73-84.
   For more studies, see Appendix: School success.
2. See Appendices: Memory, Working memory, Executive functioning, Information processing and Learning skills (concentration, listening, self-regulation).
3. See Chapter 35 on self-esteem as well as Appendix: Self-esteem.
4. See Chapter 34 on empathy as well as Appendix: Empathy.
5. Miranda, E. R., & Overy, K. (2009). Preface: The Neuroscience of Music,Contemporary Music Review, 28(3), 247-250.
   And
   Alluri, V., Toiviainen, P., Jääskeläinen, I. P., Glerean, E., Sams, M., & Brattico, E. (2011). Large-scale brain networks emerge from dynamic processing of musical timbre, key and rhythm. NeuroImage, 59(4), 3677-3689.

6. See chapter 6.
7. Miller, A., & Coen, D. (1994). The case for music in the schools. The Phi Delta Kappan, 75(6), 459-461.
8. Venerable, G. (1987). The paradox of the silicon savior: charting the reformation of the high-tech super-state. New York: American for the Arts.
9. Root-Bernstein, R. S. (2001). Music, creativity and scientific thinking. Leonardo, 34(1), 63-68.
10. White, P. (2005). Albert Einstein: The Violinist. The Physics Teacher, 43(5), 286.
11. Gerry, D., Unrau, A., & Trainor, L. J. (2012). Active music classes in infancy enhance musical, communicative and social development. Developmental Science, 15(3), 398-407.
12. Chronopoulou, E., & Riga, V. (2012). he Contribution of Music and Movement Activities to Creative Thinking in Pre-School Children. Creative Education, 3(2), 196-204.
13. Jäncke, L. (2012). The relationship between music and language. Frontiers in Psychology, 3, 123. No issue.
14. Rabinowitch, T. C., Cross, I., & Burnard, P. (2012). Long-term musical group interaction has a positive influence on empathy in children. Psychology of Music, 40(2), 131-256.
15. Rickard, N. S., Appelman, P., James, R., Murphy, F., Gill, A., & Bambrick, C. (2012). Orchestrating life skills: The effect of increased school-based music classes on children's social competence and self-esteem. International Journal of Music Education, 30(1), 3-84.
16. Steele, C. J., Bailey, J. A., Zatorre, R. J., & Penhune, V. B. (2013). Early musical training and white-matter plasticity in the corpus callosum: Evidence for a sensitive period. The Journal of Neuroscience, 33(3), 1282-1290.
17. Damien Gayle (13.2.2013). Those violin lessons weren't a waste of time after all: Learning an instrument 'makes children

grow up smarter'. Daily Mail. Retrievable at http://www.dailymail.co.uk/sciencetech/article-2277983/Those-violin-lessons-werent-waste-time-Learning-instrument-makes-children-grow-smarter.html#axzz2Kb87WbUb

18. Schellenberg, E. G. (2004). Music lessons enhance IQ. Psychological Science, 15(8), 511-514.
19. See references 16.-18. as well as the following:
    Costa-Giomi, E. (2004). Effects of three years of piano instruction on children's academic achievement, school performance and self-esteem. Psychology of Music, 32(2), 139-152.
    Rickard, N. S., Bambrick, C. J., & Gill, A. (2012). Absence of widespread psychosocial and cognitive effects of school-based music instruction in 10–13-year-old students. International Journal of Music Education, 30(1), 57-78.
20. Moreno, S., Marques, C., Santos, A., Santos, M., & Besson, M. (2009). Musical training influences linguistic abilities in 8-year-old children: more evidence for brain plasticity. Cerebral Cortex, 19(3), 712-723.
21. Degé, F., Wehrum, S., Stark, R., & Schwarzer, G. (2011). The influence of two years of school music training in secondary school on visual and auditory memory. European Journal of Developmental Psychology, 8(5), 608-623.
22. See Appendix: Benefits for pensioners.
23. Appendix: Musicality of newborn babies

Chapter 1

The Chance

1. BBC News (2010). Music tuition falling, poll suggests. Retrieved on March 18 2013 at http://www.bbc.co.uk/news/education-11179448
2. This book was Sunderland, M. (2007). What every parent

needs to know: the incredible effects of love, nurture and play on your child's development. Oxford: Dorling Kindersley.

3. Schlaug, G., Jäncke, L., Huang, Y., Staiger, J. F., & Steinmetz, H. (1995). Increased corpus callosum size in musicians. Neuropsychologia, 33(8), 1047-1055.
4. Ibid.
5. See the relevant Appendices at the end of the book – or just keep reading!
6. For now, see for instance Schellenberg, E. G. (2004). Music lessons enhance IQ. Psychological Science, 15(8), 511-514.
7. For now, see for instance Nantais, K. M., & Schellenberg, E. G. (1999). The Mozart effect: An artifact of preference. Psychological Science, 10(4), 370-373.
8. Gordon, E. E. (2011). Early childhood music abuse: Misdeeds and Neglect. Visions of Research in Music Education, 17, 1-11.
9. Gordon, E. (2003). Music Aptitude and Other Factors. In E. Gordon, A Music Learning Theory for Newborn and Young Children (pp. 22-23). Chicago: GIA Publications.
10. Ibid.
11. Less than an hour of music training per week: the amount of music training that is shown to get results in the majority of these studies that this book is built on consists of 30-60 minutes of music training a week. More than an hour a week does not yield additional general brain-boosting results, as evidenced for instance by the following study: Gruhn, W., Galley, N., & Kluth, C. (2003). Do mental speed and musical abilities interact? Annals of the New York Academy of Sciences, 999(1), 485-496.
12. Schellenberg, E. G. (2004). Music lessons enhance IQ. Psychological Science, 15(8), 511-514.

Costa-Giomi, E. (2004). Effects of three years of piano instruction on children's academic achievement, school performance and self-esteem. Psychology of Music, 32(2), 139-152.

Rickard, N. S., Bambrick, C. J., & Gill, A. (2012). Absence of widespread psychosocial and cognitive effects of school-based music instruction in 10–13-year-old students. International Journal of Music Education, 30(1), 57-78.

Steele, C. J., Bailey, J. A., Zatorre, R. J., & Penhune, V. B. (2013). Early musical training and white-matter plasticity in the corpus callosum: Evidence for a sensitive period. The Journal of Neuroscience, 33(3), 1282-1290.

13. Moffitt, T. E., Caspi, A., Harkness, A. R., & Silva, P. A. (2006). The Natural History of Change to Intellectual Performance: Who Changes? How Much? Is it Meaningful? Journal of Child Psychology and Psychiatry, 34(4), 455-506.

14. Costa-Giomi, E. (1999). The effects of three years of piano instruction on children's cognitive development. Journal of Research in Music Education, 47(3), 198-212.

Rauscher, F. H., & Zupan, M. A. (2000). Classroom keyboard instruction improves kindergarten children's spatial-temporal performance: A field experiment. Early Childhood Research Quarterly, 15(2), 215-228.

Hetland, L. (2000). Learning to make music enhances spatial reasoning. Journal of Aesthetic Education, 34(3/4), 179-238.

Zafranas, N. (2004). Piano keyboard training and the spatial–temporal development of young children attending kindergarten classes in Greece. Early Child Development and Care, 174(2), 199-211.

15. Schlaug, G., Jäncke, L., Huang, Y., Staiger, J. F., & Steinmetz, H. (1995). Increased corpus callosum size in musicians. Neuropsychologia, 33(8), 1047-1055.

Schlaug, G., Forgeard, M., Zhu, L., Norton, A., Norton, A., & Winner, E. (2009). Training-induced Neuroplasticity in Young Children. Annals of the New York Academy of Sciences, 1169(1), 205-208.

Steele, C. J., Bailey, J. A., Zatorre, R. J., & Penhune, V. B. (2013). Early Musical Training and White-Matter Plasticity in the Corpus Callosum: Evidence for a Sensitive Period. The Journal of Neuroscience, 33(3), 1282-1290.

The Finnish School System and How to Survive it

1. See Appendices Reading skills and Mathematics
2. OECD. (2010). Finland: Slow and Steady Reform for Consistently High Results. New York: OECD.
3. Nyström, S. (2011). Yhden naisen yritys: Lastenkulttuurikeskus Musikantit. Master's thesis.
4. Lillard, A., & Else-Quest, N. (2006). The early years: Evaluating Montessori education. Science, 313(5795), 1893-1894.

   Harris, M. (2008). The effects of music instruction on learning in the Montessori classroom. Montessori Life: A Publication of the American Montessori Society, 20(3), 24-31.
5. Diamond, A., & Lee, K. (2011). Interventions shown to aid executive function development in children 4 to 12 years old. Science, 333(6045), 959-964.
6. Harris, M. A. (2007). Differences in mathematics scores between students who receive traditional Montessori instruction and students who receive music enriched Montessori instruction. Journal for Learning through the Arts, 3(1), 1-50.
7. Mackenzie-Beck, Janet (2003). Is it possible to predict students' ability to develop skills in practical phonetics? In:

Proceedings of the 15th International Congress of Phonetic Sciences. Universitat AutÒnoma de Barcelona, 2833 -2836.
Dankovicová, J., House, J., Crooks, A., & Jones, K. (2007). The relationship between musical skills, music training, and intonation analysis skills. Language and Speech, 50(2), 177-225.

8. Rauscher, F. H., Shaw, G. L., Levine, L. J., Wright, E. L., Dennis, W. R., & Newcomb, R. L. (1997). Music training causes long-term enhancement of preschool children's spatial-temporal reasoning. Neurological research, 19(1), 2-8.
   See also: Moreno, S., Bialystok, E., Barac, R., Schellenberg, E. G., Cepeda, N. J., & Chau, T. (2011). Short-term music training enhances verbal intelligence and executive function. Psychological science, 22(11), 1425-1433.
9. Sunderland, M. (2007). What every parent needs to know: the incredible effects of love, nurture and play on your child's development. Oxford: Dorling Kindersley.
10. Ibid.
11. Schlaug, G., Jäncke, L., Huang, Y., Staiger, J. F., & Steinmetz, H. (1995). Increased corpus callosum size in musicians. Neuropsychologia, 33(8), 1047-1055.
12. Njiokiktjien, C., De Sonneville, L., & Vaal, J. (1994). Callosal size in children with learning disabilities. Behavioural brain research, 64(1), 213-218.
    Hynd, G. W., Semrud-Clikeman, M., Lorys, A. R., Novey, E. S., Eliopulos, D., & Lyytinen, H. (1991). Corpus callosum morphology in attention deficit-hyperactivity disorder: morphometric analysis of MRI. Journal of Learning Disabilities, 24(3), 141-146.
13. Teicher, M. H. (2000). Wounds that time won't heal: The neurobiology of child abuse. Cerebrum, 2(4), 50-67.

Teicher, M. H., Dumont, N. L., Ito, Y., Vaituzis, C., Giedd, J. N., & Andersen, S. L. (2004). Childhood neglect is associated with reduced corpus callosum area. Biological psychiatry, 56(2), 80-85.

14. Teicher, M. H., Samson, J. A., Sheu, Y. S., Polcari, A., & McGreenery, C. E. (2010). Hurtful words: association of exposure to peer verbal abuse with elevated psychiatric symptom scores and corpus callosum abnormalities. American Journal of Psychiatry, 167(12), 1464-1471.
15. Davis-Kean, P. E. (2005). The influence of parent education and family income on child achievement: the indirect role of parental expectations and the home environment. Journal of Family Psychology, 19(2), 294.
16. Fitzpatrick, K. R. (2006). The effect of instrumental music participation and socioeconomic status on Ohio fourth-, sixth-, and ninth-grade proficiency test performance. Journal of Research in Music Education, 54(1), 73-84.

Chapter 2

The Music Miracle: why it matters now more than ever

1. See, for instance, Robinson, Ken (Lecturer) (2006). Why schools kill creativity-The case for an education sytem that nurtures creativity:TED Conference talk [Motion Picture]. And
   Puttnam, L. (Director). (2009). We Are The People We've Been Waiting For [Motion Picture].
2. Chua, A. (2011). Battle hymn of the Tiger Mother. New York: Bloomsbury Publishing.
3. Venerable, G. (1987). The paradox of the silicon savior: charting the reformation of the high-tech super-state. New York: American for the Arts.

4. Miller, A., & Coen, D. (1994). The case for music in the schools. The Phi Delta Kappan, 75(6), 459-461.
5. Root-Bernstein, R. S. (2001). Music, creativity and scientific thinking. Leonardo, 34(1), 63-68.
6. White, P. (2005). Albert Einstein: The Violinist. The Physics Teacher, 43(5), 286.
7. Gruhn, W., Galley, N., & Kluth, C. (2003). Do mental speed and musical abilities interact? Annals of the New York Academy of Sciences, 999(1), 485-496.
8. Ibid.
9. Miranda, E. R., & Overy, K. (2009). Preface: The Neuroscience of Music, Contemporary Music Review, 28(3), 247-250.

   Altenmüller, E. O. (2001). How many music centers are in the brain? Annals of the New York Academy of Sciences, 930(1), 273-280.

   Gaser, C., & Schlaug, G. (2003). Brain structures differ between musicians and non-musicians. The Journal of Neuroscience, 23(27), 9240-9245.

   Alluri, V., Toiviainen, P., Jääskeläinen, I. P., Glerean, E., Sams, M., & Brattico, E. (2011). Large-scale brain networks emerge from dynamic processing of musical timbre, key and rhythm. NeuroImage, 59(4), 3677-3689.
10. Schlaug, G., Jäncke, L., Huang, Y., Staiger, J. F., & Steinmetz, H. (1995). Increased corpus callosum size in musicians. Neuropsychologia, 33(8), 1047-1055.

   Schlaug, G., Forgeard, M., Zhu, L., Norton, A., Norton, A., & Winner, E. (2009). Training induced Neuroplasticity in Young Children. Annals of the New York Academy of Sciences, 1169(1), 205-208.
11. Blood, A. J., & Zatorre, R. J. (2001). Intensely pleasurable responses to music correlate with activity in brain regions

implicated in reward and emotion. Proceedings of the National Academy of Sciences, 98(20), 11818-11823.

Pallesen, K. J., Brattico, E., Bailey, C., Korvenoja, A., Koivisto, J., Gjedde, A., & Carlson, S. (2005). Emotion processing of major, minor, and dissonant chords. Annals of the New York Academy of Sciences, 1060(1), 450-453.

Gosselin, N., Peretz, I., Johnsen, E., & Adolphs, R. (2007). Amygdala damage impairs emotion recognition from music. Neuropsychologia, 45(2), 236-244.

Koelsch, S., Fritz, T., & Schlaug, G. (2008). Amygdala activity can be modulated by unexpected chord functions during music listening. Neuroreport, 19(18), 1815-1819.

12. Munte, T. F., Altenmuller, E., & Jancke, L. (2002). The musician's brain as a model of neuroplasticity. Nature Reviews Neuroscience, 3(6), 473-477.
13. Schlaug, G., Norton, A., Overy, K., & Winner, E. (2005). Effects of music training on the child's brain and cognitive development. Annals of the New York Academy of Sciences, 1060(1), 219-230.
14. Patel, A. D. (2011). Language, music, and the brain: a resource-sharing framework. In P. Rebuschat, M. Rohmeier, J. A. Hawkins, & I. Cross, Language and Music as Cognitive Systems (pp. 1-42). Oxford: Oxford University Press.
15. Hoch, L., & Tillmann, B. (2012). Shared structural and temporal integration resources for music and arithmetic processing. Acta psychologica, 140(3), 230-235. See also Chapter 21.
16. Grahn, J. A., & Brett, M. (2007). Rhythm and beat perception in motor areas of the brain. Journal of Cognitive Neuroscience, 19(5), 893-906.
17. Appendix: Faster and more accurate processing of information.
18. Appendix: Better long-term memory.
19. Appendix: Better short-term memory.

20. Appendix: Better working memory capacity.
21. Appendix: Better thinking ability (executive functioning).
22. Luders, E., Narr, K. L., Bilder, R. M., Thompson, P. M., Szeszko, P. R., Hamilton, L., & Toga, A. W. (2007). Positive correlations between corpus callosum thickness and intelligence. Neuroimage, 37(4), 1457-1464.
    Hutchinson, A. D., Mathias, J. L., Jacobson, B. L., Ruzic, L., Bond, A. N., & Banich, M. T. (2009). Relationship between intelligence and the size and composition of the corpus callosum. Experimental Brain Research, 192(3), 455-464.
23. Hanna-Pladdy, D. (2011, April 20). Childhood Music Lessons May Provide Lifelong Boost in Brain Functioning. Retrieved from American Psychological Association: http://www.apa.org/news/press/releases/2011/04/music-lessons.aspx
24. Wan, C. Y., & Schlaug, G. (2010). Music making as a tool for promoting brain plasticity across the life span. The Neuroscientist, 16(5), 566-577.
25. Hanna-Pladdy, B., & MacKay, A. (2011). The relation between instrumental musical activity and cognitive aging. Neuropsychology, 25(3), 378.
26. Baker, K. (2011, April 20). Musical Activity May Improve Cognitive Aging. Retrieved from EMORY University: http://shared.web.emory.edu/emory/news/releases/2011/04/musical-activity-may-improve-cognitive-aging.html#.UKPZSRxlbyA
27. Hanna-Pladdy, B., & Gajewski, B. (2012). Recent and past musical activity predicts cognitive aging variability: direct comparison with general lifestyle activities. Frontiers in Human Neuroscience, 6, 198.
28. Ludlam, K. (2012, July 19). Music has big brain benefits compared to other leisure pursuits. Retrieved from EMORY News Center:

http://news.emory.edu/stories/2012/07/hanna_pladdy_music_brain/index.html

29. Chua, A. (2011). Battle hymn of the Tiger Mother. New York: Bloomsbury Publishing.
30. See, for instance, the following comparative studies: Gerry, D., Unrau, A., & Trainor, L. J. (2012). Active music classes in infancy enhance musical, communicative and social development. Developmental Science, 15(3), 398-407.
    And
    Moyeda, I., Gómez, I. C., & Flores, M. (2006). Implementing a musical program to promote preschool children's vocabulary development. Early Childhood Research & Practice, 8(1).
31. Ibid.
32. Gerry, D., Unrau, A., & Trainor, L. J. (2012). Active music classes in infancy enhance musical, communicative and social development. Developmental Science, 15(3), 398-407.
33. Winsler, A., Ducenne, L., & Koury, A. (2011). Singing One's Way to Self-Regulation: The Role of Early Music and Movement Curricula and Private Speech. Early Education and Development, 22(2), 274-304.
34. Gerry, D., Unrau, A., & Trainor, L. J. (2012). Active music classes in infancy enhance musical, communicative and social development. Developmental Science, 15(3), 398-407.
35. Nikula, M., & Rantanen, T. (2009). "Millon alkaa muskari?" Arviointitutkimus Itä-Helsingin musiikkisilta-hankkeesta.
36. Goldshtrom, Y., Korman, D., Goldshtrom, I., & Bendavid, J. (2011). The effect of rhythmic exercises on cognition and behaviour of maltreated children: A pilot study. Journal of Bodywork and Movement Therapies, 15(3), 326-334.
    Moyeda, I., Gómez, I. C., & Flores, M. (2006). Implementing a musical program to promote preschool children's vocabulary development. Early Childhood Research & Practice, 8(1).
    And

Gerry, D., Unrau, A., & Trainor, L. J. (2012). Active music classes in infancy enhance musical, communicative and social development. Developmental Science, 15(3), 398-407.

37. Ibid.
38. Asher, R. (2011). Shattered: Modern Motherhood and the Illusion of Equality. New York: Harvill Secker.
39. Mumsnet. (2012, November 4). To Think There Should Be No Such Thing As A SAHM. Retrieved from Mumsnet Talk: http://www.mumsnet.com/Talk/am_i_being_unreasonable/1604119-to-think-there-should-be-no-such-thing-as-a-SAHM?pg=21
40. Gerry, D., Unrau, A., & Trainor, L. J. (2012). Active music classes in infancy enhance musical, communicative and social development. Developmental Science, 15(3), 398-407.
41. See Appendix: The Mozart Myth as well as Chapter 11: Schellenberg, E. G. (2003). Does exposure to music have beneficial side effects? New York: Oxford University Press.
42. Zentner, M., & Eerola, T. (2010). Rhythmic engagement with music in infancy. Proceedings of the National Academy of Sciences, 107(13), 5768-5773.
43. Morgan, G., Killough, C. M., & Thompson, L. A. (2011). Does visual information influence infants' movement to music? Psychology of Music, 39(4), 402-517.
44. Register, Dena M. (2003).The Effects of Live Music Groups Versus an Educational Children's Television Program on the Emergent Literacy of Young Children. Electronic Theses, Treatises and Dissertations. Paper 1903.
45. Kim, J., Wigram, T., & Gold, C. (2008). The effects of improvisational music therapy on joint attention behaviors in autistic children: a randomized controlled study. Journal of autism and developmental disorders, 38(9), 1758-1766.
46. Kim, J., Wigram, T., & Gold, C. (2009). Emotional,

motivational and interpersonal responsiveness of children with autism in improvisational music therapy. Autism, 13(4), 389-409.

47. Hendon, C., & Bohon, L. M. (2008). Hospitalized children's mood differences during play and music therapy. Child: care, health and development, 34(2), 141-144.
48. Ibid.
49. LeMoyne, T., & Buchanan, T. (2011). Does "hovering" matter? Helicopter parenting and its effect on well-being. Sociological Spectrum, 31(4), 399-418.
50. Moore, A. (2011, May 6). Is it payback time for pushy parents? Retrieved from Daily Mail: http://www.dailymail.co.uk/home/you/article-1381201/Is-payback-time-pushy-parents.html
51. Marcon, R. A. (1992). Differential effects of three preschool models on inner-city 4-year-olds. Early Childhood Research Quarterly, 7(4), 517-530.
52. Bergen, D. (2002). The role of pretend play in children's cognitive development. Early Childhood Research and Practice, 4(1), 2-15.
53. Marcon, R. A. (2002). Moving up the grades: Relationship between preschool model and later school success. Early Childhood Research and Practice, 4(1), 1-20.

Chapter 3

The Real Secret Of Successful Children

1. Huttenlocher, P. R., & Huttenlocher, P. R. (2002). Neural plasticity: The effects of environment on the development of the cerebral cortex. Boston, Massachusetts: Harvard University Press.
2. Ibid.

3. Anvari, S. H., Trainor, L. J., Woodside, J., & Levy, B. A. (2002). Relations among musical skills, phonological processing, and early reading ability in preschool children. Journal of experimental child psychology, 83(2), 111-130.
4. Welch, G.F., Saunders, J., Papageorgi, I., Joyce, H. and Himonides. E. (2009). An instrument for the assessment of children's attitudes to singing, self and social inclusion. London: Institute of Education, University of London.
   See also: Rinta, T., Purves, R., Welch, G., Stadler Elmer, S., & Bissig, R. (2011). Connections between children's feelings of social inclusion and their musical backgrounds. Journal of Social Inclusion, 2(2), 34-57.
5. Brodsky, W., & Sulkin, I. (2011). Handclapping songs: a spontaneous platform for child development among 5–10 year old children. Early Child Development and Care, 181(8), 1111-1136.
6. Gordon, E. (2003). Music Aptitude and Other Factors. In E. Gordon, A Music Learning Theory for Newborn and Young Children (pp. 22-23). Chicago: GIA Publications.
7. Ibid.
8. See Chapter 21 on Mathematics as well as Appendix: Music Boost for Mathematics.
9. See Chapters 22-29 on language skills and reading as well as the relevant Appendices.
10. Ibid.
11. Root-Bernstein, R. S. (2001). Music, creativity and scientific thinking. Leonardo, 34(1), 63-68. Read this and be surprised at how music has played a crucial part in the works and lives of the world's top scientists and inventors.
12. Wetter, O. E., Koerner, F., & Schwaninger, A. (2009). Does musical training improve school performance? Instructional Science, 37(4), 365-374.

13. Fitzpatrick, K. R. (2006). The effect of instrumental music participation and socioeconomic status on Ohio fourth-, sixth-, and ninth-grade proficiency test performance. Journal of Research in Music Education, 54(1), 73-84.
14. Hash, P. M. (2011). Effect of Pullout Lessons on the Academic Achievement of Eighth-Grade Band Students. Update: Applications of Research in Music Education, 30(1), 16-22.
15. Spychiger, M., & Patry, J. L. (1993). Musik macht Schule: Biografie und Ergebnisse eines Schulversuchs mit erweitertem Musikunterricht. Bavaria: Verlag Die Blaue Eule.
As quoted in: Spychiger, M. B. (2001). Understanding musical activity and musical learning as sign processes: Toward a semiotic approach to music education. Journal of Aesthetic Education, 35(1), 53-67.
16. Gardiner, M. F., Fox, A., Knowles, F., & Jeffrey, D. (1996). Learning improved by arts training. Nature; Nature, 381(6580), 284.
17. See Appendix: School readiness.
18. Alexander, K. L., Entwisle, D. R., & Horsey, C. S. (1997). From first grade forward: Early foundations of high school dropout. Sociology of education, 70(2), 87-107.
19. Entwisle, D. R., Alexander, K. L., & Olson, L. S. (2005). First Grade and Educational Attainment by Age 22: A New Story1. American Journal of Sociology, 110(5), 1458-1502.
20. Wetter, O. E., Koerner, F., & Schwaninger, A. (2009). Does musical training improve school performance? Instructional Science, 37(4), 365-374.
21. Miller, A., & Coen, D. (1994). The case for music in the schools. The Phi Delta Kappan, 75(6), 459-461.
22. Parry, J., Mathers, J., Stevens, A., Parsons, A., Lilford, R., Spurgeon, P., & Thomas, H. (2006). Admissions processes

for five year medical courses at English schools: review. Bmj, 332(7548), 1005-1009.

Chapter 4

The Short History of The Music Miracle

1. Gordon, E. (1968). A study of the efficacy of general intelligence and musical aptitude tests in predicting achievement in music. Bulletin of the Council for Research in Music Education, (13), 40-45.
2. Drennan,C.B.(1984). The Relationship of Musical Aptitude, Academic Achievement and Intelligence in Merit (Gifted) Students of Murfreesboro City Schools (Tennessee). ETD Collection for Tennessee State University. Paper AAI8529568.
3. Gardiner, M. F., Fox, A., Knowles, F., & Jeffrey, D. (1996). Learning improved by arts training. Nature; Nature, 381(6580), 284.
4. Anvari, S. H., Trainor, L. J., Woodside, J., & Levy, B. A. (2002). Relations among musical skills, phonological processing, and early reading ability in preschool children. Journal of experimental child psychology, 83(2), 111-130.
5. Hetland, L. (2000). Learning to make music enhances spatial reasoning. Journal of Aesthetic Education, 34(3/4), 179-238.
6. Rauscher, F. H., & Zupan, M. A. (2000). Classroom keyboard instruction improves kindergarten children's spatial-temporal performance: A field experiment. Early Childhood Research Quarterly, 15(2), 215-228.
   And
   Costa-Giomi, E. (1999). The effects of three years of piano instruction on children's cognitive development. Journal of Research in Music Education, 47(3), 198-212.

The former study, cited above, is one of many that found the spatial-temporal intelligence boost for young children (kindergarten age) and the latter is one of many that did not find any intelligence benefits for children who started music training at age nine or later.

7. Schellenberg, E. G. (2004). Music lessons enhance IQ. Psychological Science, 15(8), 511-514.
8. Schlaug, G., Jäncke, L., Huang, Y., Staiger, J. F., & Steinmetz, H. (1995). Increased corpus callosum size in musicians. Neuropsychologia, 33(8), 1047-1055.
9. Luders, E., Narr, K. L., Bilder, R. M., Thompson, P. M., Szeszko, P. R., Hamilton, L., & Toga, A. W. (2007). Positive correlations between corpus callosum thickness and intelligence. Neuroimage, 37(4), 1457-1464.
10. Badaruddin, D. H., Andrews, G. L., Bölte, S., Schilmoeller, K. J., Schilmoeller, G., Paul, L. K., & Brown, W. S. (2007). Social and behavioral problems of children with agenesis of the corpus callosum. Child Psychiatry & Human Development, 38(4), 287-302.
11. Norton, A., Winner, E., Cronin, K., Overy, K., Lee, D. J., & Schlaug, G. (2005). Are there pre-existing neural, cognitive, or motoric markers for musical ability? Brain and cognition, 59(2), 124-134.
12. Schlaug, G., Forgeard, M., Zhu, L., Norton, A., Norton, A., & Winner, E. (2009). Training induced Neuroplasticity in Young Children. Annals of the New York Academy of Sciences, 1169(1), 205-208.

Chapter 5

How Is This Possible? The scientific explanation behind the Miracle

1. Koelsch, S., Gunter, T. C., Cramon, D. Y. V., Zysset, S., Lohmann, G., & Friederici, A. D. (2002). Bach speaks: A

cortical" language-network" serves the processing of music. Neuroimage, 17(2), 956-966.

2. Koelsch, S. (2005). Neural substrates of processing syntax and semantics in music. Current opinion in neurobiology, 15(2), 207-212.
3. Hoch, L., & Tillmann, B. (2012). Shared structural and temporal integration resources for music and arithmetic processing. Acta psychologica, 140(3), 230-235.
4. Moreno, S., Bialystok, E., Barac, R., Schellenberg, E. G., Cepeda, N. J., & Chau, T. (2011). Short-term music training enhances verbal intelligence and executive function. Psychological science, 22(11), 1425-1433.
5. Goleman, D. (1996). Emotional Intelligence: Why It Can Matter More Than IQ . Great Britain: Clays Ltd.
6. Koelsch, S., Fritz, T., Müller, K., & Friederici, A. D. (2005). Investigating emotion with music: an fMRI study. Human brain mapping, 27(3), 239-250.
   And
   Gosselin, N., Peretz, I., Johnsen, E., & Adolphs, R. (2007). Amygdala damage impairs emotion recognition from music. Neuropsychologia, 45(2), 236-244.
7. Ibid.
8. Grahn, J. A. (2009). The role of the basal ganglia in beat perception. Annals of the New York Academy of Sciences, 1169(1), 35-45.
9. Gaser, C., & Schlaug, G. (2003). Brain structures differ between musicians and non-musicians. The Journal of Neuroscience, 23(27), 9240-9245.
10. Hyde, K. L., Lerch, J., Norton, A., Forgeard, M., Winner, E., Evans, A. C., & Schlaug, G. (2009). Musical training shapes structural brain development. The Journal of Neuroscience, 29(10), 3019-3025.

11. Derri, V., Tsapakidou, A., Zachopoulou, E., & Kioumourtzoglou, E. (2001). Effect of a music and movement programme on development of locomotor skills by children 4 to 6 years of age. European journal of physical education, 6(1), 16-25.
12. Brodsky, W., & Sulkin, I. (2011). Handclapping songs: a spontaneous platform for child development among 5–10 year old children. Early Child Development and Care, 181(8), 1111-1136.
13. Krommyda, M., Papadelis, G., Chatzikallia, K., Pastiadis, K., & Kardaras, P. (2008) Does awareness of musical structure relate to general cognitive and literacy profile in children with learning disabilities? Conference on Interdisciplinary Musicology (pp. 1-10). Thessaloniki: Aristotle University of Thessaloniki.
14. Bialystok, E., & Feng, X. (2009). Language proficiency and executive control in proactive interference: Evidence from monolingual and bilingual children and adults. Brain and language, 109(2), 93-100.
15. Bialystok, E., & DePape, A. M. (2009). Musical expertise, bilingualism, and executive functioning. Journal of Experimental Psychology: Human Perception and Performance, 35(2), 565.
16. Schellenberg, E. G. (2004). Music lessons enhance IQ. Psychological Science, 15(8), 511-514.
    In comparison with:
    Bialystok, E., & Feng, X. (2009). Language proficiency and executive control in proactive interference: Evidence from monolingual and bilingual children and adults. Brain and language, 109(2), 93-100.
17. Schlaug, G., Norton, A., Overy, K., & Winner, E. (2005). Effects of music training on the child's brain and cognitive

development. Annals of the New York Academy of Sciences, 1060(1), 219-230.

18. Zimmerman, E., & Lahav, A. (2012). The multisensory brain and its ability to learn music. Annals of the New York Academy of Sciences, 1252(1), 179-184.
19. Munte, T. F., Altenmuller, E., & Jancke, L. (2002). The musician's brain as a model of neuroplasticity. Nature Reviews Neuroscience, 3(6), 473-477.
20. Conway, C. M., Pisoni, D. B., & Kronenberger, W. G. (2009). The Importance of Sound for Cognitive Sequencing Abilities: The Auditory Scaffolding Hypothesis. Current directions in psychological science, 18(5), 275-279.
21. François, C., Chobert, J., Besson, M., & Schön, D. (2012). Music training for the development of speech segmentation. Cerebral Cortex, 22(7), 1473 - 1716.
22. Appendix: Faster and more accurate processing of information
23. Dmitrieva, E. S., Gel'man, V. Y., Zaitseva, K. A., & Lan'ko, S. V. (2008). Age-related features of the interaction of learning success and characteristics of auditory operative memory. Neuroscience and behavioral physiology, 38(4), 393-398.
24. Persellin, D. C. (1992). Responses to rhythm patterns when presented to children through auditory, visual, and kinesthetic modalities. Journal of Research in Music Education, 40(4), 306-315.
25. Persellin, D. C. (1994). Effects of learning modalities on melodic and rhythmic retention and on vocal pitch-matching by preschool children. Perceptual and motor skills, 78(3c), 1231-1234.
26. Chandrasekaran, B., & Kraus, N. (2010). Music, noise-exclusion, and learning. Music Perception, 27(4), 297-306.
27. Pantev, C., Oostenveld, R., Engelien, A., Ross, B., Roberts,

L. E., & Hoke, M. (1998). Increased auditory cortical representation in musicians. Nature, 392(6678), 811-814.

28. Musacchia, G., Strait, D., & Kraus, N. (2008). Relationships between behavior, brainstem and cortical encoding of seen and heard speech in musicians and non-musicians. Hearing research, 241(1-2), 34.
29. Kraus, N. (2011). Musical training gives edge in auditory processing. The Hearing Journal, 64(2), 10.
30. Rabbitt, P. (1991). Mild hearing loss can cause apparent memory failures which increase with age and reduce with IQ. Acta Oto-laryngologica, 111(S476), 167-176.
31. Dmitrieva, E. S., Gel'man, V. Y., Zaitseva, K. A., & Lan'ko, S. V. (2008). Age-related features of the interaction of learning success and characteristics of auditory operative memory. Neuroscience and behavioral physiology, 38(4), 393-398.
32. Appendix: The Music Boost for Pensioners.

Chapter 6

The Music Miracle: Why an early start makes all the difference

1. Huttenlocher, P. R. (1999). Dendritic and synaptic development in human cerebral cortex: time course and critical periods. Developmental Neuropsychology, 16(3), 347-349.
   And
   Chechik, G., Meilijson, I., & Ruppin, E. (1998). Synaptic pruning in development: A computational account. Neural Computation, 10(7), 1759-1777.
2. Dr. Hamil R. Djalilian, in an interview with Paul Oginni (2009). UCI Research with Cochlear Implants No Longer Falling on Deaf Ears. New University News, University of California, Irvine. Retrievable at: http://www.newuniversity.

org/2009/11/news/uci-research-with-cochlear-implants-no-longer-falling-on-deaf-ears/

3. Tait, M., De Raeve, L., & Nikolopoulos, T. P. (2007). Deaf children with cochlear implants before the age of 1 year: comparison of preverbal communication with normally hearing children. International journal of pediatric otorhinolaryngology, 71(10), 1605-1611.
4. Sharma, A., Dorman, M. F., & Spahr, A. J. (2002). A sensitive period for the development of the central auditory system in children with cochlear implants: implications for age of implantation. Ear and hearing, 23(6), 532-539.
5. Ibid.
6. Schellenberg, E. G. (2004). Music lessons enhance IQ. Psychological Science, 15(8), 511-514.
7. Moreno, S., Bialystok, E., Barac, R., Schellenberg, E. G., Cepeda, N. J., & Chau, T. (2011). Short-term music training enhances verbal intelligence and executive function. Psychological science, 22(11), 1425-1433.
8. Rauscher, F. H., & Hinton, S. C. (2011). Music instruction and its diverse extra-musical benefits. Music Perception, 29(2), 215-226.
9. Ibid.
10. See, for instance, Costa-Giomi, E. (1999). The effects of three years of piano instruction on children's cognitive development. Journal of Research in Music Education, 47(3), 198-212.
11. Schlaug, G., Jäncke, L., Huang, Y., Staiger, J. F., & Steinmetz, H. (1995). Increased corpus callosum size in musicians. Neuropsychologia, 33(8), 1047-1055.
12. Schlaug, G., Forgeard, M., Zhu, L., Norton, A., Norton, A., & Winner, E. (2009). Training induced Neuroplasticity in Young Children. Annals of the New York Academy of Sciences, 1169(1), 205-208.

13. Luders, E., Narr, K. L., Bilder, R. M., Thompson, P. M., Szeszko, P. R., Hamilton, L., & Toga, A. W. (2007). Positive correlations between corpus callosum thickness and intelligence. Neuroimage, 37(4), 1457-1464.
14. Cyprien, F., Courtet, P., Malafosse, A., Maller, J., Meslin, C., Bonafé, A., & Artero, S. (2011). Suicidal behavior is associated with reduced corpus callosum area. Biological psychiatry, 70(4), 320-326.
15. Harris, M. A. (2007). Differences in mathematics scores between students who receive traditional Montessori instruction and students who receive music enriched Montessori instruction. Journal for Learning through the Arts, 3(1), 1-50.
    Although Harris studied Montessori classes with or without music training, it is crucial to note that the results apply even more within standard schools. This is because Montessori children, on average, perform significantly better on maths than their peers from the standard school, even without music training. The fact that music training further improves their Montessori advantage for maths is a case in point. Read about the Montessori advantage here:
    Miller, L. B., & Bizzell, R. P. (1983). Long-term effects of four preschool programs: Sixth, seventh, and eighth grades. Child Development, 54(3), 727-741.
    Duax, T. (1995). Report on Academic Achievement in a Private Montessori School. Namta Journal, 20(2), 145-47.
    Dohrmann, K. R., Nishida, T. K., Gartner, A., Lipsky, D. K., & Grimm, K. J. (2007). High school outcomes for students in a public Montessori program. Journal of Research in Childhood Education, 22(2), 205-217.
16. Degé, F., Wehrum, S., Stark, R., & Schwarzer, G. (2011). The influence of two years of school music training in secondary

school on visual and auditory memory. European Journal of Developmental Psychology, 8(5), 608-623.

17. Abrahamsson, N., & Hyltenstam, K. (2009). Age of onset and nativelikeness in a second language: Listener perception versus linguistic scrutiny. Language Learning, 59(2), 249-306.
18. Huttenlocher, P. R. (1999). Dendritic and synaptic development in human cerebral cortex: time course and critical periods. Developmental Neuropsychology, 16(3), 347-349.
    And
    Chechik, G., Meilijson, I., & Ruppin, E. (1998). Synaptic pruning in development: A computational account. Neural Computation, 10(7), 1759-1777.
19. Bugos, J. A., Perlstein, W. M., McCrae, C. S., Brophy, T. S., & Bedenbaugh, P. H. (2007). Individualized piano instruction enhances executive functioning and working memory in older adults. Aging and Mental Health, 11(4), 464-471.
20. Hanna-Pladdy, D. (2011, April 20). Childhood Music Lessons May Provide Lifelong Boost in Brain Functioning. Retrieved from American Psychological Association: http://www.apa.org/news/press/releases/2011/04/music-lessons.aspx
21. Wan, C. Y., & Schlaug, G. (2010). Music making as a tool for promoting brain plasticity across the life span. The Neuroscientist, 16(5), 566-577.
22. Ibid.
23. Hanna-Pladdy, B., & MacKay, A. (2011). The relation between instrumental musical activity and cognitive aging. Neuropsychology, 25(3), 378.
24. Hanna-Pladdy, B., & Gajewski, B. (2012). Recent and past musical activity predicts cognitive aging variability: direct comparison with general lifestyle activities. Frontiers in Human Neuroscience, 6, 198.

Part Two

Music Miracle for Babies and Toddlers: Gains for the baby's brain, boost for the family mood

Chapter 7

Your Baby's Brain Craves for Music Training

1. Gale, C. R., O'Callaghan, F. J., Godfrey, K. M., Law, C. M., & Martyn, C. N. (2004). Critical periods of brain growth and cognitive function in children. Brain, 127(2), 321-329.
2. Gerry, D., Unrau, A., & Trainor, L. J. (2012). Active music classes in infancy enhance musical, communicative and social development. Developmental Science. 15(3), 398-407.
3. Zentner, M., & Eerola, T. (2010). Rhythmic engagement with music in infancy. Proceedings of the National Academy of Sciences, 107(13), 5768-5773.
4. Gerry, D., Unrau, A., & Trainor, L. J. (2012). Active music classes in infancy enhance musical, communicative and social development. Developmental Science. 15(3), 398-407.
5. Ibid.
6. Brodsky, W., & Sulkin, I. (2011). Handclapping songs: a spontaneous platform for child development among 5–10 year old children. Early Child Development and Care, 181(8), 1111-1136.
7. Winsler, A., Ducenne, L., & Koury, A. (2011). Singing One's Way to Self-Regulation: The Role of Early Music and Movement Curricula and Private Speech. Early Education and Development, 22(2), 274-304.
8. Ibid.
9. Lin, H. L., Lawrence, F. R., & Gorrell, J. (2003). Kindergarten teachers' views of children's readiness for school. Early Childhood Research Quarterly, 18(2), 225-237.

10. Moffitt, T. E., Arseneault, L., Belsky, D., Dickson, N., Hancox, R. J., Harrington, H., & Caspi, A. (2011). A gradient of childhood self-control predicts health, wealth, and public safety. Proceedings of the National Academy of Sciences, 108(7), 2693-2698.
11. Winsler, A., Ducenne, L., & Koury, A. (2011). Singing One's Way to Self-Regulation: The Role of Early Music and Movement Curricula and Private Speech. Early Education and Development, 22(2), 274-304.
12. Casey, B. J., Somerville, L. H., Gotlib, I. H., Ayduk, O., Franklin, N. T., Askren, M. K., & Shoda, Y. (2011). Behavioral and neural correlates of delay of gratification 40 years later. Proceedings of the National Academy of Sciences, 108(36), 14998-15003.
13. Moffitt, T. E., Arseneault, L., Belsky, D., Dickson, N., Hancox, R. J., Harrington, H., & Caspi, A. (2011). A gradient of childhood self-control predicts health, wealth, and public safety. Proceedings of the National Academy of Sciences, 108(7), 2693-2698.
14. Moreno, S., Bialystok, E., Barac, R., Schellenberg, E. G., Cepeda, N. J., & Chau, T. (2011). Short-term music training enhances verbal intelligence and executive function. Psychological science, 22(11), 1425-1433.
15. Shore, R. A. (2010). Music and Cognitive Development: From Notes to Neural Networks. NHSA DIALOG, 13(1), 53-65.
16. See Appendix: Music training compared with other activities
17. Nikula, M., & Rantanen, T. (2009). "Millon alkaa muskari?": Arviointitutkimus Itä-Helsingin musiikkisilta-hankkeesta päiväkoti. Helsinki: Laakavuoressa.
18. Ibid.

Chapter 8

Harmony in the Household

1. Nakata, T., & Trehub, S. E. (2004). Infants' responsiveness to maternal speech and singing. Infant Behavior and Development, 27(4), 455-464.
2. Trainor, L. J., & Zacharias, C. A. (1998). Infants prefer higher-pitched singing. Infant Behavior and Development, 21(4), 799-805.
3. Zentner, M., & Eerola, T. (2010). Rhythmic engagement with music in infancy. Proceedings of the National Academy of Sciences, 107(13), 5768-5773.
4. Tafuri, Infant Musicality, new research.....2008. Page 46
5. Ibid.
6. Masataka, N. (2005). Preference for consonance over dissonance by hearing newborns of deaf parents and of hearing parents. Developmental science, 9(1), 46-50.
7. Perani, D. (2012). Functional and structural connectivity for language and music processing at birth. Rendiconti Lincei, 22(3), 1-10.
8. Brandt, A., Gebrian, M., & Slevc, L. R. (2012). Music and early language acquisition. Frontiers in Psychology, 3, 327.
9. Ibid.
10. Zentner, M., & Eerola, T. (2010). Rhythmic engagement with music in infancy. Proceedings of the National Academy of Sciences, 107(13), 5768-5773.
11. Ibid.
12. See Chapters 17-19

    And

    Krommyda, M., Papadelis, G., Chatzikallia, K., Pastiadis, K., & Kardaras, P. (2008) Does awareness of musical structure relate to general cognitive and literacy profile in children with learning disabilities? Conference on Interdisciplinary Musicology (pp. 1-10). Thessaloniki: Aristotle University of Thessaloniki.

Yunxia, C. U. I. (2010). Research on the Effect of Rhythm Training on Chidren's Intelligence. Journal of Sports and Science, 3, 018.

Brodsky, W., & Sulkin, I. (2011). Handclapping songs: a spontaneous platform for child development among 5–10 year old children. Early Child Development and Care, 181(8), 1111-1136.

Waber, D. P., Weiler, M. D., Bellinger, D. C., Marcus, D. J., Forbes, P. W., Wypij, D., & Wolff, P. H. (2000). Diminished motor timing control in children referred for diagnosis of learning problems. Developmental neuropsychology, 17(2), 181-197.

13. See, for instance, the following studies:
Waber, D. P., Weiler, M. D., Bellinger, D. C., Marcus, D. J., Forbes, P. W., Wypij, D., & Wolff, P. H. (2000). Diminished motor timing control in children referred for diagnosis of learning problems. Developmental neuropsychology, 17(2), 181-197.
And
Krommyda, M., Papadelis, G., Chatzikallia, K., Pastiadis, K., & Kardaras, P. (2008) Does awareness of musical structure relate to general cognitive and literacy profile in children with learning disabilities? Conference on Interdisciplinary Musicology (pp. 1-10). Thessaloniki: Aristotle University of Thessaloniki.
14. Zentner, M., & Eerola, T. (2010). Rhythmic engagement with music in infancy. Proceedings of the National Academy of Sciences, 107(13), 5768-5773.
15. Nicholson, J. M., Berthelsen, D., Abad, V., Williams, K., & Bradley, J. (2008). Impact of music therapy to promote positive parenting and child development. Journal of Health Psychology, 13(2), 226-238.
16. Walworth, D. D. (2007). The Effect of Developmental Music

Groups for Parents and Premature Or Typical Infants Under Two Years On Parental responsiveness And Infant Social Development. Ann Arbor: ProQuest LCC.

Chapter 9

And Your Baby Can Sing: Unleashing Your Baby's Inner Vocalist and Wordsmith

1. Brandt, A., Gebrian, M., & Slevc, L. R. (2012). Music and early language acquisition. Frontiers in Psychology, 3, 327.
2. Tafuri, Infant Musicality – New Research for Educators and Parents, 2008.
3. Tafuri, Infant Musicality – New Research for Educators and Parents, 2008.
4. Tafuri, Infant Musicality – New Research for Educators and Parents, 2008, pages 87-88.
5. Gerry, D., Unrau, A., & Trainor, L. J. (2012). Active music classes in infancy enhance musical, communicative and social development. Developmental Science. 15(3), 398-407.
6. Brandt, A., Gebrian, M., & Slevc, L. R. (2012). Music and early language acquisition. Frontiers in Psychology, 3, 327.
7. Nakata, T., & Trehub, S. E. (2004). Infants' responsiveness to maternal speech and singing. Infant Behavior and Development, 27(4), 455-464.
8. Gordon, E. (2003). Music Aptitude and Other Factors. In E. Gordon, A Music Learning Theory for Newborn and Young Children (pp. 22-23). Chicago: GIA Publications.
9. Brandt, A., Gebrian, M., & Slevc, L. R. (2012). Music and early language acquisition. Frontiers in Psychology, 3, 327. No issue.
10. Ibid.

11. Malloch, S. N. (2000). Mothers and infants and communicative musicality. Musicae scientiae, 3(1 suppl), 29-57.
12. Ibid.
13. Trainor, L. J., Austin, C. M., & Desjardins, R. N. (2000). Is infant-directed speech prosody a result of the vocal expression of emotion?. Psychological science, 11(3), 188-195.

Part Three

The Many Myths of Music Education

Chapter 10

The Culture Myth - Tuning into Human Nature

1. Miller, G. (2000). Evolution of human music through sexual selection. The origins of music, 329-360.
2. Weinberger, N. M. (1998). Brain, behavior, biology, and music: Some research findings and their implications for educational policy. Arts Education Policy Review, 99(3), 28-36.
3. Patel, A. D., Iversen, J. R., Bregman, M. R., & Schulz, I. (2009). Experimental evidence for synchronization to a musical beat in a nonhuman animal. Current Biology, 19(10), 827-830.
4. Buck, J. & Buck, E., (1966). Biology of Synchronous Flashing of Fireflies. Nature, 211, 562 - 564.
5. Buck, J., & Buck, E. (1968). Mechanism of rhythmic synchronous flashing of fireflies. Fireflies of Southeast Asia may use anticipatory time-measuring in synchronizing their flashing. Science, 159(3821), 1319-1327.
6. Hannon, E. E., & Trainor, L. J. (2007). Music acquisition: effects of enculturation and formal training on development. Trends in Cognitive Sciences, 11(11), 466-472.

7. Ibid.
8. Blood, A. J., & Zatorre, R. J. (2001). Intensely pleasurable responses to music correlate with activity in brain regions implicated in reward and emotion. Proceedings of the National Academy of Sciences, 98(20), 11818-11823.
9. Ibid.
10. Ibid.
11. See Appendix: Music Training increases IQ as well as Appendix: Faster and more accurate processing of information
12. Appendix: Spatial-temporal intelligence.
13. Better memory – appendices.
14. Jennifer viegar, darwin's wife influenced theories ADDITION
15. Ibid.
16. Darwin, 1871
17. Ibid.
18. Ibid addition double check
19. Dunbar, R. I., Kaskatis, K., MacDonald, I., & Barra, V. (2012). Performance of music elevates pain threshold and positive affect: Implications for the evolutionary function of music. Evolutionary psychology: an international journal of evolutionary approaches to psychology and behavior, 10(4), 688.
20. Ibid.
21. General intelligence & rhythm see chapter X (link T 2002, Madison 2007/8?).
22. Brodsky, W., & Sulkin, I. (2011). Handclapping songs: a spontaneous platform for child development among 5–10 year old children. Early Child Development and Care, 181(8), 1111-1136.

Chapter 11

The Mozart Myth: Why listening to a genius will not make your child one

1. Rauscher, F. H., Shaw, G., & Ky, K. (1993). Mozart and spatial reasoning. Nature, 365, 611.
2. An array of studies has shown the incorrect design of the original 'Mozart Effect' study. The following 5 papers together make the point clearly for the curious reader, although many more exist in the scientific literature: Thompson, W. F., Schellenberg, E. G., & Husain, G. (2001). Arousal, mood, and the Mozart effect. Psychological Science, 12(3), 248-251.
   Steele, K. M., Bass, K. E., & Crook, M. D. (1999). The mystery of the Mozart effect: Failure to replicate. Psychological Science, 10(4), 366-369.
   McKelvie, P., & Low, J. (2002). Listening to Mozart does not improve children's spatial ability: Final curtains for the Mozart effect. British Journal of Developmental Psychology, 20(2), 241-258.
   Lynn, E. M. (2000). Another failure to generalize the Mozart effect. Psychological reports, 87(1), 325-330.
   Pietschnig, J., Voracek, M., & Formann, A. K. (2010). Mozart effect–Shmozart effect: A meta-analysis. Intelligence, 38(3), 314-323.
3. Schellenberg, E. G. (2005). Music and cognitive abilities. Current Directions in Psychological Science, 14(6), 317-320.
4. Schellenberg, E. G., & Hallam, S. (2005). Music Listening and Cognitive Abilities in 10 and 11 Year Olds: The Blur Effect. Annals of the New York Academy of Sciences, 1060(1), 202-209.
5. Schellenberg, E. G. (2005). Music and cognitive abilities. Current Directions in Psychological Science, 14(6), 317-320.
6. Estrada, C. A., Isen, A. M., & Young, M. J. (1997). Positive

affect facilitates integration of information and decreases anchoring in reasoning among physicians. Organizational behavior and human decision processes, 72(1), 117-135.

7. Blood, A. J., & Zatorre, R. J. (2001). Intensely pleasurable responses to music correlate with activity in brain regions implicated in reward and emotion. Proceedings of the National Academy of Sciences, 98(20), 11818-11823.
8. Schellenberg, E. G., Nakata, T., Hunter, P. G., & Tamoto, S. (2007). Exposure to music and cognitive performance: Tests of children and adults. Psychology of Music, 35(1), 5-19. For the isolated effect of a short-term boost for cognitive tests produced by mood-boosting visualization alone, see Bryan, T., & Bryan, J. (1991). Positive mood and math performance. Journal of Learning Disabilities, 24(8), 490-494.
9. Schellenberg, E. G., Nakata, T., Hunter, P. G., & Tamoto, S. (2007). Exposure to music and cognitive performance: Tests of children and adults. Psychology of Music, 35(1), 5-19.
10. Druckerman, P. (2012). French Children Don't Throw Food. Parenting Secrets From Paris. Black Swan.
11. Rauscher, F. (2002). Mozart and the mind:Factual and fictional effects of musical enrichment. In J. M. Aronson, Improving Academic Achievement: Impact of Psychological Factors on Education (pp. 267-278). New York: Emerald Group Publishing.
12. Schellenberg, E. G., Nakata, T., Hunter, P. G., & Tamoto, S. (2007). Exposure to music and cognitive performance: Tests of children and adults. Psychology of Music, 35(1), 5-19.
13. Schellenberg, E. G., & Hallam, S. (2005). Music Listening and Cognitive Abilities in 10 and 11 Year Olds: The Blur Effect. Annals of the New York Academy of Sciences, 1060(1), 202-209.
14. Ibid.

15. Nantais, K. M., & Schellenberg, E. G. (1999). The Mozart effect: An artifact of preference. Psychological Science, 10(4), 370-373.
See also: Husain, G., Thompson, W. F., & Schellenberg, E. G. (2002). Effects of musical tempo and mode on arousal, mood, and spatial abilities. Music Perception, 20(2), 151-171.
16. Zentner, M., & Eerola, T. (2010). Rhythmic engagement with music in infancy. Proceedings of the National Academy of Sciences, 107(13), 5768-5773.
17. See Chapters 17-19
And
Krommyda, M., Papadelis, G., Chatzikallia, K., Pastiadis, K., & Kardaras, P. (2008) Does awareness of musical structure relate to general cognitive and literacy profile in children with learning disabilities? Conference on Interdisciplinary Musicology (pp. 1-10). Thessaloniki: Aristotle University of Thessaloniki.
Yunxia, C. U. I. (2010). Research on the Effect of Rhythm Training on Chidren's Intelligence. Journal of Sports and Science, 3, 018.
Brodsky, W., & Sulkin, I. (2011). Handclapping songs: a spontaneous platform for child development among 5–10 year old children. Early Child Development and Care, 181(8), 1111-1136.
Waber, D. P., Weiler, M. D., Bellinger, D. C., Marcus, D. J., Forbes, P. W., Wypij, D., & Wolff, P. H. (2000). Diminished motor timing control in children referred for diagnosis of learning problems. Developmental neuropsychology, 17(2), 181-197.

1. University of York (2010, March 16). Babies are born to dance, new research shows. ScienceDaily. Retrieved January 12, 2013, from http://www.sciencedaily.com / releases/2010/03/100315161925.htm
2. Kanazawa, S., & Perina, K. (2012). Why More Intelligent Individuals Like Classical Music. Journal of Behavioral Decision Making, 25(3), 264–275.
18. Ibid.

Background Music or Music Background

1. See, for instance, Salamé, P., & Baddeley, A. (1989). Effects of background music on phonological short-term memory. The Quarterly Journal of Experimental Psychology, 41(1), 107-122.
   And
   Ransdell, S. E., & Gilroy, L. (2001). The effects of background music on word processed writing. Computers in Human Behavior, 17(2), 141-148.
2. Crawford, H. J., & Strapp, C. M. (1994). Effects of vocal and instrumental music on visuospatial and verbal performance as moderated by studying preference and personality. Personality and individual differences, 16(2), 237-245.
3. Salamé, P., & Baddeley, A. (1989). Effects of background music on phonological short-term memory. The Quarterly Journal of Experimental Psychology, 41(1), 107-122.
4. Ibid.
5. Parbery-Clark, A., Skoe, E., & Kraus, N. (2009). Musical experience limits the degradative effects of background noise on the neural processing of sound. The Journal of Neuroscience, 29(45), 14100-14107.

Chapter 12

When Listening Helps: The Four Exceptions

Early Enculturation

1. Gordon, E. E. (2011). Early childhood music abuse: Misdeeds and Neglect.Visions of Research in Music Education, 17, 1-11.
2. Hart, B., & Risley, T. (1999). The Social World of Children: Learning To Talk. Baltimore: Paul H.Brookes Publishing Co. And
   Hart, B., & Risley, T. R. (2003). The early catastrophe: The 30 million word gap by age 3. American Educator, 27(1), 4-9.
3. Stewart, L., & Walsh, V. (2005). Infant learning: music and the baby brain. Current biology, 15(21), R882-R884.
4. Ibid.
5. Hannon, E. E., & Trehub, S. E. (2005). Tuning in to musical rhythms: Infants learn more readily than adults. Proceedings of the National Academy of Sciences of the United States of America, 102(35), 12639-12643.
6. Gordon, E. E. (2011). Early childhood music abuse: Misdeeds and Neglect. Visions of Research in Music Education, 17, 1-11.
7. Hannon, E. E., & Trehub, S. E. (2005). Tuning in to musical rhythms: Infants learn more readily than adults. Proceedings of the National Academy of Sciences of the United States of America, 102(35), 12639-12643.
8. Hannon, E. E., & Trehub, S. E. (2005). Metrical categories in infancy and adulthood. Psychological Science, 16(1), 48-55.
   Soley, G., & Hannon, E. E. (2010). Infants prefer the musical meter of their own culture: a cross-cultural comparison. Developmental psychology, 46(1), 286.
9. Gerry, D. W., Faux, A. L., & Trainor, L. J. (2010). Effects

of Kindermusik training on infants' rhythmic enculturation. Developmental science, 13(3), 545-551.

10. Peery, J. C., & Peery, I. W. (1986). Effects of exposure to classical music on the musical preferences of preschool children. Journal of Research in Music Education, 34(1), 24-33.
11. ter Bogt, T. F., Delsing, M. J., van Zalk, M., Christenson, P. G., & Meeus, W. H. (2011). Intergenerational Continuity of Taste: Parental and Adolescent Music Preferences. Social Forces, 90(1), 297-319.
12. Zentner, M., & Eerola, T. (2010). Rhythmic engagement with music in infancy. Proceedings of the National Academy of Sciences, 107(13), 5768-5773.
13. See Chapters 17-19

    And

    Krommyda, M., Papadelis, G., Chatzikallia, K., Pastiadis, K., & Kardaras, P. (2008) Does awareness of musical structure relate to general cognitive and literacy profile in children with learning disabilities? Conference on Interdisciplinary Musicology (pp. 1-10). Thessaloniki: Aristotle University of Thessaloniki.

    Yunxia, C. U. I. (2010). Research on the Effect of Rhythm Training on Chidren's Intelligence. Journal of Sports and Science, 3, 018.

    Brodsky, W., & Sulkin, I. (2011). Handclapping songs: a spontaneous platform for child development among 5–10 year old children. Early Child Development and Care, 181(8), 1111-1136.

    Waber, D. P., Weiler, M. D., Bellinger, D. C., Marcus, D. J., Forbes, P. W., Wypij, D., & Wolff, P. H. (2000). Diminished motor timing control in children referred for diagnosis of learning problems. Developmental neuropsychology, 17(2), 181-197.

Songs as Learning Tools

1. Medina, S. L. (1990). The Effects of Music upon Second Language Vocabulary Acquisition. San Francisco.
   Schön, D., Boyer, M., Moreno, S., Besson, M., Peretz, I., & Kolinsky, R. (2008). Songs as an aid for language acquisition. Cognition, 106(2), 975-983.
   Šišková, D. (2008). Teaching Vocabulary through Music. Unpublished Diploma's Thesis, Masaryk University,Brno, Czech Republic.
2. Schön, D., Boyer, M., Moreno, S., Besson, M., Peretz, I., & Kolinsky, R. (2008). Songs as an aid for language acquisition. Cognition, 106(2), 975-983.
3. See Appendix: Songs as Learning Tools.
4. Campabello, N., De Carlo, M. J., O'Neil, J., & Vacek, M. J. (2002). Music Enhances Learning. Unpublished Master's Theses, Chicago, Saint Xavier University.

The Health Benefits of Listening to Music

1. Phumdoung, S., & Good, M. (2003). Music reduces sensation and distress of labor pain. Pain Management Nursing, 4(2), 54-61.
2. Särkämö, T., Tervaniemi, M., Laitinen, S., Forsblom, A., Soinila, S., Mikkonen, M., & Hietanen, M. (2008). Music listening enhances cognitive recovery and mood after middle cerebral artery stroke. Brain, 131(3), 866-876.
3. Schwartz, F. J., & Ritchie, R. (2004). Music listening in neonatal intensive care units. Music therapy and medicine, theoretical and clinical applications, 13-23.
4. Ibid.

5. Thayer, R. E., Newman, J. R., & McClain, T. M. (1994). Self-regulation of mood: Strategies for changing a bad mood, raising energy, and reducing tension. Journal of personality and social psychology, 67(5), 910.
6. Nantais, K. M., & Schellenberg, E. G. (1999). The Mozart effect: An artifact of preference. Psychological Science, 10(4), 370-373.
7. Dunbar, R. I., Kaskatis, K., MacDonald, I., & Barra, V. (2012). Performance of music elevates pain threshold and positive affect: Implications for the evolutionary function of music. Evolutionary psychology: an international journal of evolutionary approaches to psychology and behavior, 10(4), 688.

Music as a Form of Beneficial Entertainment

1. Saarikallio, S. (2009). Emotional self-regulation through music in 3-8-year-old children. Proceedings of the 7th Triennial Conference of European Society for the Cognitive Sciences of Music (ESCOM 2009) (pp. 452–462). Jyväskylä: University of Jyväskylä Press.
2. Giomo, C. J. (1993). An experimental study of children's sensitivity to mood in music. Psychology of Music, 21(2), 141-162.
3. Brand, M. (1986). Relationship between home musical environment and selected musical attributes of second-grade children. Journal of Research in Music Education, 34(2), 111-120.
4. Swing, E. L., Gentile, D. A., Anderson, C. A., & Walsh, D. A. (2010). Television and video game exposure and the development of attention problems. Pediatrics, 126(2), 214-221.
5. Zimmerman, F. J., Christakis, D. A., & Meltzoff, A. N. (2007).

Associations between media viewing and language development in children under age 2 years. The Journal of pediatrics, 151(4), 364-368.
6. Lillard, A. S., & Peterson, J. (2011). The immediate impact of different types of television on young children's executive function. Pediatrics, 128(4), 644-649.
7. Manganello, J. A., & Taylor, C. A. (2009). Television exposure as a risk factor for aggressive behavior among 3-year-old children. Archives of pediatrics & adolescent medicine, 163(11), 1037.
8. Zimmerman, F. J., Christakis, D. A., & Meltzoff, A. N. (2007). Associations between media viewing and language development in children under age 2 years. The Journal of pediatrics, 151(4), 364-368.

Chapter 13

Musicality, 'Talent Shows' and the Biggest Myth of All

1. Perani, D., Saccuman, M. C., Scifo, P., Spada, D., Andreolli, G., Rovelli, R., & Koelsch, S. (2010). Functional specializations for music processing in the human newborn brain. Proceedings of the National Academy of Sciences, 107(10), 4758-4763. See also the earlier study before the very recent brain imaging of newborn children: Trainor, L. J., Tsang, C. D., & Cheung, V. H. (2002). Preference for sensory consonance in 2-and 4-month-old infants. Music Perception, 20(2), 187-194.
2. Sugimoto, T., Kobayashi, H., Nobuyoshi, N., Kiriyama, Y., Takeshita, H., Nakamura, T., & Hashiya, K. (2010). Preference for consonant music over dissonant music by an infant chimpanzee. Primates, 51(1), 7-12.
3. Chiandetti, C., & Vallortigara, G. (2011). Chicks like consonant music. Psychological science, 22(10), 1270-1273.
4. Winkler, I., Háden, G. P., Ladinig, O., Sziller, I., & Honing, H.

(2009). Newborn infants detect the beat in music. Proceedings of the National Academy of Sciences, 106(7), 2468-2471.

5. Welch, G. (2001). The misunderstanding of music. London: Institute of Education Publications, University of London.
6. Tafuri, J. (2008). Infant Musicality – New Research for Educators and Parents (pp. 18). Ashgate.
7. Tafuri, J. (2008). Infant Musicality – New Research for Educators and Parents. Ashgate.
8. Gerry, D., Unrau, A., & Trainor, L. J. (2012). Active music classes in infancy enhance musical, communicative and social development. Developmental Science. 15(3), 398-407.
9. Juvonen, A., Lehtonen, K, & Ruismaki, H. Musically restricted under the pressure of postmodern society, 1-11.
10. Ibid.
11. Welch, G. (2001). The misunderstanding of music. London: Institute of Education Publications, University of London.
12. Gordon, E. E. (2011). Early childhood music abuse: Misdeeds and Neglect. Visions of Research in Music Education, 17, 1-11.
13. Juvonen, A., Lehtonen, K, & Ruismaki, H. Musically restricted under the pressure of postmodern society, 1-11.
14. Ibid.

Part Four

IQ or Multiple Intelligences? Music training boosts them all

Introduction

1. See Appendix: Faster and more accurate processing of information
2. Ibid.
3. Neisser, U., Boodoo, G., Bouchard Jr, T. J., Boykin, A. W.,

Brody, N., Ceci, S. J., & Urbina, S. (1996). Intelligence: Knowns and unknowns. American psychologist, 51(2), 77.
Gottfredson, L. S. (1997). Mainstream science on intelligence: An editorial with 52 signatories, history, and bibliography. Intelligence, 24(1), 13-23.

4. Batty, G. D., Deary, I. J., & Gottfredson, L. S. (2007). Premorbid (early life) IQ and later mortality risk: systematic review. Annals of epidemiology, 17(4), 278-288.
   Batty, G. D., Wennerstad, K. M., Smith, G. D., Gunnell, D., Deary, I. J., Tynelius, P., & Rasmussen, F. (2009). IQ in early adulthood and mortality by middle age: cohort study of 1 million Swedish men. Epidemiology, 20(1), 100-109.
5. Gottfredson, L. S., & Deary, I. J. (2004). Intelligence predicts health and longevity, but why? Current Directions in Psychological Science, 13(1), 1-4.
6. Zagorsky, J. L. (2007). Do you have to be smart to be rich? The impact of IQ on wealth, income and financial distress. Intelligence, 35(5), 489-501.

Chapter 14

IQ: Why it matters and how to raise it

1. Batty, G. D., Deary, I. J., & Gottfredson, L. S. (2007). Premorbid (early life) IQ and later mortality risk: systematic review. Annals of epidemiology, 17(4), 278-288.
2. Gottfredson, L. S., & Deary, I. J. (2004). Intelligence predicts health and longevity, but why? Current Directions in Psychological Science, 13(1), 1-4.
3. Gottfredson, L. S. (1997). Why g matters: The complexity of everyday life. Intelligence, 24(1), 79-132.
4. Moffitt, T. E., Caspi, A., Harkness, A. R., & Silva, P. A. (2006). The Natural History of Change to Intellectual Performance:

Who Changes? How Much? Is it Meaningful? Journal of Child Psychology and Psychiatry, 34(4), 455-506.

5. Streissguth, A. P., Barr, H. M., Sampson, P. D., Darby, B. L., & Martin, D. C. (1989). IQ at age 4 in relation to maternal alcohol use and smoking during pregnancy. Developmental Psychology, 25(1), 3.
6. Koenen, K. C., Moffitt, T. E., Caspi, A., Taylor, A., & Purcell, S. (2003). Domestic violence is associated with environmental suppression of IQ in young children. Development and psychopathology, 15(02), 297-311.
7. Canfield, R. L., Henderson Jr, C. R., Cory-Slechta, D. A., Cox, C., Jusko, T. A., & Lanphear, B. P. (2003). Intellectual impairment in children with blood lead concentrations below 10 μg per deciliter. New England Journal of Medicine, 348(16), 1517-1526.
8. Liu, J., Raine, A., Venables, P. H., Dalais, C., & Mednick, S. A. (2003). Malnutrition at age 3 years and lower cognitive ability at age 11 years: independence from psychosocial adversity. Archives of pediatrics & adolescent medicine, 157(6), 593.
9. Anderson, J. W., Johnstone, B. M., & Remley, D. T. (1999). Breast-feeding and cognitive development: a meta-analysis. The American journal of clinical nutrition, 70(4), 525-535.
10. Geoff Der, G., & Deary, I. J. (2006). Effect of breastfeeding on intelligence in children: prospective study, sibling pairs analysis, and meta-analysis. BMJ: British Medical Journal, 333(7575), 945.
11. Caspi, A., Williams, B., Kim-Cohen, J., Craig, I. W., Milne, B. J., Poulton, R., & Moffitt, T. E. (2007). Moderation of breastfeeding effects on the IQ by genetic variation in fatty acid metabolism. Proceedings of the National Academy of Sciences, 104(47), 18860-18865.
12. Schellenberg, E. G. (2006). Long-term positive associations

between music lessons and IQ. Journal of Educational Psychology, 98(2), 457.

13. Schellenberg, E. G. (2004). Music lessons enhance IQ. Psychological Science, 15(8), 511-514.

Chapter 15

Building IQ

1. Appendix: Music Boost for Quicker Thinking and Faster Information Processing
2. Deary, I. J., Penke, L., & Johnson, W. (2010). The neuroscience of human intelligence differences. Nature Reviews Neuroscience, 11(3), 201-211.
3. McDaniel, M. A. (2005). Big-brained people are smarter: A meta-analysis of the relationship between in vivo brain volume and intelligence. Intelligence, 33(4), 337-346.
4. Luders, E., Narr, K. L., Bilder, R. M., Thompson, P. M., Szeszko, P. R., Hamilton, L., & Toga, A. W. (2007). Positive correlations between corpus callosum thickness and intelligence. Neuroimage, 37(4), 1457-1464.
5. Paradiso, S., Andreasen, N. C., O'Leary, D. S., Arndt, S., & Robinson, R. G. (1997). Cerebellar size and cognition: correlations with IQ, verbal memory and motor dexterity. Neuropsychiatry, neuropsychology, and behavioral neurology, 10(1), 1.
6. Reiss, A. L., Abrams, M. T., Singer, H. S., Ross, J. L., & Denckla, M. B. (1996). Brain development, gender and IQ in children A volumetric imaging study. Brain, 119(5), 1763-1774.
7. Moffitt, T. E., Caspi, A., Harkness, A. R., & Silva, P. A. (2006). The Natural History of Change to Intellectual Performance:

Who Changes? How Much? Is it Meaningful? Journal of Child Psychology and Psychiatry, 34(4), 455-506.

8. Schlaug, G., Jäncke, L., Huang, Y., Staiger, J. F., & Steinmetz, H. (1995). Increased corpus callosum size in musicians. Neuropsychologia, 33(8), 1047-1055.
9. Rauscher, F. H., & Hinton, S. C. (2011). Music instruction and its diverse extra-musical benefits. Music Perception, 29(2), 215-226.
10. Harris, M. A. (2007). Differences in mathematics scores between students who receive traditional Montessori instruction and students who receive music enriched Montessori instruction. Journal for Learning through the Arts, 3(1), 1-50.

Chapter 16

IQ Controversy: One or Multiple Intelligences?

1. Neisser, U., Boodoo, G., Bouchard Jr, T. J., Boykin, A. W., Brody, N., Ceci, S. J., & Urbina, S. (1996). Intelligence: Knowns and unknowns. American psychologist, 51(2), 77. Gottfredson, L. S. (1997). Mainstream science on intelligence: An editorial with 52 signatories, history, and bibliography. Intelligence, 24(1), 13-23.
2. Gardner, H., & Moran, S. (2006). The science of multiple intelligences theory: A response to Lynn Waterhouse. Educational psychologist, 41(4), 227-232.
3. Ibid.
4. Hatch, T. C., & Gardner, H. (1986). From testing intelligence to assessing competences: A pluralistic view of intellect. Roeper Review, 8(3), 147-150. ~~*Howard Gardner's Multiple Intelligences*

5. Gardner, H. (2006). Multiple Intelligences: New Horizons in Theory and Practice. Basic Books.
6. Ibid.
7. Ibid.
8. Ibid.
9. Ibid.
10. Ibid.
11. Gardner, H. (2006). Multiple Intelligences: New Horizons in Theory and Practice (pp.17). Basic Books.
12. Gardner, H. (2006). Multiple Intelligences: New Horizons in Theory and Practice. Basic Books.
13. Ibid.
14. Waterhouse, L. (2006). Multiple intelligences, the Mozart effect, and emotional intelligence: A critical review. Educational Psychologist, 41(4), 207-225.
15. Gardner, H., & Moran, S. (2006). The science of multiple intelligences theory: A response to Lynn Waterhouse. Educational psychologist, 41(4), 227-232.
16. Back cover of Gardner, H. (2006). Multiple Intelligences: New Horizons in Theory and Practice. Basic Books.
17. Appendix: Rhythm Skills and IQ. See also Chapters 17 and 18 of this book.
18. See Appendix: Music Boost for Movement and Physical Ability. See also Chapter 19.
19. Brown, S., Martinez, M. J., & Parsons, L. M. (2006). Music and language side by side in the brain: a PET study of the generation of melodies and sentences. European journal of neuroscience, 23(10), 2791-2803. See also Chapters 22-24 of this book. ~~*The Music Boost for Multiple Intelligences*
20. Gardner, H. (2006). Multiple Intelligences: New Horizons in Theory and Practice. Basic Books.
21. Moreno, S., Bialystok, E., Barac, R., Schellenberg, E.

G., Cepeda, N. J., & Chau, T. (2011). Short-term music training enhances verbal intelligence and executive function. Psychological science, 22(11), 1425-1433.

22. Gardner, H. (2006). Multiple Intelligences: New Horizons in Theory and Practice. Basic Books.
23. See Appendix: Music Boost for IQ and Intelligence
24. Watanabe, D., Savion-Lemieux, T., & Penhune, V. B. (2007). The effect of early musical training on adult motor performance: evidence for a sensitive period in motor learning. Experimental Brain Research, 176(2), 332-340.

    Penhune, V. B. (2011). Sensitive periods in human development: Evidence from musical training. Cortex, 47(9), 1126-1137.

    Bailey, J., & Penhune, V. B. (2012). A sensitive period for musical training: contributions of age of onset and cognitive abilities. Annals of the New York Academy of Sciences, 1252(1), 163-170.
25. Gordon, E. E. (2011). Early childhood music abuse: Misdeeds and Neglect. Visions of Research in Music Education, 17, 1-11.
26. See Chapter 20 on skills in music and movement as well as the following studies:

    Brown, J., Sherrill, C., & Gench, B. (1981). Effects of an Integrated Physical Education / Music Program in Changing Early Childhood Perceptual-Motor Performance. Perceptual and Motor Skills, 53(1), 151-154.

    Derri, V., Tsapakidou, A., Zachopoulou, E., & Kioumourtzoglou, E. (2001). Effect of a music and movement programme on development of locomotor skills by children 4 to 6 years of age. European journal of physical education, 6(1), 16-25.

    Zachopoulou, E., Tsapakidou, A., & Derri, V. (2004). The effects of a developmentally appropriate music and movement program on motor performance. Early Childhood Research Quarterly, 19(4), 631-642.

27. Klein, S. A., & Winkelstein, M. L. (1996). Enhancing pediatric health care with music. Journal of pediatric health care, 10(2), 74-81.
28. Brochard, R., Dufour, A., & Despres, O. (2004). Effect of musical expertise on visuospatial abilities: Evidence from reaction times and mental imagery. Brain and cognition, 54(2), 103-109.

    Jakobson, L. S., Lewycky, S. T., Kilgour, A. R., & Stoesz, B. M. (2008). Memory for verbal and visual material in highly trained musicians. Music Perception, 26(1), 41-55.

    Pietsch, S., & Jansen, P. (2011). Different mental rotation performance in students of music, sport and education. Learning and Individual Differences, 22(1), 159-163.
29. Peterson, J. M., & Leonard, M. L. (1974). Left-handedness among architects: Some facts and speculation. Perceptual and Motor Skills, 38(2), 547-550.
30. Ibid.
31. Pietsch, S., & Jansen, P. (2011). Different mental rotation performance in students of music, sport and education. Learning and Individual Differences, 22(1), 159-163.
32. Dmitrieva, E. S., Gel'man, V. Y., Zaitseva, K. A., & Orlov, A. M. (2006). Ontogenetic features of the psychophysiological mechanisms of perception of the emotional component of speech in musically gifted children. Neuroscience and behavioral physiology, 36(1), 53-62.
33. See Appendices Music Boost for Self-Esteem and Confidence and Music Boost for Emotional Well-being
34. Gardner, H. (2006). Multiple intelligences: New horizons (rev. ed). New York: Basic Books
35. Bugos, J., & Mostafa, W. (2011). Musical Training Enhances

Information Processing Speed. Bulletin of the Council for Research in Music Education, 187, 7-18.

36. Patston, L. L., Corballis, M. C., Hogg, S. L., & Tippett, L. J. (2006). The Neglect of Musicians Line Bisection Reveals an Opposite Bias. Psychological Science, 17(12), 1029-1031.
    Patston, L. L., Hogg, S. L., & Tippett, L. J. (2007). Attention in musicians is more bilateral than in non-musicians. Laterality, 12(3), 262-272.
    Patston, L. L., Kirk, I. J., Rolfe, M. H. S., Corballis, M. C., & Tippett, L. J. (2007). The unusual symmetry of musicians: Musicians have equilateral interhemispheric transfer for visual information. Neuropsychologia, 45(9), 2059-2065.
    Brochard, R., Dufour, A., & Despres, O. (2004). Effect of musical expertise on visuospatial abilities: Evidence from reaction times and mental imagery. Brain and cognition, 54(2), 103-109.
37. Kraus, N., & Chandrasekaran, B. (2010). Music training for the development of auditory skills. Nature Reviews Neuroscience, 11(8), 599-605.
38. Hanna-Pladdy, B., & MacKay, A. (2011). The relation between instrumental musical activity and cognitive aging. Neuropsychology, 25(3), 378.
39. Gardner, H. (2006). Multiple intelligences: New horizons (rev. ed). New York: Basic Books.
40. Gottfredson, L. S., & Deary, I. J. (2004). Intelligence predicts health and longevity, but why? Current Directions in Psychological Science, 13(1), 1-4.
41. Kalmar, M. (1982). The effects of music education based on Kodaly's directives in nursery school children: From a psychologist's point of view. Psychology of Music, 63-68.
42. Robinson, S. K. (Director). (2006). Why schools kill creativity-

The case for an education sytem that nurtures creativity:TED Conference talk [Motion Picture].

Puttnam, L. (Director). (2009). We Are The People We've Been Waiting For [Motion Picture].

Chapter 17

The Surprise Link Between Music Skills and IQ

1. Jensen, A. R., & Munro, E. (1979). Reaction time, movement time, and intelligence. Intelligence, 3(2), 121-126.
2. Appendix: IQ: What's Rhythm Got to Do With It?
3. Rammsayer, T. H., & Brandler, S. (2002). On the relationship between general fluid intelligence and psychophysical indicators of temporal resolution in the brain. Journal of Research in Personality, 36(5), 507-530.
4. Rammsayer, T. H., & Brandler, S. (2007). Performance on temporal information processing as an index of general intelligence. Intelligence, 35(2), 123-139.

   Troche, S. J., & Rammsayer, T. H. (2009). Temporal and non-temporal sensory discrimination and their predictions of capacity-and speed-related aspects of psychometric intelligence. Personality and Individual Differences, 47(1), 52-57.
5. Phillips, D. (1976). An investigation of the relationship between musicality and intelligence. Psychology of Music, 4(2), 16-31.
6. Lynn, R., Graham Wilson, R., & Gault, A. (1989). Simple musical tests as measures of Spearman's g. Personality and Individual Differences, 10(1), 25-28.
7. Kilgour, A. R., Jakobson, L. S., & Cuddy, L. L. (2000). Music training and rate of presentation as mediators of text and song recall. Memory & Cognition, 28(5), 700-710.

8. Jakobson, L. S., Cuddy, L. L., & Kilgour, A. R. (2003). Time tagging: A key to musicians' superior memory. Music Perception, 20(3), 307-313.
9. Ullén, F., Forsman, L., Blom, Ö., Karabanov, A., & Madison, G. (2008). Intelligence and variability in a simple timing task share neural substrates in the prefrontal white matter. The Journal of Neuroscience, 28(16), 4238-4243.
10. Cleland, G. (2008, April 17.) Drummers are natural intellectuals. *The Telegraph*. Retrieved from http://www.telegraph.co.uk/news/uknews/1895839/Drummers-are-natural-intellectuals.html
11. Ullén, F., Söderlund, T., Kääriä, L., & Madison, G. (2012). Bottom–up mechanisms are involved in the relation between accuracy in timing tasks and intelligence—Further evidence using manipulations of state motivation. Intelligence, 40(2), 100-106.
12. Holm, L., Ullén, F., & Madison, G. (2012). Motor and Executive Control in Repetitive Timing of Brief Intervals. Journal of Experimental Psychology: Human Perception and Performance.
13. Moreno, S., Bialystok, E., Barac, R., Schellenberg, E. G., Cepeda, N. J., & Chau, T. (2011). Short-term music training enhances verbal intelligence and executive function. Psychological science, 22(11), 1425-1433.
14. Fujioka, T., Ross, B., Kakigi, R., Pantev, C., & Trainor, L. J. (2006). One year of musical training affects development of auditory cortical-evoked fields in young children. Brain, 129(10), 2593-2608.
15. Krommyda, M., Papadelis, G., Chatzikallia, K., Pastiadis, K., & Kardaras, P. (2008) Does awareness of musical structure relate to general cognitive and literacy profile in children with learning disabilities? Conference on Interdisciplinary

Musicology (pp. 1-10). Thessaloniki: Aristotle University of Thessaloniki.

16. Yunxia, C. U. I. (2010). Research on the Effect of Rhythm Training on Children's Intelligence. Journal of Sports and Science, 3, 018.
17. Brodsky, W., & Sulkin, I. (2011). Handclapping songs: a spontaneous platform for child development among 5–10 year old children. Early Child Development and Care, 181(8), 1111-1136.
18. Waber, D. P., Weiler, M. D., Bellinger, D. C., Marcus, D. J., Forbes, P. W., Wypij, D., & Wolff, P. H. (2000). Diminished motor timing control in children referred for diagnosis of learning problems. Developmental neuropsychology, 17(2), 181-197.
19. Moffitt, T. E., Caspi, A., Harkness, A. R., & Silva, P. A. (2006). The Natural History of Change to Intellectual Performance: Who Changes? How Much? Is it Meaningful? Journal of Child Psychology and Psychiatry, 34(4), 455-506.
20. Reiss, A. L., Abrams, M. T., Singer, H. S., Ross, J. L., & Denckla, M. B. (1996). Brain development, gender and IQ in children A volumetric imaging study. Brain, 119(5), 1763-1774.
21. Rauscher, F. H. (2003). Effects of piano, rhythm, and singing instruction on the spatial reasoning of at-risk children. Proceedings of the European Society for the Cognitive Sciences of Music, Hannover, Germany: Hannover University Press.

    Rauscher, F. H., & Hinton, S. C. (2011). Music instruction and its diverse extra-musical benefits. Music Perception, 29(2), 215-226.
22. Watanabe, D., Savion-Lemieux, T., & Penhune, V. B. (2007). The effect of early musical training on adult motor

performance: evidence for a sensitive period in motor learning. Experimental Brain Research, 176(2), 332-340.

Penhune, V. B. (2011). Sensitive periods in human development: Evidence from musical training. Cortex, 47(9), 1126-1137.

23. Rauscher, F. H., & Hinton, S. C. (2011). Music instruction and its diverse extra-musical benefits. Music Perception, 29(2), 215-226.
24. Ibid.
25. Brodsky, W., & Sulkin, I. (2011). Handclapping songs: a spontaneous platform for child development among 5–10 year old children. Early Child Development and Care, 181(8), 1111-1136.
26. Dege, F., Wehrum, S., Stark, R., & Schwarzer, G. (2011). The influence of two years of school music training in secondary school on visual and auditory memory. European Journal of Developmental Psychology, 8(5), 608-623.
27. See Appendix: Music Boost for the Elderly
28. No study has found an IQ boost from music training for children who start learning music after the age of seven. For instance, compare the results in the following two research papers, where the first one concerns the benefits for children who start before this watershed age, and the second one finds no cognitive benefits for children who start later than age seven.

    Rauscher, F. H. (2003). Can Music Instruction Affect Children's Cognitive Development? Developmental Psychology, 20(4), 615-636.

And

Costa-Giomi, E. (2004). Effects of three years of piano instruction on children's academic achievement, school performance and self-esteem. Psychology of Music, 32(2), 139-152.

Chapter 18

Rhythm at Birth, Skills through Practice

1. For a scientifically accurate yet easily understandable account on infant brain development see Nash, J. M. (1997). Fertile minds. Special Report, Time, 149(5), 52.
2. Tafuri, J. (2008). Infant Musicality (pp.87). Ashgate Publishing.
3. Zentner, M., & Eerola, T. (2010). Rhythmic engagement with music in infancy. Proceedings of the National Academy of Sciences, 107(13), 5768-5773.
4. Winkler, I., Háden, G. P., Ladinig, O., Sziller, I., & Honing, H. (2009). Newborn infants detect the beat in music. Proceedings of the National Academy of Sciences, 106(7), 2468-2471.
5. Phillips-Silver, J., & Trainor, L. J. (2005). Feeling the beat: Movement influences infant rhythm perception. Science, 308(5727), 1430-1430.
6. Koester, L. S., Papousek, H., & Papousek, M. (1989). Patterns of rhythmic stimulation by mothers with three-month-olds: A cross-modal comparison. International Journal of Behavioral Development, 12(2), 143-154.
7. Nolan, K. (2007). The Comparative Effectiveness of Teaching Beat Detection through Movement and Singing among Kindergarten Students. Unpublished Master's Theses, Tucson, University of Arizona.
8. Persellin, D. C. (1992). Responses to rhythm patterns when presented to children through auditory, visual, and kinesthetic modalities. Journal of Research in Music Education, 40(4), 306-315.

9. Persellin, D. C., & Pierce, C. (1988). Association of preference for modality to learning of rhythm patterns in music. Perceptual and Motor Skills, 67(3), 825-826
10. Gerry, D. W., Faux, A. L., & Trainor, L. J. (2010). Effects of Kindermusik training on infants' rhythmic enculturation. Developmental science, 13(3), 545-551.
11. Brodsky, W., & Sulkin, I. (2011). Handclapping songs: a spontaneous platform for child development among 5–10 year old children. Early Child Development and Care, 181(8), 1111-1136.
12. Kuhlman, K., & Schweinhart, L. J. (1999). Timing in child development. High Scope Inspiring Educators to Inspire Children Retrieved December 16, 2012 from http://www.highscope.org/Content.asp?ContentId=234
13. See Appendix: Lack of rhythm skills predicts learning disability
14. Ullén, F., Forsman, L., Blom, Ö., Karabanov, A., & Madison, G. (2008). Intelligence and variability in a simple timing task share neural substrates in the prefrontal white matter. The Journal of Neuroscience, 28(16), 4238-4243.
15. See the introduction to Part Four of this book as well as the Chapter 14, with the respective references.

Chapter 19

Rhythm's Made to Make You Move

1. Chen, J. L., Penhune, V. B., & Zatorre, R. J. (2008). Listening to musical rhythms recruits motor regions of the brain. Cerebral Cortex, 18(12), 2844-2854.
2. Phillips-Silver, J., & Trainor, L. J. (2007). Hearing what the body feels: Auditory encoding of rhythmic movement. Cognition, 105(3), 533-546. ~~ Su, Y. H. (2012). The influence of external and internal motor processes on

human auditory rhythm perception .Unpublished Doctoral dissertation, Ludwig-Maximilians-Universität München, Munich, Germany.

3. Zentner, M., & Eerola, T. (2010). Rhythmic engagement with music in infancy. Proceedings of the National Academy of Sciences, 107(13), 5768-5773.
4. Dunbar, R. I., Kaskatis, K., MacDonald, I., & Barra, V. (2012). Performance of music elevates pain threshold and positive affect: Implications for the evolutionary function of music. Evolutionary psychology: an international journal of evolutionary approaches to psychology and behavior, 10(4), 688.
5. Zentner, M., & Eerola, T. (2010). Rhythmic engagement with music in infancy. Proceedings of the National Academy of Sciences, 107(13), 5768-5773.

Chapter 20

How Music Boosts Fitness and Physical Ability

1. Nethery, V. M. (2002). Competition between internal and external sources of information during exercise: influence on RPE and the impact of the exercise load. Journal of Sports Medicine and Physical Fitness, 42(2), 172-178.
2. Chipman L. (1966). The Effects of Selected Music on Endurance. Unpublished Master's Thesis, Springfield College, Massachusetts, United States.
3. Kravitz, L. (1994). The Effects of Music on Exercise. The University of New Mexico. Retrieved December 16, 2012 from http://www.unm.edu/~lkravitz/Article%20folder/musicexercise.html
4. Beckett, A. (1990). The effects of music on exercise as

determined by physiological recovery heart rates and distances. Journal of Music Therapy, 27(3), 126-136.

5. Barnett, L. M., Van Beurden, E., Morgan, P. J., Brooks, L. O., & Beard, J. R. (2009). Childhood motor skill proficiency as a predictor of adolescent physical activity. Journal of adolescent health, 44(3), 252-259.
6. Beisman G.L. (1967). Effect of Rhythm Accompaniment upon learning fundamental motor skills. Research Quarterly, 38(2), 172-176.
7. Ibid.
8. Zachopoulou, E., Tsapakidou, A., & Derri, V. (2004). The effects of a developmentally appropriate music and movement program on motor performance. Early Childhood Research Quarterly, 19(4), 631-642.
9. Pollatou, E., Liapa, E., Diggelidis, N., & Zachopoulou, E. (2005). Measure of rhythmic ability in high school students who are involved in motor activities accompanied or not by music. Inquiries in Sport & Physical Education, 3(1), 7-22.
10. Brodsky, W., & Sulkin, I. (2011). Handclapping songs: a spontaneous platform for child development among 5–10 year old children. Early Child Development and Care, 181(8), 1111-1136.

Chapter 21

Mastering Mathematics with Music Training

1. Gottfried, L. In a letter to Christian Goldbach, April 17, 1712.
2. See Appendix: Music Boost for Mathematics
3. Gardiner, M. F., Fox, A., Knowles, F., & Jeffrey, D. (1996). Learning improved by arts training. Nature; Nature, 381(6580), 284.
4. Schlaug, G., Norton, A., Overy, K., & Winner, E. (2005).

Effects of music training on the child's brain and cognitive development. Annals of the New York Academy of Sciences, 1060(1), 219-230.

5. Scripp, L. (2003). Critical Links, Next Steps: An Evolving Conception of Music and Learning in Public School Education. Adapted from a presentation at Columbia University, Chicago, 2002. Retrievable at http://www.music-in-education.org/articles/2-AF.pdf
6. Sortor, J. M., & Kulp, M. T. (2003). Are the results of the Beery-Buktenica Developmental Test of Visual-Motor Integration and its subtests related to achievement test scores? Optometry & Vision Science, 80(11), 758-763.
7. Brown, J., Sherrill, C., & Gench, B. (1981). Effects of an Integrated Physical Education / Music Program in Changing Early Childhood Perceptual-Motor Performance. Perceptual and Motor Skills, 53(1), 151-154.
8. Ibid.
9. On the brains of mathematicians: Aydin, K., Ucar, A., Oguz, K. K., Okur, O. O., Agayev, A., Unal, Z., ... & Ozturk, C. (2007). Increased gray matter density in the parietal cortex of mathematicians: a voxel-based morphometry study. American Journal of Neuroradiology, 28(10), 1859-1864.

   On the music boost for this mathematical region:

   Stewart, L., Henson, R., Kampe, K., Walsh, V., Turner, R., & Frith, U. (2003). Brain changes after learning to read and play music. Neuroimage, 20(1), 71-83.

   Sluming, V., Brooks, J., Howard, M., Downes, J. J., & Roberts, N. (2007). Broca's area supports enhanced visuospatial cognition in orchestral musicians. The Journal of Neuroscience, 27(14), 3799-3806.

   See also:

   Hoenig, K., Müller, C., Herrnberger, B., Sim, E. J., Spitzer,

M., Ehret, G., & Kiefer, M. (2011). Neuroplasticity of semantic representations for musical instruments in professional musicians. Neuroimage, 56(3), 1714-1725.

10. Haimson, J., Swain, D., & Winner, E. (2011). Do Mathematicians Have Above Average Musical Skill? Music Perception, 29(2), 203-213.
11. Conway, C. M., Pisoni, D. B., & Kronenberger, W. G. (2009). The Importance of Sound for Cognitive Sequencing Abilities The Auditory Scaffolding Hypothesis. Current directions in psychological science, 18(5), 275-279.
12. Jordan, N. C., Kaplan, D., Ramineni, C., & Locuniak, M. N. (2009). Early math matters: Kindergarten number competence and later mathematics outcomes. Developmental Psychology, 45(3), 850.
13. Bailey, D. H., Hoard, M. K., Nugent, L., & Geary, D. C. (2012). Competence with fractions predicts gains in mathematics achievement. Journal of Experimental Child Psychology, 113(3), 447-455.
    Flawn, T. (2008). Foundations for success:The Final Report of the National Mathematics Advisory Panel. Washington: US. Department of education.
14. Kelstrom, J. M. (1998). The untapped power of music: Its role in the curriculum and its effect on academic achievement. NASSP Bulletin, 82(597), 34-43.
    San Francisco State University (2012, March 22). Getting in rhythm helps children grasp fractions, study finds. ScienceDaily. Retrieved December 16, 2012 from http://www.sciencedaily.com /releases/2012/03/120322100209.htm
15. Graziano, A. B., Peterson, M., & Shaw, G. L. (1999). Enhanced learning of proportional math through music training and spatial-temporal training. Neurological Research, 21(2), 139.
16. An, S. A., Kulm, G. O., & Ma, T. (2008). The Effects of a

Music Composition Activity on Chinese Students' Attitudes and Beliefs towards Mathematics: An Exploratory Study. Journal of Mathematics Education, 1(1), 96-113.

Part Five

Linguistic Intelligence

Introduction

1. Gordon, E. E. (2011). Early childhood music abuse: Misdeeds and Neglect. Visions of Research in Music Education, 17, 1-11.
2. Gardner, H. (2006). Multiple intelligences: New horizons (rev. ed). New York: Basic Books

Chapter 22

The Astonishing Secret of Language Skills

1. Piro, J. M., & Ortiz, C. (2009). The effect of piano lessons on the vocabulary and verbal sequencing skills of primary grade students. Psychology of Music, 37(3), 325-347.
2. Hurwitz, I., Wolff, P. H., Bortnick, B. D., & Kokas, K. (1975). Nonmusicol Effects of the Kodaly Music Curriculum in Primary Grade Children. Journal of learning Disabilities, 8(3), 167-174.
3. Stringer, L. S. (2004). The effects of" Music Play" instruction on language behaviors of children with developmental disabilities, ages three to six.
4. Moreno, S., Bialystok, E., Barac, R., Schellenberg, E. G., Cepeda, N. J., & Chau, T. (2011). Short-term music training enhances verbal intelligence and executive function. Psychological science, 22(11), 1425-1433.
5. Koelsch, S., Gunter, T. C., Cramon, D. Y. V., Zysset, S.,

Lohmann, G., & Friederici, A. D. (2002). Bach speaks: A cortical" language-network" serves the processing of music. Neuroimage, 17(2), 956-966.

Patel, A. D. (2003). Language, music, syntax and the brain. Nature neuroscience, 6(7), 674-681.

Fedorenko, E., Patel, A., Casasanto, D., Winawer, J., & Gibson, E. (2009). Structural integration in language and music: Evidence for a shared system. Memory & cognition, 37(1), 1-9.

Schön, D., Gordon, R., Campagne, A., Magne, C., Astésano, C., Anton, J. L., & Besson, M. (2010). Similar cerebral networks in language, music and song perception. Neuroimage, 51(1), 450-461.

6. Chen-Hafteck, L., & Mang, E. (2012). Music And Language In Early Childhood Development And Learning. In G. E. McPherson, & G. F. Welch, The Oxford Handbook of Music Education (p. 261). New York: Oxford University Press.
7. Magne, C., Schön, D., & Besson, M. (2006). Musician children detect pitch violations in both music and language better than nonmusician children: behavioral and electrophysiological approaches. Journal of Cognitive Neuroscience, 18(2), 199-211.
8. Dunbar, R., Barrett, L. & Lycett, J. (2005). Evolutionary Psychology: A Beginner's Guide. Oneworld Publications.
9. Brandt, A., Gebrian, M., & Slevc, L. R. (2012). Music and early language acquisition. Frontiers in Psychology, 3, 327.
10. Moreno, S., Bialystok, E., Barac, R., Schellenberg, E. G., Cepeda, N. J., & Chau, T. (2011). Short-term music training enhances verbal intelligence and executive function. Psychological science, 22(11), 1425-1433.

Chapter 23

Melody: The Basis for Communication and Vocabulary

1. Johnson, E. K., & Jusczyk, P. W. (2001). Word segmentation by 8-month-olds: When speech cues count more than statistics. Journal of Memory and Language, 44(4), 548-567.
2. Tsao, F. M., Liu, H. M., & Kuhl, P. K. (2004). Speech perception in infancy predicts language development in the second year of life: a longitudinal study. Child development, 75(4), 1067-1084.
   Gerry, D., Unrau, A., & Trainor, L. J. (2012). Active music classes in infancy enhance musical, communicative and social development. Developmental Science. 15(3), 398-407.
   Moyeda, I., Gómez, I. C., & Flores, M. (2006). Implementing a musical program to promote preschool children's vocabulary development. Early Childhood Research & Practice, 8(1).
3. Research by Marilee Mommott, as quoted in: Dunbar, R., Barrett, L. & Lycett, J. (2005). Evolutionary Psychology: A Beginner's Guide (pp. 48). Oneworld Publications.
4. Moyeda, I., Gómez, I. C., & Flores, M. (2006). Implementing a musical program to promote preschool children's vocabulary development. Early Childhood Research & Practice, 8(1).
5. Gathercole, S. E., & Baddeley, A. D. (1989). Evaluation of the role of phonological STM in the development of vocabulary in children: A longitudinal study. Journal of memory and language, 28(2), 200-213.
   Tsao, F. M., Liu, H. M., & Kuhl, P. K. (2004). Speech perception in infancy predicts language development in the second year of life: a longitudinal study. Child development, 75(4), 1067-1084.
6. Marin, M. M. (2009). Effects of early musical training on

musical and linguistic syntactic abilities. Annals of the New York Academy of Sciences, 1169(1), 187-190.

7. Schön, D., Magne, C., & Besson, M. (2004). The music of speech: Music training facilitates pitch processing in both music and language. Psychophysiology, 41(3), 341-349.
   Magne, C., Schön, D., & Besson, M. (2006). Musician children detect pitch violations in both music and language better than nonmusician children: behavioral and electrophysiological approaches. Journal of Cognitive Neuroscience, 18(2), 199-211.
   Besson, M., Schön, D., Moreno, S., Santos, A., & Magne, C. (2007). Influence of musical expertise and musical training on pitch processing in music and language. Restorative Neurology and Neuroscience, 25(3), 399-410.
8. Ibid.
9. Snow, D. (2000). The emotional basis of linguistic and nonlinguistic intonation: Implications for hemispheric specialization. Developmental neuropsychology, 17(1), 1-28.
10. Moreno, S., & Besson, M. (2006). Musical training and language related brain electrical activity in children. Psychophysiology, 43(3), 287-291.
11. Besson, M., Schön, D., Moreno, S., Santos, A., & Magne, C. (2007). Influence of musical expertise and musical training on pitch processing in music and language. Restorative Neurology and Neuroscience, 25(3), 399-410.
12. Santos, A., Joly-Pottuz, B., Moreno, S., Habib, M., & Besson, M. (2007). Behavioural and event-related potentials evidence for pitch discrimination deficits in dyslexic children: Improvement after intensive phonic intervention. Neuropsychologia, 45(5), 1080-1090.
13. Loui, P., Kroog, K., Zuk, J., Winner, E., & Schlaug, G. (2011). Relating pitch awareness to phonemic awareness in children:

implications for tone-deafness and dyslexia. Frontiers in psychology, 2,111.

14. Santos, A., Joly-Pottuz, B., Moreno, S., Habib, M., & Besson, M. (2007). Behavioural and event-related potentials evidence for pitch discrimination deficits in dyslexic children: Improvement after intensive phonic intervention. Neuropsychologia, 45(5), 1080-1090.

Chapter 24

What Explains the Music Boost for Language?

Structures of Language, Information and Understanding

1. Marin, M. M. (2009). Effects of early musical training on musical and linguistic syntactic abilities. Annals of the New York Academy of Sciences, 1169(1), 187-190.
2. Jentschke, S., & Koelsch, S. (2009). Musical training modulates the development of syntax processing in children. Neuroimage, 47(2), 735-744.
3. Francois, C., & Schön, D. (2011). Musical expertise boosts implicit learning of both musical and linguistic structures. Cerebral Cortex, 21(10), 2357-2365.
4. Schön, D., Boyer, M., Moreno, S., Besson, M., Peretz, I., & Kolinsky, R. (2008). Songs as an aid for language acquisition. Cognition, 106(2), 975-983.
   Schön, D., & François, C. (2011). Musical expertise and statistical learning of musical and linguistic structures. Frontiers in Psychology, 2,167.
5. Heim, S., Opitz, B., & Friederici, A. D. (2003). Distributed cortical networks for syntax processing: Broca's area as the common denominator. Brain and language, 85(3), 402-408.
6. Flöel, A., de Vries, M. H., Scholz, J., Breitenstein, C., &

Johansen-Berg, H. (2009). White matter integrity in the vicinity of Broca's area predicts grammar learning success. Neuroimage, 47(4), 1974.

7. Maess, B., Koelsch, S., Gunter, T. C., & Friederici, A. D. (2001). Musical syntax is processed in Broca's area: an MEG study. Nature neuroscience, 4(5), 540-545.
8. Sluming, V., Barrick, T., Howard, M., Cezayirli, E., Mayes, A., & Roberts, N. (2002). Voxel-based morphometry reveals increased gray matter density in Broca's area in male symphony orchestra musicians. Neuroimage, 17(3), 1613-1622.
9. François, C., Tillmann, B., & Schön, D. (2012). Cognitive and methodological considerations on the effects of musical expertise on speech segmentation. Annals of the New York Academy of Sciences, 1252(1), 108-115.
10. Conway, C. M., Pisoni, D. B., & Kronenberger, W. G. (2009). The Importance of Sound for Cognitive Sequencing Abilities: The Auditory Scaffolding Hypothesis. Current directions in psychological science, 18(5), 275-279.

'What Do You Mean?' Semantics: The meaning of words and phrases

1. Koelsch, S. (2005). Neural substrates of processing syntax and semantics in music. Current opinion in neurobiology, 15(2), 207-212.
2. Koelsch, S., Kasper, E., Sammler, D., Schulze, K., Gunter, T., & Friederici, A. D. (2004). Music, language and meaning: brain signatures of semantic processing. Nature neuroscience, 7(3), 302-307.

Steinbeis, N., & Koelsch, S. (2008). Shared neural resources between music and language indicate semantic processing of musical tension-resolution patterns. Cerebral Cortex, 18(5), 1169-1178.

3. Kutas, M., & Federmeier, K. D. (2000). Electrophysiology reveals semantic memory use in language comprehension. Trends in cognitive sciences, 4(12), 463-470.
4. Hsieh, S., Hornberger, M., Piguet, O., & Hodges, J. R. (2011). Neural basis of music knowledge: evidence from the dementias. Brain, 134(9), 2523-2534.

Chapter 25

Music as the Key to Foreign Languages

1. Milovanov, R., Huotilainen, M., Välimäki, V., Esquef, P. A., & Tervaniemi, M. (2008). Musical aptitude and second language pronunciation skills in school-aged children: neural and behavioral evidence. Brain research, 1194, 81-89.
2. Appendix: Music Boost for Foreign Languages and their Pronounciation.
3. Marques, C., Moreno, S., Luís Castro, S., & Besson, M. (2007). Musicians detect pitch violation in a foreign language better than nonmusicians: Behavioral and electrophysiological evidence. Journal of Cognitive Neuroscience, 19(9), 1453-1463.
4. Shook, A., Marian, V., Bartolotti, J., & Schroeder, S. R. (2013). Musical Experience Influences Statistical Learning of a Novel Language. The American journal of psychology, 126(1), 95-104.

Part Six

Don't Believe The Rhyme: Music Skills as the Route to Literacy

Introduction

1. Appendix: Music Boost for Reading

2. Reading skills can be predicted based on auditory abilities; Hornickel, J., Chandrasekaran, B., Zecker, S., & Kraus, N. (2011). Auditory brainstem measures predict reading and speech-in-noise perception in school-aged children. Behavioural brain research, 216(2), 597-605. ~~ Bhide, A., Power, A., & Goswami, U. (2013). A Rhythmic Musical Intervention for Poor Readers: A Comparison of Efficacy With a Letter Based Intervention. Mind, Brain, and Education, 7(2), 113-123.
3. Duncan, L. G., Seymour, P. H., & Hill, S. (1997). How important are rhyme and analogy in beginning reading? Cognition, 63(2), 171-208.

   Nation, K., & Hulme, C. (1997). Phonemic segmentation, not onset rime segmentation, predicts early reading and spelling skills. Reading Research Quarterly, 32(2), 154-167.

   Muter, V., Hulme, C., Snowling, M., & Taylor, S. (1998). Segmentation, not rhyming, predicts early progress in learning to read. Journal of Experimental Child Psychology, 71(1), 3-27.
4. Melby-Lervåg, M. (2012). The Relative Predictive Contribution and Causal Role of Phoneme Awareness, Rhyme Awareness, and Verbal Short-Term Memory in Reading Skills: A Review. Scandinavian Journal of Educational Research, 56(1), 101-118.

   See also the following:

   Hulme, C., Hatcher, P. J., Nation, K., Brown, A., Adams, J., & Stuart, G. (2002). Phoneme awareness is a better predictor of early reading skill than onset-rime awareness. Journal of experimental child psychology, 82(1), 2-28.

   Caravolas, M., Volín, J., & Hulme, C. (2005). Phoneme awareness is a key component of alphabetic literacy skills in consistent and inconsistent orthographies: Evidence from

Czech and English children. Journal of Experimental Child Psychology, 92(2), 107-139.

5. Murphy, C. F. B., & Schochat, E. (2011). Effect of nonlinguistic auditory training on phonological and reading skills. Folia Phoniatrica et Logopaedica, 63(3), 147-153.
6. Movsesian, E. A. (1967). The influence of teaching music reading skills on the development of basic reading skills in the primary grades. Unpublished Doctoral dissertation, University of Southern California, Los Angeles, United States.

   Nicholson, D. L. (1971). Music as an aid to learning. Unpublished Doctoral dissertation, New York University, New York, United States.

   Klemish, J. (1973). A review of recent research in elementary music education. Bulletin of the Council for Research in Music Education, 34, 23-40.

   Hurwitz, I., Wolff, P. H., Bortnick, B. D., & Kokas, K. (1975). Nonmusicol Effects of the Kodaly Music Curriculum in Primary Grade Children. Journal of learning Disabilities, 8(3), 167-174.
7. Barwick, J., Valentine, E., West, R., & Wilding, J. (1989). Relations between reading and musical abilities. British Journal of Educational Psychology, 59(2), 253-257.
8. Lamb, S. J., & Gregory, A. H. (1993). The relationship between music and reading in beginning readers. Educational Psychology, 13(1), 19-27.
9. Ibid.
10. Butzlaff, R. (2000). Can music be used to teach reading? Journal of Aesthetic Education, 34(3/4), 167-178.
11. Ciares, J. & Borgese P. (n.d.). The Benefits of Music on Child Development. PaulBorgese.com. Retrieved December 16, 2012 from http://www.paulborgese.com/report_benefitofmusic.html

12. Moreno, S., Marques, C., Santos, A., Santos, M., & Besson, M. (2009). Musical training influences linguistic abilities in 8-year-old children: more evidence for brain plasticity. Cerebral Cortex, 19(3), 712-723.

Chapter 26

Phonological Awareness

1. Appendix: Music Boost for Reading
2. Anvari, S. H., Trainor, L. J., Woodside, J., & Levy, B. A. (2002). Relations among musical skills, phonological processing, and early reading ability in preschool children. Journal of experimental child psychology, 83(2), 111-130.
3. Fawcett, A. J., & Nicolson, R. I. (1995). Persistence of phonological awareness deficits in older children with dyslexia. Reading and Writing, 7(4), 361-376.
4. François, C., Chobert, J., Besson, M., & Schön, D. (2012). Music training for the development of speech segmentation. Cerebral Cortex, 22(7), 1473 - 1716.

Chapter 27

Music training: The foundation for reading

1. Most, T., Al-Yagon, M., Tur-Kaspa, H., & Margalit, M. (2000). Phonological awareness, peer nominations, and social competence among preschool children at risk for developing learning disabilities. International Journal of Disability, Development and Education, 47(1), 89-105.
2. Ibid.
3. Mackenzie-Beck, Janet (2003) Is it possible to predict students'

ability to develop skills in practical phonetics? Proceedings of the 15th International Congress of Phonetic Sciences (pp. 2833 -2836). Barcelona: Universitat AutÒnoma de Barcelona Press Dankovicová, J., House, J., Crooks, A., & Jones, K. (2007). The relationship between musical skills, music training, and intonation analysis skills. Language and Speech, 50(2), 177-225.

4. Reading skills can be predicted based on auditory abilities: Hornickel, J., Chandrasekaran, B., Zecker, S., & Kraus, N. (2011). Auditory brainstem measures predict reading and speech-in-noise perception in school-aged children. Behavioural brain research, 216(2), 597-605. Bhide, A., Power, A., & Goswami, U. (2013). A Rhythmic Musical Intervention for Poor Readers: A Comparison of Efficacy With a Letter Based Intervention. Mind, Brain, and Education, 7(2), 113-123.
5. Register, D. (2001). The effects of an early intervention music curriculum on prereading/writing. Journal of Music Therapy, 38(3), 239.
6. Register, Dena M. (2003).The Effects of Live Music Groups Versus an Educational Children's Television Program on the Emergent Literacy of Young Children. Unpublished Doctoral Theses, Florida State University, Florida, United States.
7. Spychiger, M., & Patry, J. L. (1993). Musik macht Schule: Biografie und Ergebnisse eines Schulversuchs mit erweitertem Musikunterricht. Hilzinger: Verlag Die Blaue Eule.
   As quoted in:
   Spychiger, M. B. (2001). Understanding musical activity and musical learning as sign processes: Toward a semiotic approach to music education. Journal of Aesthetic Education, 35(1), 53-67.

Chapter 28:

What Are Little Words Made Of? The Three Components of Phonological Awareness

1. Chobert, J., Marie, C., François, C., Schön, D., & Besson, M. (2011). Enhanced passive and active processing of syllables in musician children. Journal of cognitive neuroscience, 23(12), 3874-3887.
2. Parbery-Clark, A., Tierney, A., Strait, D. L., & Kraus, N. (2012). Musicians have fine-tuned neural distinction of speech syllables. Neuroscience, 219(6), 111-119.
3. See, for instance, the following studies: ~~ Duncan, L. G., Seymour, P. H., & Hill, S. (1997). How important are rhyme and analogy in beginning reading? Cognition, 63(2), 171-208.
   Nation, K., & Hulme, C. (1997). Phonemic segmentation, not onset rime segmentation, predicts early reading and spelling skills. Reading Research Quarterly, 32(2), 154-167.
   Muter, V., Hulme, C., Snowling, M., & Taylor, S. (1998). Segmentation, not rhyming, predicts early progress in learning to read. Journal of Experimental Child Psychology, 71(1), 3-27.
   Melby-Lervåg, M. (2012). The Relative Predictive Contribution and Causal Role of Phoneme Awareness, Rhyme Awareness, and Verbal Short-Term Memory in Reading Skills: A Review. Scandinavian Journal of Educational Research, 56(1), 101-118.
   Hulme, C., Hatcher, P. J., Nation, K., Brown, A., Adams, J., & Stuart, G. (2002). Phoneme awareness is a better predictor of early reading skill than onset-rime awareness. Journal of experimental child psychology, 82(1), 2-28.
   Caravolas, M., Volín, J., & Hulme, C. (2005). Phoneme awareness is a key component of alphabetic literacy skills in

consistent and inconsistent orthographies: Evidence from Czech and English children. Journal of Experimental Child Psychology, 92(2), 107-139.

4. Hulme, C., Hatcher, P. J., Nation, K., Brown, A., Adams, J., & Stuart, G. (2002). Phoneme awareness is a better predictor of early reading skill than onset-rime awareness. Journal of experimental child psychology, 82(1), 2-28.
5. Verni, L. (2011, October 21). Ofsted: 'Getting them reading early' *Guidance and training for inspectors.* Department of Education. Retrieved December 16,2012 from https://www.education.gov.uk/publications/standard/publicationDetail/Page1/110122
6. Branch, Hannele (1984). The Finnish Language. Finnish Language and Culture. Guide: 8. London (Centre for Information on Language Teaching and Research).
7. Lundberg, I., Olofsson, Å., & Wall, S. (1980). Reading and spelling skills in the first school years predicted from phonemic awareness skills in kindergarten. Scandinavian Journal of Psychology, 21(1), 159-173.
8. Entwisle, D. R., Alexander, K. L., & Olson, L. S. (2005). First Grade and Educational Attainment by Age 22: A New Story1. American Journal of Sociology, 110(5), 1458-1502.
9. Lyon, G. R., Shaywitz, S. E., & Shaywitz, B. A. (2003). A definition of dyslexia. Annals of dyslexia, 53(1), 1-14.
10. Hatcher, P. J., Hulme, C., & Snowling, M. J. (2004). Explicit phoneme training combined with phonic reading instruction helps young children at risk of reading failure. Journal of Child Psychology and Psychiatry, 45(2), 338-358.
11. Gromko, J. E. (2005). The effect of music instruction on phonemic awareness in beginning readers. Journal of Research in Music Education, 53(3), 199-209.
12. Douglas, S., & Willatts, P. (2005). The relationship between

musical ability and literacy skills. Journal of Research in Reading, 17(2), 99-107.

Chapter 29

The Curious Case of Dyslexia

1. Atterbury, B. W. (1983). A comparison of rhythm pattern perception and performance in normal and learning-disabled readers, age seven and eight. Journal of Research in Music Education, 31(4), 259-270.
   Overy, K., Nicolson, R. I., Fawcett, A. J., & Clarke, E. F. (2003). Dyslexia and music: measuring musical timing skills. Dyslexia, 9(1), 18-36.
2. Overy, K. (2003). Dyslexia and music. Annals of the New York Academy of Sciences, 999(1), 497-505.
3. David, D., Wade Woolley, L., Kirby, J. R., & Smithrim, K. (2006). Rhythm and reading development in school age children: a longitudinal study. Journal of Research in Reading, 30(2), 169-183.
4. Bruck, M. (1992). Persistence of dyslexics' phonological awareness deficits. Developmental psychology, 28(5), 874.
5. Besson, M., Schön, D., Moreno, S., Santos, A., & Magne, C. (2007). Influence of musical expertise and musical training on pitch processing in music and language. Restorative Neurology and Neuroscience, 25(3), 399-410.
   Forgeard, M., Schlaug, G., Norton, A., Rosam, C., Iyengar, U., & Winner, E. (2008). The relation between music and phonological processing in normal-reading children and children with dyslexia. Music Perception, 25(4), 383-390.
6. Loui, P., Kroog, K., Zuk, J., Winner, E., & Schlaug, G. (2011).

Relating pitch awareness to phonemic awareness in children: implications for tone-deafness and dyslexia. Frontiers in psychology, 2,111.

7. Ibid.

Part Seven

The Sense of Sensibility: Emotional Intelligence, Social Skills, Well-being and Confidence

Introduction

1. Welch, G.F., Saunders, J., Papageorgi, I., Joyce, H. and Himonides. E. (2009). An instrument for the assessment of children's attitudes to singing, self and social inclusion. London: Institute of Education, University of London
   And
   Rinta, T., Purves, R., Welch, G., Stadler Elmer, S., & Bissig, R. (2011). Connections between children's feelings of social inclusion and their musical backgrounds. Journal of Social Inclusion, 2(2), 34-57.
2. Most, T., Al-Yagon, M., Tur-Kaspa, H., & Margalit, M. (2000). Phonological awareness, peer nominations, and social competence among preschool children at risk for developing learning disabilities. International Journal of Disability, Development and Education, 47(1), 89-105.
3. Koelsch, S. (2010). Towards a neural basis of music-evoked emotions. Trends in cognitive sciences, 14(3), 131-137.
4. Goleman, D. (1996). Emotional Intelligence: Why It Can Matter More Than IQ . Great Britain: Clays Ltd.
5. Sänger, J., Müller, V., & Lindenberger, U. (2012). Intra-and interbrain synchronization and network properties when playing guitar in duets. Frontiers in human neuroscience, 6.

6. Molnar-Szakacs, I., & Overy, K. (2006). Music and mirror neurons: from motion to'e'motion. Social cognitive and affective neuroscience, 1(3), 235-241.
7. Koelsch, S. (2010). Towards a neural basis of music-evoked emotions. Trends in cognitive sciences, 14(3), 131-137.

Chapter 30
Learning Music, Learning Emotion

1. Hunter, P. G., & Schellenberg, E. G. (2010). Music and emotion. In Music perception (pp. 129-164). Springer New York. ★★★★★★ See also the following: Koelsch, S., Fritz, T., Müller, K., & Friederici, A. D. (2006). Investigating emotion with music: an fMRI study. Human brain mapping, 27(3), 239-250. ★★★★ Panksepp, J., & Bernatzky, G. (2002). Emotional sounds and the brain: the neuro-affective foundations of musical appreciation. Behavioural processes, 60(2), 133-155.
   Trainor, L. J., & Schmidt, L. A. (2003). Processing emotions induced by music. The cognitive neuroscience of music, 310-324.
2. Winsler, A., Ducenne, L., & Koury, A. (2011). Singing One's Way to Self-Regulation: The Role of Early Music and Movement Curricula and Private Speech. Early Education and Development, 22(2), 274-304.
   Gerry, D., Unrau, A., & Trainor, L. J. (2012). Active music classes in infancy enhance musical, communicative and social development. Developmental Science. 15(3), 398-407.
3. Denham, S. A., Bassett, H. H., Way, E., Mincic, M., Zinsser, K., & Graling, K. (2012). Preschoolers' emotion knowledge: Self-regulatory foundations, and predictions of early school success. Cognition & Emotion, 26(4), 667-679.
4. Goleman, D. (1996). Emotional Intelligence: Why It Can Matter More Than IQ . Great Britain: Clays Ltd.

5. Damasio, A. (1994). Descartes' Error: Emotion, Reason and the Human Brain. Vintage Publishing.
6. Balkwill, L. L., & Thompson, W. F. (1999). A cross-cultural investigation of the perception of emotion in music: Psychophysical and cultural cues. Music perception, 17(1), 43-64.
7. Fritz, T., Jentschke, S., Gosselin, N., Sammler, D., Peretz, I., Turner, R., & Koelsch, S. (2009). Universal recognition of three basic emotions in music. Current Biology, 19(7), 573-576.
8. Tafuri, J. (2008). Infant Musicality – New Research for Educators and Parents. Ashgate.
9. Gerry, D., Unrau, A., & Trainor, L. J. (2012). Active music classes in infancy enhance musical, communicative and social development. Developmental Science. 15(3), 398-407.
10. Ibid.
11. Winsler, A., Ducenne, L., & Koury, A. (2011). Singing One's Way to Self-Regulation: The Role of Early Music and Movement Curricula and Private Speech. Early Education and Development, 22(2), 274-304.
12. Moffitt, T. E., Arseneault, L., Belsky, D., Dickson, N., Hancox, R. J., Harrington, H., ... & Caspi, A. (2011). A gradient of childhood self-control predicts health, wealth, and public safety. Proceedings of the National Academy of Sciences, 108(7), 2693-2698.

Chapter 31

Do You Hear What I Feel? Music Training and Emotion Recognition

1. Musacchia, G., Sams, M., Skoe, E., & Kraus, N. (2007). Musicians have enhanced subcortical auditory and audiovisual

processing of speech and music. Proceedings of the National Academy of Sciences, 104(40), 15894-15898.

Strait, D. L., Kraus, N., Skoe, E., & Ashley, R. (2009). Musical experience and neural efficiency–effects of training on subcortical processing of vocal expressions of emotion. European Journal of Neuroscience, 29(3), 661-668.

2. Thompson, W. F., Schellenberg, E. G., & Husain, G. (2004). Decoding speech prosody: do music lessons help? Emotion, 4(1), 46.
3. Resnicow, J. E., Salovey, P., & Repp, B. H. (2004). Is recognition of emotion in music performance an aspect of emotional intelligence? Music Perception, 22(1), 145-158.
4. Lima, C. F., & Castro, S. L. (2011). Speaking to the trained ear: Musical expertise enhances the recognition of emotions in speech prosody. Emotion, 11(5), 1021.

   Bhatara, A., Tirovolas, A. K., Duan, L. M., Levy, B., & Levitin, D. J. (2011). Perception of emotional expression in musical performance. Journal of Experimental Psychology: Human Perception and Performance, 37(3), 921.
5. Strait, D. L., Kraus, N., Skoe, E., & Ashley, R. (2009). Musical experience and neural efficiency–effects of training on subcortical processing of vocal expressions of emotion. European Journal of Neuroscience, 29(3), 661-668.
6. Giomo, C. J. (1993). An experimental study of children's sensitivity to mood in music. Psychology of Music, 21(2), 141-162.
7. Gerry, D., Unrau, A., & Trainor, L. J. (2012). Active music classes in infancy enhance musical, communicative and social development. Developmental Science. 15(3), 398-407.
8. Juslin, P. N., & Laukka, P. (2003). Communication of emotions in vocal expression and music performance: Different channels, same code?. Psychological bulletin, 129(5), 770.

Laukka, P., & Juslin, P. N. (2007). Similar patterns of age-related differences in emotion recognition from speech and music. Motivation and Emotion, 31(3), 182-191.

9. Magne, C., Schön, D., & Besson, M. (2006). Musician children detect pitch violations in both music and language better than nonmusician children: behavioral and electrophysiological approaches. Journal of Cognitive Neuroscience, 18(2), 199-211.
10. Dmitrieva, E. S., Gel'man, V. Y., Zaitseva, K. A., & Orlov, A. M. (2006). Ontogenetic features of the psychophysiological mechanisms of perception of the emotional component of speech in musically gifted children. Neuroscience and behavioral physiology, 36(1), 53-62.
11. Petrides, K. V., Niven, L., & Mouskounti, T. (2006). The trait emotional intelligence of ballet dancers and musicians. Psicothema, 18(Suplemento), 101-107.
    Petrides, K. V., & Furnham, A. (2002). Trait emotional intelligence: Behavioural validation in two studies of emotion recognition and reactivity to mood induction. European Journal of Personality, 17(1), 39-57.
12. Hsieh, S., Hornberger, M., Piguet, O., & Hodges, J. R. (2012). Brain correlates of musical and facial emotion recognition: Evidence from the dementias. Neuropsychologia, 50(8), 1814-1822.
13. Spilka, M. J., Steele, C. J., & Penhune, V. B. (2010). Gesture imitation in musicians and non-musicians. Experimental brain research, 204(4), 549-558.
14. Ambady, N., & Rosenthal, R. (1992). Thin slices of expressive behavior as predictors of interpersonal consequences: A meta-analysis. Psychological Bulletin; Psychological Bulletin, 111(2), 256.

Chapter 32

Taming the Wild Horses: Managing and Appreciating Emotion

1. Winsler, A., Ducenne, L., & Koury, A. (2011). Singing One's Way to Self-Regulation: The Role of Early Music and Movement Curricula and Private Speech. Early Education and Development, 22(2), 274-304.
2. Gruhn, W., Galley, N., & Kluth, C. (2003). Do mental speed and musical abilities interact? Annals of the New York Academy of Sciences, 999(1), 485-496.
3. Snow, D. (2000). The emotional basis of linguistic and nonlinguistic intonation: Implications for hemispheric specialization. Developmental neuropsychology, 17(1), 1-28.
4. Bhatara, A., Tirovolas, A. K., Duan, L. M., Levy, B., & Levitin, D. J. (2011). Perception of emotional expression in musical performance. Journal of Experimental Psychology: Human Perception and Performance, 37(3), 921.
5. Juslin, P. N., & Laukka, P. (2004). Expression, perception, and induction of musical emotions: A review and a questionnaire study of everyday listening. Journal of New Music Research, 33(3), 217-238.

Chapter 33

Harmony in School

1. Dake, J. A., Price, J. H., & Telljohann, S. K. (2003). The nature and extent of bullying at school. Journal of School Health, 73(5), 173-180.
2. Dmitrieva, E. S., Gel'man, V. Y., Zaitseva, K. A., & Orlov, A. M. (2006). Ontogenetic features of the psychophysiological mechanisms of perception of the emotional component

of speech in musically gifted children. Neuroscience and behavioral physiology, 36(1), 53-62.

3. Ursache, A., Blair, C., & Raver, C. C. (2012). The Promotion of Self Regulation as a Means of Enhancing School Readiness and Early Achievement in Children at Risk for School Failure. Child Development Perspectives, 6(2), 122-128.
4. Dake, J. A., Price, J. H., & Telljohann, S. K. (2003). The nature and extent of bullying at school. Journal of School Health, 73(5), 173-180.
5. Staubli, S., & Killias, M. (2011). Long-term outcomes of passive bullying during childhood: Suicide attempts, victimization and offending. European Journal of Criminology, 8(5), 377-385.
6. Whitney, I., & Smith, P. K. (1993). A survey of the nature and extent of bullying in junior/middle and secondary schools. Educational research, 35(1), 3-25.

   Wolke, D., Woods, S., Stanford, K., & Schulz, H. (2001). Bullying and victimization of primary school children in England and Germany: Prevalence and school factors. British Journal of Psychology, 92(4), 673-696.
7. Teicher, M. H., Samson, J. A., Sheu, Y. S., Polcari, A., & McGreenery, C. E. (2010). Hurtful words: association of exposure to peer verbal abuse with elevated psychiatric symptom scores and corpus callosum abnormalities. American Journal of Psychiatry, 167(12), 1464-1471.
8. Dake, J. A., Price, J. H., & Telljohann, S. K. (2003). The nature and extent of bullying at school. Journal of School Health, 73(5), 173-180.
9. Lobo, Y. B., & Winsler, A. (2006). The effects of a creative dance and movement program on the social competence of Head Start preschoolers. Social Development, 15(3), 501-519.

   Lau, W. C. M. (2008). Using singing games in music lessons

to enhance young children's social skills. Asia-Pacific Journal for Arts Education, 6(2), 1-30.

10. Choi, A. N., Lee, M. S., & Lee, J. S. (2010). Group music intervention reduces aggression and improves self-esteem in children with highly aggressive behavior: A pilot controlled trial. Evidence-Based Complementary and Alternative Medicine, 7(2), 213-217.

Chapter 34

Empathy: The Missing Link Between Emotional Intelligence and Real Life

1. Stout, M. (2005). The Sociopath Next Door. New York: Three Rivers Press.
2. O'Moore, M., & Kirkham, C. (2001). Self esteem and its relationship to bullying behaviour. Aggressive behavior, 27(4), 269-283.
3. Baumeister, R. F., Campbell, J. D., Krueger, J. I., & Vohs, K. D. (2003). Does high self-esteem cause better performance, interpersonal success, happiness, or healthier lifestyles? Psychological science in the public interest, 4(1), 1-44.

   Brown, R. P., & Zeigler-Hill, V. (2004). Narcissism and the non-equivalence of self-esteem measures: A matter of dominance? Journal of Research in Personality, 38(6), 585-592.
4. Baumeister, R. F., Campbell, J. D., Krueger, J. I., & Vohs, K. D. (2003). Does high self-esteem cause better performance, interpersonal success, happiness, or healthier lifestyles? Psychological science in the public interest, 4(1), 1-44.

   And

   Penney, L. M., & Spector, P. E. (2002). Narcissism and counterproductive work behavior: Do bigger egos mean bigger problems? International Journal of Selection and Assessment, 10(1 2), 126-134.

5. Bushman, B. J., & Baumeister, R. F. (1998). Threatened egotism, narcissism, self-esteem, and direct and displaced aggression: Does self-love or self-hate lead to violence? Journal of personality and social psychology, 75(1), 219-229.
6. Reidy, D. E., Zeichner, A., Foster, J. D., & Martinez, M. A. (2008). Effects of narcissistic entitlement and exploitativeness on human physical aggression. Personality and Individual Differences, 44(4), 865-875.
7. Bushman, B. J., Bonacci, A. M., Van Dijk, M., & Baumeister, R. F. (2003). Narcissism, sexual refusal, and aggression: Testing a narcissistic reactance model of sexual coercion. Journal of Personality and Social Psychology, 84(5), 1027.

Music Training is Empathy Training

1. Brand, E., & Bar-Gil, O. R. A. (2008). Improving interpersonal communication through music. Proceedings of the 22nd International Society of Music (pp. 71-79). Bologna:ISME
2. Kirschner, S., & Tomasello, M. (2010). Joint music making promotes prosocial behavior in 4-year-old children. Evolution and Human Behavior, 31(5), 354-364.
3. Rabinowitch, T. C., Cross, I., & Burnard, P. (2012). Long-term musical group interaction has a positive influence on empathy in children. Psychology of Music, 40(2), 131-256.
4. Kalliopuska, M., & Ruokonen, I. (1986). Effects of music education on development of holistic empathy. Perceptual and motor skills, 62(1), 187-191.
5. Kalliopuska, M., & Ruokonen, I. (1993). A study with a follow-up of the effects of music education on holistic development of empathy. Perceptual and motor skills, 76(1), 131-137.

6. Hietolahti-Ansten, M., & Kalliopuska, M. (1990). Self-esteem and empathy among children actively involved in music. Perceptual and motor skills, 71(3f), 1364-1366.
7. Ibid.

Chapter 35

Self-Esteem, Confidence and the Musical Key to Happiness

1. Baumeister, R. F., Campbell, J. D., Krueger, J. I., & Vohs, K. D. (2003). Does high self-esteem cause better performance, interpersonal success, happiness, or healthier lifestyles? Psychological science in the public interest, 4(1), 1-44.
2. Ibid.
3. Furnham, A., & Cheng, H. (2000). Perceived parental behaviour, self-esteem and happiness. Social psychiatry and psychiatric epidemiology, 35(10), 463-470.
4. Baumeister, R. F., Campbell, J. D., Krueger, J. I., & Vohs, K. D. (2003). Does high self-esteem cause better performance, interpersonal success, happiness, or healthier lifestyles? Psychological science in the public interest, 4(1), 1-44.
5. See, for instance, the following studies (also in Appendix: Self-esteem and confidence):
   Hietolahti-Ansten, M., & Kalliopuska, M. (1990). Self-esteem and empathy among children actively involved in music. Perceptual and motor skills, 71(3f), 1364-1366.
   Choi, A. N., Lee, M. S., & Lee, J. S. (2010). Group music intervention reduces aggression and improves self-esteem in children with highly aggressive behavior: A pilot controlled trial. Evidence-Based Complementary and Alternative Medicine, 7(2), 213-217.
   Dalgas-Pelish, P. (2006). Effects of a self-esteem intervention

program on school-age children. Pediatric nursing, 32(4), 341-348.

Kokotsaki, D., & Hallam, S. (2007). Higher education music students' perceptions of the benefits of participative music making. Music Education Research, 9(1), 93-109.

Rickard, N. S., Appelman, P., James, R., Murphy, F., Gill, A., & Bambrick, C. (2012). Orchestrating life skills: The effect of increased school-based music classes on children's social competence and self-esteem. International Journal of Music Education, 30(1), 3-84.

Hallam, S. (2010). The power of music: its impact on the intellectual, social and personal development of children and young people. International Journal of Music Education, 28(3), 269-289.

Michel, D. E. (1971). Self-esteem and academic achievement in black junior high school students: Effects of automated guitar instruction. Bulletin of the Council for Research in Music Education, 24, 15-23.

Warner, L. (1999). Self-esteem: A byproduct of quality classroom music. Childhood Education, 76(1), 19-23.

6. Baumeister, R. F., Campbell, J. D., Krueger, J. I., & Vohs, K. D. (2003). Does high self-esteem cause better performance, interpersonal success, happiness, or healthier lifestyles? Psychological science in the public interest, 4(1), 1-44.
7. Costa-Giomi, E. (2004). Effects of three years of piano instruction on children's academic achievement, school performance and self-esteem. Psychology of Music, 32(2), 139-152.
8. Ibid.
9. Jutras, P. J. (2006). The benefits of adult piano study as self-reported by selected adult piano students. Journal of Research in Music Education, 54(2), 97-110.

10. Varvarigou, M., Creech, A., Hallam, S., & McQueen, H. (2012). Benefits experienced by older people in group music-making activities. Journal of Applied Arts & Health, 3(2), 133-148.
11. Gerry, D., Unrau, A., & Trainor, L. J. (2012). Active music classes in infancy enhance musical, communicative and social development. Developmental Science. 15(3), 398-407.
12. Rickard, N. S., Appelman, P., James, R., Murphy, F., Gill, A., & Bambrick, C. (2012). Orchestrating life skills: The effect of increased school-based music classes on children's social competence and self-esteem. International Journal of Music Education, 30(1), 3-84.
13. Hietolahti-Ansten, M., & Kalliopuska, M. (1990). Self-esteem and empathy among children actively involved in music. Perceptual and motor skills, 71(3f), 1364-1366.
14. Rickard, N. S., Appelman, P., James, R., Murphy, F., Gill, A., & Bambrick, C. (2012). Orchestrating life skills: The effect of increased school-based music classes on children's social competence and self-esteem. International Journal of Music Education, 30(1), 3-84.
15. Burkhardt, J., & Brennan, C. (2012). The effects of recreational dance interventions on the health and well-being of children and young people: A systematic review. Arts & Health, 4(2), 148-161.
16. Larson, R. (1994). Youth organizations, hobbies, and sports as developmental contexts. Adolescence in context: The interplay of family, school, peers, and work in adjustment, 46-65.
17. Mahoney, J. L., & Cairns, R. B. (1997). Do extracurricular activities protect against early school dropout? Developmental psychology, 33(2), 241.
18. Eccles, J. S., & Barber, B. L. (1999). Student Council, Volunteering, Basketball, or Marching Band What Kind of

Extracurricular Involvement Matters? Journal of adolescent research, 14(1), 10-43.

19. Wilbum, V. R., & Smith, D. E. (2005). Stress, self-esteem, and suicidal ideation in late adolescents. Adolescence, 40(157), 33-45.
20. Ibid.
21. Toyoshima, K., Fukui, H., & Kuda, K. (2011). Piano playing reduces stress more than other creative art activities. International Journal of Music Education, 29(3), 257-263.

Part Eight

Creativity and New Learning - Remedies In The Face Of the Challenges of Today and Tomorrow

Introduction

1. Wurman, R. S. (1989). Information Anxiety. New York: Doubleday.
2. Varian, H., & Lyman, P. (2000). How much information. University of California, Berkeley: UC Press.

Chapter 36

The Brain Upgrade: How Music Training Increases Memory and Brainpower

Swimming In the Sea Of Information

1. Varian, H., & Lyman, P. (2003, October 27). "How Much Information?". Regents of the University of California. Retrieved December 16,2012 from http://www2.sims.berkeley.edu/research/projects/how-much-info-2003/
2. See Appendix: Music Boost for Brainpower, regarding working memory and information processing

3. George, E. M., & Coch, D. (2011). Music training and working memory: an ERP study. Neuropsychologia, 49(5), 1083-1094.
4. See Appendix: Music Boost for Long-term Memory

Chapter 37

The Boss of the Brain: Executive Functioning

1. Anderson, P. (2002). Assessment and development of executive function (EF) during childhood. Child Neuropsychology, 8(2), 71-82.
   Funahashi, S. (2001). Neuronal mechanisms of executive control by the prefrontal cortex. Neuroscience research, 39(2), 147-165.
2. Bialystok, E. (2007). Cognitive effects of bilingualism: How linguistic experience leads to cognitive change. International Journal of Bilingual Education and Bilingualism, 10(3), 210-223.
3. Bialystok, E., & DePape, A. M. (2009). Musical expertise, bilingualism, and executive functioning. Journal of Experimental Psychology: Human Perception and Performance, 35(2), 565.
4. Delis, D. C., Lansing, A., Houston, W. S., Wetter, S., Han, S. D., Jacobson, M., & Kramer, J. (2007). Creativity Lost: The Importance of Testing Higher-Level Executive Functions in School-Age Children and Adolescents. Journal of Psychoeducational Assessment, 25(1), 29-40.
5. Moreno, S., Bialystok, E., Barac, R., Schellenberg, E. G., Cepeda, N. J., & Chau, T. (2011). Short-term music training enhances verbal intelligence and executive function. Psychological science, 22(11), 1425-1433.
6. Schellenberg, E. G. (2006). Long-term positive associations

between music lessons and IQ. Journal of Educational Psychology, 98(2), 457.

Chapter 38

The Creativity Crisis of Children

1. Tomasco, S. (2010, May 18). IBM 2010 Global CEO Study: Creativity Selected as Most Crucial Factor for Future Success. IBM. Retrieved 16 December 2012 from http://www-03.ibm.com/press/us/en/pressrelease/31670.wss
2. Torgovnick, K. (2012, August 21). The 20 most-watched TED Talks to date. TED Ideas Worth Spreading. Retrieved from http://blog.ted.com/2012/08/21/the-20-most-watched-ted-talks-to-date/
3. Land, G., & Jarman, B. (1993). Breakpoint and beyond: Mastering the future--today. HarperCollins.
4. Ibid.
5. Kim, K. H. (2011). The Creativity Crisis: The Decrease in Creative Thinking Scores on the Torrance Tests of Creative Thinking. Creativity Research Journal, 23(4), 285-295.

Chapter 39

How to Preserve Your Child's Creative Genius

1. Richard, E., & Frank, B. (1962). Caution in comparing creativity and IQ. Psychological Reports, 10(1), 229-230.
2. Britannica. (2010, December 23). Explaining the Decline of Creativity in American Children: A Reply to Readers . Encyclopedia Britannica Blog Facts Matter. Retrieved 16 December 2012 from http://www.britannica.com/

blogs/2010/12/explaining-the-decline-of-creativity-in-american-children-a-reply-to-readers/

3. Nicol, J. J., & Long, B. C. (1996). Creativity and perceived stress of female music therapists and hobbyists. Creativity Research Journal, 9(1), 1-10.
4. Gold, R., Faust, M., & Ben-Artzi, E. (2012). Metaphors and verbal creativity: The role of the right hemisphere. Laterality: Asymmetries of Body, Brain and Cognition, 17(5), 602-614.
5. Kowatari, Y., Lee, S. H., Yamamura, H., Nagamori, Y., Levy, P., Yamane, S., & Yamamoto, M. (2009). Neural networks involved in artistic creativity. Human brain mapping, 30(5), 1678-1690.
6. Gibson, C., Folley, B. S., & Park, S. (2009). Enhanced divergent thinking and creativity in musicians: A behavioral and near-infrared spectroscopy study. Brain and Cognition, 69(1), 162-169.
7. Shamay-Tsoory, S. G., Adler, N., Aharon-Peretz, J., Perry, D., & Mayseless, N. (2011). The origins of originality: The neural bases of creative thinking and originality. Neuropsychologia, 49(2), 178-185.
8. Hyde, K. L., Lerch, J., Norton, A., Forgeard, M., Winner, E., Evans, A. C., & Schlaug, G. (2009). Musical training shapes structural brain development. The Journal of Neuroscience, 29(10), 3019-3025.

   Schlaug, G., Forgeard, M., Zhu, L., Norton, A., Norton, A., & Winner, E. (2009). Training-induced Neuroplasticity in Young Children. Annals of the New York Academy of Sciences, 1169(1), 205-208.
9. Ibid.
10. Chronopoulou, E., & Riga, V. (2012). The Contribution of Music and Movement Activities to Creative Thinking in Pre-School Children. Creative Education, 3(2), 196-204.

11. Brown, S., Martinez, M. J., & Parsons, L. M. (2006). Music and language side by side in the brain: a PET study of the generation of melodies and sentences. European Journal of Neuroscience, 23(10), 2791-2803.
12. Chronopoulou, E., & Riga, V. (2012). The Contribution of Music and Movement Activities to Creative Thinking in Pre-School Children. Creative Education, 3(2), 196-204.
13. Bachtold, L. M. (1974). The Creative Personality and the Ideal Pupil Revisited*. The Journal of Creative Behavior, 8(1), 47-54.

    Cropley, A. J. (1992). More ways than one: Fostering creativity. Norwood: Ablex Publishing.

    Dettmer, P. (1981). Improving Teacher Attitudes toward Characteristics of the Creatively Gifted. Gifted Child Quarterly, 25(1), 11-16.

    Getzels, J. W., & Jackson, P. W. (1962). Creativity and intelligence: Explorations with gifted students. Oxford: Willey.

    Torrance, E. (1963). The creative personality and the ideal pupil. The Teachers College Record, 65(3), 220-226.
14. Westby, E. L., & Dawson, V. L. (1995). Creativity: Asset or burden in the classroom? Creativity Research Journal, 8(1), 1-10.
15. Westby, E. L., & Dawson, V. L. (1995). Creativity: Asset or burden in the classroom? Creativity Research Journal, 8(1), 1-10. In reference to Dettmer 1981

Part Nine

What Next? Music Education and its Obstacles and Opportunities

Chapter 40

Navigating the Maze to the Music Miracle: the three elements of music training

1. See, for instance, these comparative studies between different educational and non-educational music groups:
   Gerry, D., Unrau, A., & Trainor, L. J. (2012). Active music classes in infancy enhance musical, communicative and social development. Developmental Science. 15(3), 398-407.
   Moyeda, I., Gómez, I. C., & Flores, M. (2006). Implementing a musical program to promote preschool children's vocabulary development. Early Childhood Research & Practice, 8(1).
   Brodsky, W., & Sulkin, I. (2011). Handclapping songs: a spontaneous platform for child development among 5–10 year old children. Early Child Development and Care, 181(8), 1111-1136.
2. Gordon, E. (2003). Music Aptitude and Other Factors. In E. Gordon, A Music Learning Theory for Newborn and Young Children (pp. 22-23). Chicago: GIA Publications.
3. Gerry, D., Unrau, A., & Trainor, L. J. (2012). Active music classes in infancy enhance musical, communicative and social development. Developmental Science. 15(3), 398-407.
   See also: Register, Dena M. (2003).The Effects of Live Music Groups Versus an Educational Children's Television Program on the Emergent Literacy of Young Children. Unpublished Doctoral Theses, Florida State University, Florida, United States.
4. Hendon, C., & Bohon, L. M. (2008). Hospitalized children's mood differences during play and music therapy. Child: care, health and development, 34(2), 141-144.

5. Gordon, E. (2003). Music Aptitude and Other Factors. In E. Gordon, A Music Learning Theory for Newborn and Young Children (pp. 22-23). Chicago: GIA Publications.
6. Hennessy, S. (2000). Overcoming the red-feeling: The development of confidence to teach music in primary school amongst student teachers. British Journal of Music Education, 17(2), 183-196.
7. Lamb, S. J., & Gregory, A. H. (1993). The relationship between music and reading in beginning readers. Educational Psychology, 13(1), 19-27.

Rhythm: Clap your hands for a higher IQ

1. Winkler, I., Háden, G. P., Ladinig, O., Sziller, I., & Honing, H. (2009). Newborn infants detect the beat in music. Proceedings of the National Academy of Sciences, 106(7), 2468-2471.
2. Brodsky, W., & Sulkin, I. (2011). Handclapping songs: a spontaneous platform for child development among 5–10 year old children. Early Child Development and Care, 181(8), 1111-1136.
3. Ibid.
4. Ibid.
5. Chen, J. L., Penhune, V. B., & Zatorre, R. J. (2008). Listening to musical rhythms recruits motor regions of the brain. Cerebral Cortex, 18(12), 2844-2854.
6. Zentner, M., & Eerola, T. (2010). Rhythmic engagement with music in infancy. Proceedings of the National Academy of Sciences, 107(13), 5768-5773.
   See also: University of York (2010, March 16). Babies are born to dance, new research shows. ScienceDaily. Retrieved

April 8, 2013, from http://www.sciencedaily.com / releases/2010/03/100315161925.htm

7. Ibid.
8. See Appendix: Rhythm Skills and IQ (See also previous Chapters 18-19)
9. Waber, D. P., Weiler, M. D., Bellinger, D. C., Marcus, D. J., Forbes, P. W., Wypij, D., & Wolff, P. H. (2000). Diminished motor timing control in children referred for diagnosis of learning problems. Developmental neuropsychology, 17(2), 181-197.

   See also: Krommyda, M., Papadelis, G., Chatzikallia, K., Pastiadis, K., & Kardaras, P. (2008) Does awareness of musical structure relate to general cognitive and literacy profile in children with learning disabilities? Conference on Interdisciplinary Musicology (pp. 1-10). Thessaloniki: Aristotle University of Thessaloniki.
10. See, for instance, this rhythm training programme that shows the correlation from an improvement of rhythm skills to an improvement of academic skills: Brodsky, W., & Sulkin, I. (2011). Handclapping songs: a spontaneous platform for child development among 5–10 year old children. Early Child Development and Care, 181(8), 1111-1136.
11. Waber, D. P., Weiler, M. D., Bellinger, D. C., Marcus, D. J., Forbes, P. W., Wypij, D., & Wolff, P. H. (2000). Diminished motor timing control in children referred for diagnosis of learning problems. Developmental neuropsychology, 17(2), 181-197.

    Krommyda, M., Papadelis, G., Chatzikallia, K., Pastiadis, K., & Kardaras, P. (2008) Does awareness of musical structure relate to general cognitive and literacy profile in children with learning disabilities? Conference on Interdisciplinary

Musicology (pp. 1-10). Thessaloniki: Aristotle University of Thessaloniki.

Brodsky, W., & Sulkin, I. (2011). Handclapping songs: a spontaneous platform for child development among 5–10 year old children. Early Child Development and Care, 181(8), 1111-1136.

Melody: Tune your way to success

1. Perani, D., Saccuman, M. C., Scifo, P., Spada, D., Andreolli, G., Rovelli, R., & Koelsch, S. (2010). Functional specializations for music processing in the human newborn brain. Proceedings of the National Academy of Sciences, 107(10), 4758-4763. See also: Trainor, L. J., Tsang, C. D., & Cheung, V. H. (2002). Preference for sensory consonance in 2-and 4-month-old infants. Music Perception, 20(2), 187-194.
2. Nakata, T., & Trehub, S. E. (2004). Infants' responsiveness to maternal speech and singing. Infant Behavior and Development, 27(4), 455-464.
3. Brandt, A., Gebrian, M., & Slevc, L. R. (2012). Music and early language acquisition. Frontiers in Psychology, 3, 327.
4. See Chapter 13.
5. Juvonen, A., Lehtonen, K, & Ruismaki, H. Musically restricted under the pressure of postmodern society, 1-11.
6. Welch, G. (2001). The misunderstanding of music. London: Institute of Education Publications, University of London.
7. Ibid.
8. Ibid.
9. Forgeard, M., Schlaug, G., Norton, A., Rosam, C., Iyengar, U., & Winner, E. (2008). The relation between music and phonological processing in normal-reading children and children with dyslexia. Music Perception, 25(4), 383-390.

See also: Lamb, S. J., & Gregory, A. H. (1993). The relationship between music and reading in beginning readers. Educational Psychology, 13(1), 19-27.

And

Anvari, S. H., Trainor, L. J., Woodside, J., & Levy, B. A. (2002). Relations among musical skills, phonological processing, and early reading ability in preschool children. Journal of experimental child psychology, 83(2), 111-130.

10. See Appendix: Music Boost for Reading Skills
11. See Chapters 26-28
12. Kraus, N., & Chandrasekaran, B. (2010). Music training for the development of auditory skills. Nature Reviews Neuroscience, 11(8), 599-605.
13. See, for instance, the following studies:

    Bolduc, J., & Montésinos-Gelet, I. (2005). Pitch processing and phonological awareness. Psychomusicology: Music, Mind & Brain, 19(1), 3-14.

    Lamb, S. J., & Gregory, A. H. (1993). The relationship between music and reading in beginning readers. Educational Psychology, 13(1), 19-27.

    Beattie, R. L., & Manis, F. R. (2011). The relationship between prosodic perception, phonological awareness and vocabulary in emergent literacy. Journal of Research in Reading.
14. Reading skills can be predicted based on auditory abilities; Hornickel, J., Chandrasekaran, B., Zecker, S., & Kraus, N. (2011). Auditory brainstem measures predict reading and speech-in-noise perception in school-aged children. Behavioural brain research, 216(2), 597-605. ~~ Bhide, A., Power, A., & Goswami, U. (2013). A Rhythmic Musical Intervention for Poor Readers: A Comparison of Efficacy With a Letter Based Intervention. Mind, Brain, and Education, 7(2), 113-123.

15. Mackenzie-Beck, Janet (2003) *Is it possible to predict students' ability to develop skills in practical phonetics?* Proceedings of the 15th International Congress of Phonetic Sciences (pp. 2833 -2836). Barcelona: Universitat Autonoma de Barcelona Press
    Dankovicová, J., House, J., Crooks, A., & Jones, K. (2007). The relationship between musical skills, music training, and intonation analysis skills. Language and Speech, 50(2), 177-225.
16. Loui, P., Kroog, K., Zuk, J., Winner, E., & Schlaug, G. (2011). Relating pitch awareness to phonemic awareness in children: implications for tone-deafness and dyslexia. Frontiers in psychology, 2,111.
17. Musacchia, G., Sams, M., Skoe, E., & Kraus, N. (2007). Musicians have enhanced subcortical auditory and audiovisual processing of speech and music. Proceedings of the National Academy of Sciences, 104(40), 15894-15898.
    Strait, D. L., Kraus, N., Skoe, E., & Ashley, R. (2009). Musical experience and neural efficiency–effects of training on subcortical processing of vocal expressions of emotion. European Journal of Neuroscience, 29(3), 661-668.
    Thompson, W. F., Schellenberg, E. G., & Husain, G. (2004). Decoding speech prosody: do music lessons help? Emotion, 4(1), 46.

Notation: Reading Music, Counting Maths

1. Scripp, L. (2003). Critical links, next steps: an evolving conception of music and learning in public school education. Journal of Learning Through Music, 119-140.
2. Graziano, A. B., Peterson, M., & Shaw, G. L. (1999). Enhanced learning of proportional math through music training and spatial-temporal training. Neurological research, 21(2), 139.

And
San Francisco State University (2012, March 22). Getting in rhythm helps children grasp fractions, study finds. ScienceDaily. Retrieved April 8, 2013, from http://www.sciencedaily.com / releases/2012/03/120322100209.htm

3. Hodges, D. A. (1992). The acquisition of music reading skills. In Handbook of research on music teaching and learning: A project of the Music Educators National Conference (pp. 466-471).
4. Rogers, G. L. (1996). Effect of colored rhythmic notation on music-reading skills of elementary students. Journal of Research in Music Education, 44(1), 15-25.
5. Ibid.
6. Kyme, G. H. (1960). An experiment in teaching children to read music with shape notes. Journal of Research in Music Education, 8(1), 3-8.
7. Hodges, D. A. (1992). The acquisition of music reading skills. In Handbook of research on music teaching and learning: A project of the Music Educators National Conference (pp. 466-471).
8. Autry, M. R. (1976). A study of the effect of hand signs in the development of sight singing skills (Doctoral dissertation, University of Texas, Austin, 1975). Dissertation Abstracts International, 37.
   And
   Klemish, J. J. (1970). A comparative study of two methods of teaching music reading to first-grade children. Journal of Research in Music Education, 18(4), 355-364.
   Both as cited in: Hodges, D. A. (1992). The acquisition of music reading skills. In Handbook of research on music teaching and learning: A project of the Music Educators National Conference (pp. 466-471).

9. Hodges, D. A. (1992). The acquisition of music reading skills. In Handbook of research on music teaching and learning: A project of the Music Educators National Conference (pp. 466-471).
10. Ibid.
11. Lloyd, M. J. (1978). Teach music to aid beginning readers. The Reading Teacher, 32(3), 323-327.
12. Hallam, S. (2010). The power of music: its impact on the intellectual, social and personal development of children and young people. International Journal of Music Education, 28(3), 269-289.
13. Persellin, D. C. (1994). Effects of learning modalities on melodic and rhythmic retention and on vocal pitch-matching by preschool children. Perceptual and motor skills, 78(3c), 1231-1234.
14. Gordon, E. (2003). Music Aptitude and Other Factors. In E. Gordon, A Music Learning Theory for Newborn and Young Children (pp. 22-23). Chicago: GIA Publications.
15. Sloboda, J. (1978), as quoted in McPherson, G. E., & Gabrielsson, A. (2002). From sound to sign. The science and psychology of music performance: Creative strategies for teaching and learning, 99-116.
16. Hargreaves, D. J. (1986). The developmental psychology of music. Cambridge University Press. ~~ Chapter 41 ~~ All instruments and genres lead to the Music Miracle

Chapter 41

All instruments and genres lead to the Music Miracle

1. Chua, A. (2011). Battle hymn of the tiger mother. New York: Bloomsbury Publishing.
2. Rauscher, F. H., & Hinton, S. C. (2011). Music instruction

and its diverse extra-musical benefits. Music Perception, 29(2), 215-226.

3. Ibid.
4. Ibid.
5. Tai, T. C. (2010). The effect of violin, keyboard, and singing instruction on the spatial ability and music aptitude of young children. Unpublished Master's Theses, University of Maryland, Maryland, United States.
6. Ibid. See also Schellenberg's study, where singing produced an IQ boost equivalent, or even slightly larger, to that of piano instruction. As in Tai's study, Schellenberg's test children received professional music training by professional musicians. Singalong groups are fun but it would be unrealistic to expect an IQ boost from them.
7. Schellenberg, E. G. (2004). Music lessons enhance IQ. Psychological Science, 15(8), 511-514.
8. Winkelman, M. (2003). Complementary therapy for addiction: "drumming out drugs". Journal Information, 93(4), 647-651.

Informal and formal learning, classical and popular music

9. Green, L. (2008). Music, informal learning and the school: A new classroom pedagogy. Hamsphire: Ashgate Publishing.
10. Ibid.
11. See, for instance, the following studies: Woody, R. H., & Lehmann, A. C. (2010). Student musicians' ear-playing ability as a function of vernacular music experiences. Journal of Research in Music Education, 58(2), 101-115.

    Davidson, L., Scripp, L., & Welsh, P. (1988). " Happy Birthday": Evidence for Conflicts of Perceptual Knowledge and Conceptual Understanding. Journal of Aesthetic Education, 22(1), 65-74.

    McPherson, G. E., & Gabrielsson, A. (2002). From sound

to sign. The science and psychology of music performance: Creative strategies for teaching and learning, 99-116.

12. Ruismäki, H., & Tereska, T. (2008). Students' assessments of music learning experiences from kindergarten to university. British Journal of Music Education, 25(01), 23-39.
13. Levitin, D. J. (2006). This is your brain on music: The science of a human obsession. In D. J. Levitin, This is your brain on music: The science of a human obsession. (p. 212). New York: Dutton Adult.
14. See, for instance, this revealing study of an overtly formal music training that ends up reducing its participants' musicality: Davidson, L., Scripp, L., & Welsh, P. (1988). " Happy Birthday": Evidence for Conflicts of Perceptual Knowledge and Conceptual Understanding. Journal of Aesthetic Education, 22(1), 65-74.
For further discussion, see also: McPherson, G. E., & Gabrielsson, A. (2002). From sound to sign. The science and psychology of music performance: Creative strategies for teaching and learning, 99-116.

Chapter 42

The Personal Touch and Feeling the Invisible: The 'sixth sense' of music education

1. Whidden, C. (2008). The injustice of singer/non-singer labels by music educators. GEMS (Gender, Education, Music, and Society), 5, 1-15.
2. Juslin, P. N., & Laukka, P. (2004). Expression, perception, and induction of musical emotions: A review and a questionnaire study of everyday listening. Journal of New Music Research, 33(3), 217-238.

3. Sloboda, J. A. (1993). Musical ability. The origins and development of high ability, 106-118.
4. Juvonen, A., Lehtonen, K., & Ruismäki, H. Musically restricted under the pressure of postmodern society.
5. Ruismäki, H. and Tereska, T. in Saccone, C. (2005). A Preface: Neothemi Metaphors and Crossed Paths. ICT and Communicating Cultures, 9.
6. Sloboda, J. A. (1993). Musical ability. The origins and development of high ability, 106-118.
   And
   Davidson, J. W., Moore, D. G., Sloboda, J. A., & Howe, M. J. (1998). Characteristics of music teachers and the progress of young instrumentalists. Journal of Research in Music Education, 46(1), 141-160.
7. Juvonen, A., Lehtonen, K., & Ruismäki, H. Musically restricted under the pressure of postmodern society.
8. Appendix: We Are All Born Musical The Musicality of Newborn Babies (See also Chapter 13 of this book).

Epilogue: Training For Happiness

1. Csikszentmihalyi, M. (2008). Flow: The Psychology of Optimal Experience. In M. Csikszentmihalyi, Flow: The Psychology of Optimal Experience (p. 11). New York: Harper&Row.
2. Csikszentmihalyi, M. (2008). Flow: The Psychology of Optimal Experience. In M. Csikszentmihalyi, Flow: The Psychology of Optimal Experience (p. 45-46). New York: Harper&Row.
3. Csikszentmihalyi, M. (2008). Flow: The Psychology of Optimal Experience. In M. Csikszentmihalyi, Flow: The

Psychology of Optimal Experience (p. 53). New York: Harper&Row.

4. Csikszentmihalyi, M. (2008). Flow: The Psychology of Optimal Experience. In M. Csikszentmihalyi, Flow: The Psychology of Optimal Experience (p. 52). New York: Harper&Row.
5. Csikszentmihalyi, M. (2008). Flow: The Psychology of Optimal Experience. In M. Csikszentmihalyi, Flow: The Psychology of Optimal Experience (p. 54). New York: Harper&Row.
6. Custodero, L. A. (2005). Observable indicators of flow experience: A developmental perspective on musical engagement in young children from infancy to school age. Music Education Research, 7(2), 185-209.
7. Csikszentmihalyi, M. (2008). Flow: The Psychology of Optimal Experience. In M. Csikszentmihalyi, Flow: The Psychology of Optimal Experience. New York: Harper&Row.
8. Shersnoff, D. J., & Csikszentmihalyi, M. (2009). Flow in Schools : Cultivating Engaged Learners and Optimal Learning Environments. In M. J. Furlong, Handbook Of Positive Psychology In Schools (pp. 131-146). New York: Routledge.
   Csikszentmihalyi, M. (2008). Flow: The Psychology of Optimal Experience. In M. Csikszentmihalyi, Flow: The Psychology of Optimal Experience (p. 47). New York: Harper&Row.
9. Land, G. Jarman, B. (1992). Breakpoint and beyond: Mastering the future today. Harper Collins.
10. Csikszentmihalyi, M. (1997). Creativity: Flow and the psychology of discovery and invention. Harper perennial.
11. Ibid.
12. Zentner, M., & Eerola, T. (2010). Rhythmic engagement

with music in infancy. Proceedings of the National Academy of Sciences, 107(13), 5768-5773.

Hendon, C., & Bohon, L. M. (2008). Hospitalized children's mood differences during play and music therapy. Child: care, health and development, 34(2), 141-144.

13. Nicholson, J. M., Berthelsen, D., Abad, V., Williams, K., & Bradley, J. (2008). Impact of music therapy to promote positive parenting and child development. Journal of Health Psychology, 13(2), 226-238.
14. Ibid.
15. Rauscher, F. H., LeMieux, M., & Hinton, S. C. (2006). Quality piano instruction affects at-risk elementary school children's cognitive abilities and self-esteem. Ninth International Conference on Music Perception and Cognition. Bologna: University of Bologna Press.

    Lau, W. C. M. (2008). Using singing games in music lessons to enhance young children's social skills. Asia-Pacific Journal for Arts Education, 6(2), 1-30.
16. Hietolahti-Ansten, M., & Kalliopuska, M. (1990). Self-esteem and empathy among children actively involved in music. Perceptual and motor skills, 71(3f), 1364-1366.

    Costa-Giomi, E. (2004). Effects of three years of piano instruction on children's academic achievement, school performance and self-esteem. Psychology of Music, 32(2), 139-152.

Box 1 references

1. Luders, E., Narr, K. L., Bilder, R. M., Thompson, P. M., Szeszko, P. R., Hamilton, L., & Toga, A. W. (2007). Positive correlations between corpus callosum thickness and intelligence. Neuroimage, 37(4), 1457-1464.
2. Takeuchi, H., Taki, Y., Sassa, Y., Hashizume, H., Sekiguchi, A., Fukushima, A., & Kawashima, R. (2010). White matter structures associated with creativity: Evidence from diffusion tensor imaging. Neuroimage, 51(1), 11-18.
3. The original Schlaug study: Schlaug, G., Jäncke, L., Huang, Y., Staiger, J. F., & Steinmetz, H. (1995). Increased corpus callosum size in musicians. Neuropsychologia, 33(8), 1047-1055.

   Recent research concerning children and the corpus callosum boost via music training:

   Hyde, K. L., Lerch, J., Norton, A., Forgeard, M., Winner, E., Evans, A. C., & Schlaug, G. (2009). Musical training shapes structural brain development. *The Journal of Neuroscience, 29*(10), 3019-3025.

   And

   Steele, C. J., Bailey, J. A., Zatorre, R. J., & Penhune, V. B. (2013). Early Musical Training and White-Matter Plasticity in the Corpus Callosum: Evidence for a Sensitive Period. *The Journal of Neuroscience, 33*(3), 1282-1290.
4. Patston, L. L., Hogg, S. L., & Tippett, L. J. (2007). Attention in musicians is more bilateral than in non-musicians. *Laterality, 12*(3), 262-272.
5. See Chapters 14-18 on intelligence as well as Appendix: Music Boost for IQ.
6. See Chapter 38-39 on creativity as well as Appendix: Music Boost for Creativity.

Box 2 references

7. Schlaug, G., Norton, A., Overy, K., & Winner, E. (2005). Effects of music training on the child's brain and cognitive development. Annals of the New York Academy of Sciences, 1060(1), 219-230. See also: Gaser, C., & Schlaug, G. (2003). Brain structures differ between musicians and non-musicians. The Journal of Neuroscience, 23(27), 9240-9245.
8. Schlaug, G., Norton, A., Overy, K., & Winner, E. (2005). Effects of music training on the child's brain and cognitive development. Annals of the New York Academy of Sciences, 1060(1), 219-230.
9. See Appendix: Music Boost for the Elderly
10. Huang, Z., Zhang, J. X., Yang, Z., Dong, G., Wu, J., Chan, A. S., & Weng, X. (2010). Verbal memory retrieval engages visual cortex in musicians. Neuroscience, 168(1), 179-189.
11. Schmithorst, V. J., & Holland, S. K. (2003). The effect of musical training on music processing: A functional magnetic resonance imaging study in humans. Neuroscience Letters, 348(2), 65-68.
12. Gaser, C., & Schlaug, G. (2003). Brain structures differ between musicians and non-musicians. The Journal of Neuroscience, 23(27), 9240-9245.
13. Grahn, J. A., & Rowe, J. B. (2009). Feeling the beat: premotor and striatal interactions in musicians and nonmusicians during beat perception. The Journal of Neuroscience, 29(23), 7540-7548.
14. Hyde, K. L., Lerch, J., Norton, A., Forgeard, M., Winner, E., Evans, A. C., & Schlaug, G. (2009). The effects of musical training on structural brain development. Annals of the New York Academy of Sciences, 1169(1), 182-186.
15. Li, S., Han, Y., Wang, D., Yang, H., Fan, Y., Lv, Y., ... & He,

Y. (2010). Mapping surface variability of the central sulcus in musicians. Cerebral Cortex, 20(1), 25-33.

16. Pantev, C., Lappe, C., Herholz, S. C., & Trainor, L. (2009). Auditory Somatosensory Integration and Cortical Plasticity in Musical Training. Annals of the New York Academy of Sciences, 1169(1), 143-150.

See also: Gaser, C., & Schlaug, G. (2003). Brain structures differ between musicians and non-musicians. The Journal of Neuroscience, 23(27), 9240-9245.

11. Stewart, L., Henson, R., Kampe, K., Walsh, V., Turner, R., & Frith, U. (2003). Brain changes after learning to read and play music. Neuroimage, 20(1), 71-83.

See also: Gaser, C., & Schlaug, G. (2003). Brain structures differ between musicians and non-musicians. The Journal of Neuroscience, 23(27), 9240-9245.

12. See Appendix: Music Boost for Spatial-temporal intelligence, as well as discussion in Chapter 16.

13.Stewart, L., Henson, R., Kampe, K., Walsh, V., Turner, R., & Frith, U. (2003). Brain changes after learning to read and play music. Neuroimage, 20(1), 71-83.

14. Seghier, M. L. (2013). The Angular Gyrus: Multiple Functions and Multiple Subdivisions. The Neuroscientist, 19(1), 43-61.

15. Sluming, V., Brooks, J., Howard, M., Downes, J. J., & Roberts, N. (2007). Broca's area supports enhanced visuospatial cognition in orchestral musicians. The Journal of Neuroscience, 27(14), 3799-3806.

See also:

Hoenig, K., Müller, C., Herrnberger, B., Sim, E. J., Spitzer, M., Ehret, G., & Kiefer, M. (2011). Neuroplasticity of semantic representations for musical instruments in professional musicians. Neuroimage, 56(3), 1714-1725.

16. Kawamura, M., Midorikawa, A., & Kezuka, M. (2000). Cerebral localization of the center for reading and writing music. Neuroreport, 11(14), 3299-3303.

17. Aydin, K., Ucar, A., Oguz, K. K., Okur, O. O., Agayev, A., Unal, Z., ... & Ozturk, C. (2007). Increased gray matter density in the parietal cortex of mathematicians: a voxel-based morphometry study. American Journal of Neuroradiology, 28(10), 1859-1864

18.See Chapter 21 as well as Appendix: Music Boost for Mathematics

19. Schlaug, G., Norton, A., Overy, K., & Winner, E. (2005). Effects of music training on the child's brain and cognitive development. Annals of the New York Academy of Sciences, 1060(1), 219-230.

20. Huang, Z., Zhang, J. X., Yang, Z., Dong, G., Wu, J., Chan, A. S., & Weng, X. (2010). Verbal memory retrieval engages visual cortex in musicians. Neuroscience, 168(1), 179-189.

21. See Appendix: Music Boost for Memory.

22.Gaser, C., & Schlaug, G. (2003). Brain structures differ between musicians and non-musicians. The Journal of Neuroscience, 23(27), 9240-9245.

23.Ibid.

24.Peretz, I., & Zatorre, R. J. (2005). Brain organization for music processing. Annu. Rev. Psychol., 56, 89-114.

25. Seung, Y., Kyong, J. S., Woo, S. H., Lee, B. T., & Lee, K. M. (2005). Brain activation during music listening in individuals with or without prior music training. Neuroscience research, 52(4), 323-329.

26. Schlaug, G., Norton, A., Overy, K., & Winner, E. (2005). Effects of music training on the child's brain and cognitive

development. Annals of the New York Academy of Sciences, 1060(1), 219-230.
27. See Appendix on working memory.
28. See Chapters 22-25.
29.See Chapters 30-31 as well as Appendix: Emotional Recognition
30. See Part Seven of the book.
31. Halwani, G. F., Loui, P., Rüber, T., & Schlaug, G. (2011). Effects of practice and experience on the arcuate fasciculus: comparing singers, instrumentalists, and non-musicians. Frontiers in psychology, 2.
32. See Chapters 22-25.

Box 3 references

1. Groussard, M., La Joie, R., Rauchs, G., Landeau, B., Chételat, G., Viader, F., ... & Platel, H. (2010). When music and long-term memory interact: effects of musicåal expertise on functional and structural plasticity in the hippocampus. PloS one, 5(10), e13225.
2. Herdener, M., Esposito, F., di Salle, F., Boller, C., Hilti, C. C., Habermeyer, B., ... & Cattapan-Ludewig, K. (2010). Musical training induces functional plasticity in human hippocampus. The Journal of Neuroscience, 30(4), 1377-1384.
3. Oechslin, M. S., Descloux, C., Croquelois, A., Chanal, J., Van De Ville, D., Lazeyras, F., & James, C. E. (2013). Hippocampal volume predicts fluid intelligence in musically trained people. Hippocampus.
4. See Appendices Music Boost for Memory and Music Boost for Spatial-Visual Skills.
5. Strick, P. L., Dum, R. P., & Fiez, J. A. (2009). Cerebellum

and nonmotor function. Annual review of neuroscience, 32, 413-434.

6. Bengtsson, S. L., & Ullén, F. (2006). Dissociation between melodic and rhythmic processing during piano performance from musical scores. Neuroimage, 30(1), 272.
7. Hutchinson, S., Lee, L. H. L., Gaab, N., & Schlaug, G. (2003). Cerebellar volume of musicians. Cerebral cortex, 13(9), 943-949.
8. See, for instance, these pioneering studies:
9. Wong, P. C., Skoe, E., Russo, N. M., Dees, T., & Kraus, N. (2007). Musical experience shapes human brainstem encoding of linguistic pitch patterns. Nature neuroscience, 10(4), 420-422.
10. Strait, D. L., Kraus, N., Skoe, E., & Ashley, R. (2009). Musical experience and neural efficiency–effects of training on subcortical processing of vocal expressions of emotion. European Journal of Neuroscience, 29(3), 661-668.
11. Strait, D. L., Kraus, N., Skoe, E., & Ashley, R. (2009). Musical experience promotes subcortical efficiency in processing emotional vocal sounds. Annals of the New York Academy of Sciences, 1169(1), 209-213.
12. Imfeld, A., Oechslin, M. S., Meyer, M., Loenneker, T., & Jancke, L. (2009). White matter plasticity in the corticospinal tract of musicians: a diffusion tensor imaging study. Neuroimage, 46(3), 600-607.
13. Patston, L. L., Hogg, S. L., & Tippett, L. J. (2007). Attention in musicians is more bilateral than in non-musicians. Laterality, 12(3), 262-272.
14. Jensen, A. R. (1993). Why is reaction time correlated with psychometric g?. Current Directions in Psychological Science, 2(2), 53-56.

15. See Appendices 'Music Boost for IQ' and Music Boost for Information Processing'.
16. Imfeld, A., Oechslin, M. S., Meyer, M., Loenneker, T., & Jancke, L. (2009). White matter plasticity in the corticospinal tract of musicians: a diffusion tensor imaging study. Neuroimage, 46(3), 600-607.

Appendices:

Music Boost for School Success

Wetter, O. E., Koerner, F., & Schwaninger, A. (2009). Does musical training improve school performance? Instructional Science, 37(4), 365-374.

Fitzpatrick, K. R. (2006). The effect of instrumental music participation and socioeconomic status on Ohio fourth-, sixth-, and ninth-grade proficiency test performance. Journal of Research in Music Education, 54(1), 73-84.

Brodsky, W., & Sulkin, I. (2011). Handclapping songs: a spontaneous platform for child development among 5–10 year old children. Early Child Development and Care, 181(8), 1111-1136.

Hash, P. M. (2011). Effect of Pullout Lessons on the Academic Achievement of Eighth-Grade Band Students. *Update: Applications of Research in Music Education*, *30*(1), 16-22.

Spychiger, M., & Patry, J. L. (1993). Musik macht Schule: Biografie und Ergebnisse eines Schulversuchs mit erweitertem Musikunterricht. Bavaria: Verlag Die Blaue Eule. As quoted in: Spychiger, M. B. (2001). Understanding musical activity and musical learning as sign processes: Toward a semiotic approach to music education. Journal of Aesthetic Education, 35(1), 53-67.

Gardiner, M. F., Fox, A., Knowles, F., & Jeffrey, D. (1996). Learning improved by arts training. *Nature; Nature, 381*(6580), 284.

Chandrasekaran, B., & Kraus, N. (2010). Music, noise-exclusion, and learning. *Music Perception, 27*(4), 297-306.

Music Boost for Memory and Working Memory

Degé, F., Wehrum, S., Stark, R., & Schwarzer, G. (2011). The influence of two years of school music training in secondary school on visual and auditory memory. European Journal of Developmental Psychology, 8(5), 608-623.

Bugos, J. A., Perlstein, W. M., McCrae, C. S., Brophy, T. S., & Bedenbaugh, P. H. (2007). Individualized piano instruction enhances executive functioning and working memory in older adults. Aging and Mental Health, 11(4), 464-471.

Gruhn, W., Galley, N., & Kluth, C. (2003). Do mental speed and musical abilities interact?. Annals of the New York Academy of Sciences, 999(1), 485-496.

Jakobson, L. S., Lewycky, S. T., Kilgour, A. R., & Stoesz, B. M. (2008). Memory for verbal and visual material in highly trained musicians. Music Perception, 26(1), 41-55.

George, E. M., & Coch, D. (2011). Music training and working memory: an ERP study. Neuropsychologia, 49(5), 1083-1094.

Music Boost for Better Thinking Ability (Executive functioning)

Diamond, A., & Lee, K. (2011). Interventions shown to aid executive function development in children 4 to 12 years old. Science, 333(6045), 959-964.

Moreno, S., Bialystok, E., Barac, R., Schellenberg, E. G., Cepeda, N. J., & Chau, T. (2011). Short-term music training enhances verbal intelligence and executive function. Psychological science, 22(11), 1425-1433.

Bialystok, E., & DePape, A. M. (2009). Musical expertise, bilingualism, and executive functioning. Journal of Experimental Psychology: Human Perception and Performance, 35(2), 565.

Music Boost for Learning Ability (concentration, listening, self-regulation)

Winsler, A., Ducenne, L., & Koury, A. (2011). Singing One's Way to Self-Regulation: The Role of Early Music and Movement Curricula and Private Speech. Early Education and Development, 22(2), 274-304.

Chandrasekaran, B., & Kraus, N. (2010). Music, noise-exclusion, and learning. Music Perception, 27(4), 297-306.

Parbery-Clark, A., Skoe, E., & Kraus, N. (2009). Musical experience limits the degradative effects of background noise on the neural processing of sound. The Journal of Neuroscience, 29(45), 14100-14107.

Music Boost for Faster and More Accurate Information processing

Brochard, R., Dufour, A., & Despres, O. (2004). Effect of musical expertise on visuospatial abilities: Evidence from reaction times and mental imagery. Brain and cognition, 54(2), 103-109.

Bugos, J., & Mostafa, W. (2011). Musical Training Enhances Information Processing Speed. Bulletin of the Council for Research in Music Education, 187, 7-18.

Music boost for school readiness

Winsler, A., Ducenne, L., & Koury, A. (2011). Singing One's Way to Self-Regulation: The Role of Early Music and Movement Curricula and Private Speech. Early Education and Development, 22(2), 274-304.

Denham, S. A., Bassett, H. H., Way, E., Mincic, M., Zinsser, K., & Graling, K. (2012). Preschoolers' emotion knowledge: Self-regulatory foundations, and predictions of early school success. Cognition & Emotion, 26(4), 667-679.

Ursache, A., Blair, C., & Raver, C. C. (2012). The Promotion of Self Regulation as a Means of Enhancing School Readiness and Early Achievement in Children at Risk for School Failure. Child Development Perspectives, 6(2), 122-128.

Duncan, G. J., Dowsett, C. J., Claessens, A., Magnuson, K., Huston, A. C., Klebanov, P., ... & Japel, C. (2007). School readiness and later achievement. Developmental psychology, 43(6), 1428.

Music Boost for Self-esteem and Confidence

Rickard, N. S., Appelman, P., James, R., Murphy, F., Gill, A., & Bambrick, C. (2012). Orchestrating life skills: The effect of increased school-based music classes on children's social competence and self-esteem. International Journal of Music Education, 30(1), 3-84.

Hietolahti-Ansten, M., & Kalliopuska, M. (1990). Self-esteem and empathy among children actively involved in music. Perceptual and motor skills, 71(3f), 1364-1366.

Choi, A. N., Lee, M. S., & Lee, J. S. (2010). Group music intervention reduces aggression and improves self-esteem in children with highly aggressive behavior: A pilot controlled trial. Evidence-Based Complementary and Alternative Medicine, 7(2), 213-217.

Dalgas-Pelish, P. (2006). Effects of a self-esteem intervention program on school-age children. Pediatric nursing, 32(4), 341-348.

Kokotsaki, D., & Hallam, S. (2007). Higher education music students' perceptions of the benefits of participative music making. Music Education Research, 9(1), 93-109.

Hallam, S. (2010). The power of music: its impact on the intellectual, social and personal development of children and young people. International Journal of Music Education, 28(3), 269-289.

Michel, D. E. (1971). Self-esteem and academic achievement in black junior high school students: Effects of automated guitar instruction. Bulletin of the Council for Research in Music Education, 24, 15-23.

Warner, L. (1999). Self-esteem: A byproduct of quality classroom music. Childhood Education, 76(1), 19-23.

Welch, G.F., Saunders, J., Papageorgi, I., Joyce, H. and Himonides. E. (2009). An instrument for the assessment of children's attitudes to singing, self and social inclusion. London: Institute of Education, University of London.

Rinta, T., Purves, R., Welch, G., Stadler Elmer, S., & Bissig, R. (2011). Connections between children's feelings of social inclusion and their musical backgrounds. *Journal of Social Inclusion, 2*(2), 34-57.

Music Boost for Emotional Skills

Lobo, Y. B., & Winsler, A. (2006). The effects of a creative dance and movement program on the social competence of Head Start preschoolers. Social Development, 15(3), 501-519.

Lau, W. C. M. (2008). Using singing games in music lessons to enhance young children's social skills. *Asia-Pacific Journal for Arts Education, 6*(2), 1-30.

Choi, A. N., Lee, M. S., & Lee, J. S. (2010). Group music intervention reduces aggression and improves self-esteem in children with highly aggressive behavior: A pilot controlled trial. *Evidence-Based Complementary and Alternative Medicine*, 7(2), 213-217.

Dmitrieva, E. S., Gel'man, V. Y., Zaitseva, K. A., & Orlov, A. M. (2006). Ontogenetic features of the psychophysiological mechanisms of perception of the emotional component of speech in musically gifted children. *Neuroscience and behavioral physiology, 36*(1), 53-62.

Musacchia, G., Sams, M., Skoe, E., & Kraus, N. (2007). Musicians have enhanced subcortical auditory and audiovisual processing of speech and music. *Proceedings of the National Academy of Sciences, 104*(40), 15894-15898.

Thompson, W. F., Schellenberg, E. G., & Husain, G. (2004). Decoding speech prosody: do music lessons help? *Emotion*, *4*(1), 46.

Resnicow, J. E., Salovey, P., & Repp, B. H. (2004). Is recognition of emotion in music performance an aspect of emotional intelligence? *Music Perception*, *22*(1), 145-158.

Lima, C. F., & Castro, S. L. (2011). Speaking to the trained ear: Musical expertise enhances the recognition of emotions in speech prosody. *Emotion*, *11*(5), 1021.

Bhatara, A., Tirovolas, A. K., Duan, L. M., Levy, B., & Levitin, D. J. (2011). Perception of emotional expression in musical performance. *Journal of Experimental Psychology: Human Perception and Performance, 37*(3), 921.

Strait, D. L., Kraus, N., Skoe, E., & Ashley, R. (2009). Musical experience and neural efficiency–effects of training on subcortical processing of vocal expressions of emotion. *European Journal of Neuroscience*, *29*(3), 661-668.

Giomo, C. J. (1993). An experimental study of children's sensitivity to mood in music. *Psychology of Music*, *21*(2), 141-162.

Petrides, K. V., Niven, L., & Mouskounti, T. (2006). The trait emotional intelligence of ballet dancers and musicians. *Psicothema*, *18*(Suplemento), 101-107.

Petrides, K. V., & Furnham, A. (2002). Trait emotional intelligence: Behavioural validation in two studies of emotion recognition and reactivity to mood induction. *European Journal of Personality, 17*(1), 39-57.

Hsieh, S., Hornberger, M., Piguet, O., & Hodges, J. R. (2012). Brain correlates of musical and facial emotion recognition: Evidence from the dementias. *Neuropsychologia, 50*(8), 1814-1822.

Spilka, M. J., Steele, C. J., & Penhune, V. B. (2010). Gesture imitation in musicians and non-musicians. *Experimental brain research, 204*(4), 549-558.

Music Boost for Empathy

Rabinowitch, T. C., Cross, I., & Burnard, P. (2012). Long-term musical group interaction has a positive influence on empathy in children. *Psychology of Music, 40*(2), 131-256.

Brand, E., & Bar-Gil, O. R. A. (2008). Improving interpersonal communication through music. *Proceedings of the 22nd International Society of Music* (pp. 71-79). Bologna:ISME

Kirschner, S., & Tomasello, M. (2010). Joint music making promotes prosocial behavior in 4-year-old children. *Evolution and Human Behavior, 31*(5), 354-364.

Kalliopuska, M., & Ruokonen, I. (1986). Effects of music education on development of holistic empathy. *Perceptual and motor skills, 62*(1), 187-191.

Kalliopuska, M., & Ruokonen, I. (1993). A study with a follow-up of the effects of music education on holistic development of empathy. *Perceptual and motor skills, 76*(1), 131-137.

Hietolahti-Ansten, M., & Kalliopuska, M. (1990). Self-esteem and empathy among children actively involved in music. *Perceptual and motor skills, 71*(3f), 1364-1366.*Music Boost for Creativity*

Chronopoulou, E., & Riga, V. (2012). The Contribution of Music and Movement Activities to Creative Thinking in Pre-School Children. *Creative Education, 3*(2), 196-204.

Root-Bernstein, R. S. (2001). Music, creativity and scientific thinking. *Leonardo, 34*(1), 63-68.

Kalmar, M. (1982). The effects of music education based on Kodaly's directives in nursery school children: From a psychologist's point of view. *Psychology of Music*, 63-68.

Music Boost for Babies

Gerry, D., Unrau, A., & Trainor, L. J. (2012). Active music classes in infancy enhance musical, communicative and social development. *Developmental Science, 15*(3), 398-407.

Zentner, M., & Eerola, T. (2010). Rhythmic engagement with music in infancy. *Proceedings of the National Academy of Sciences, 107*(13), 5768-5773.

Tafuri, J. (2008). Infant Musicality - New Research for Educators and Parents. Ashgate.

Trainor, L. J., Wu, L., & Tsang, C. D. (2004). Long term memory for music: Infants remember tempo and timbre. Developmental Science, 7(3), 289-296.

Gordon, E. E. (2011). Early childhood music abuse: Misdeeds and Neglect. Visions of Research in Music Education, 17,1-11.

Music and the brain's language networks

Jäncke, L. (2012). The relationship between music and language. *Frontiers in Psychology, 3*, 123.

Patel, A. D. (2011). Language, music, and the brain: a resource-sharing framework. In P. Rebuschat, M. Rohmeier, J. A. Hawkins, & I. Cross, Language and Music as Cognitive Systems (pp. 1-42). Oxford: Oxford University Press.

Koelsch, S., Gunter, T. C., Cramon, D. Y. V., Zysset, S., Lohmann, G., & Friederici, A. D. (2002). Bach speaks: A cortical" language-network" serves the processing of music. *Neuroimage, 17*(2), 956-966.

Koelsch, S. (2005). Neural substrates of processing syntax and semantics in music. *Current opinion in neurobiology, 15*(2), 207-212.
Koelsch, S., Gunter, T. C., Cramon, D. Y. V., Zysset, S., Lohmann, G., & Friederici, A. D. (2002). Bach speaks: A cortical" language-network" serves the processing of music. *Neuroimage, 17*(2), 956-966.

Patel, A. D. (2003). Language, music, syntax and the brain. *Nature neuroscience, 6*(7), 674-681.

Fedorenko, E., Patel, A., Casasanto, D., Winawer, J., & Gibson, E. (2009). Structural integration in language and music: Evidence for a shared system. *Memory & cognition, 37*(1), 1-9.

Schön, D., Gordon, R., Campagne, A., Magne, C., Astésano, C., Anton, J. L., & Besson, M. (2010). Similar cerebral networks in language, music and song perception. *Neuroimage*, *51*(1), 450-461.

Music Boost for IQ

Schellenberg, E. G. (2004). Music lessons enhance IQ. *Psychological Science*, *15*(8), 511-514.

Moreno, S., Bialystok, E., Barac, R., Schellenberg, E. G., Cepeda, N. J., & Chau, T. (2011). Short-term music training enhances verbal intelligence and executive function. *Psychological science*, *22*(11), 1425-1433.

Gruhn, W., Galley, N., & Kluth, C. (2003). Do mental speed and musical abilities interact? *Annals of the New York Academy of Sciences*, *999*(1), 485-496.

Lynn, R., Graham Wilson, R., & Gault, A. (1989). Simple musical tests as measures of Spearman's g. *Personality and Individual Differences*, *10*(1), 25-28.

Ullén, F., Forsman, L., Blom, Ö., Karabanov, A., & Madison, G. (2008). Intelligence and variability in a simple timing task share neural substrates in the prefrontal white matter. *The Journal of Neuroscience*, *28*(16), 4238-4243.

Various links between music skills and intelligence

Schlaug, G., Jäncke, L., Huang, Y., Staiger, J. F., & Steinmetz, H. (1995). Increased corpus callosum size in musicians. *Neuropsychologia*, *33*(8), 1047-1055.

Luders, E., Narr, K. L., Bilder, R. M., Thompson, P. M., Szeszko, P. R., Hamilton, L., & Toga, A. W. (2007). Positive correlations between corpus callosum thickness and intelligence. *Neuroimage*, *37*(4), 1457-1464.

Conway, C. M., Pisoni, D. B., & Kronenberger, W. G. (2009). The Importance of Sound for Cognitive Sequencing Abilities: The Auditory Scaffolding Hypothesis. *Current directions in psychological science*, *18*(5), 275-279.

Rammsayer, T. H., & Brandler, S. (2007). Performance on temporal information processing as an index of general intelligence. *Intelligence*, *35*(2), 123-139.

Critical Age 0-7

Costa-Giomi, E. (2004). Effects of three years of piano instruction on children's academic achievement, school performance and self-esteem. Psychology of Music, 32(2), 139-152.

Rickard, N. S., Bambrick, C. J., & Gill, A. (2012). Absence of widespread psychosocial and cognitive effects of school-based music instruction in 10–13-year-old students. International Journal of Music Education, 30(1), 57-78

Steele, C. J., Bailey, J. A., Zatorre, R. J., & Penhune, V. B. (2013). Early musical training and white-matter plasticity in the corpus callosum: Evidence for a sensitive period. The Journal of Neuroscience, 33(3), 1282-1290.

Watanabe, D., Savion-Lemieux, T., & Penhune, V. B. (2007). The effect of early musical training on adult motor performance: evidence for a sensitive period in motor learning. *Experimental Brain Research, 176*(2), 332-340.

Penhune, V. B. (2011). Sensitive periods in human development: Evidence from musical training. *Cortex*, *47*(9), 1126-1137.

Bailey, J., & Penhune, V. B. (2012). A sensitive period for musical training: contributions of age of onset and cognitive abilities. *Annals of the New York Academy of Sciences, 1252*(1), 163-170.

Moffitt, T. E., Caspi, A., Harkness, A. R., & Silva, P. A. (2006). The Natural History of Change to Intellectual Performance: Who Changes? How Much? Is it Meaningful? Journal of Child Psychology and Psychiatry, 34(4), 455-506.

Abrahamsson, N., & Hyltenstam, K. (2009). Age of onset and nativelikeness in a second language: Listener perception versus linguistic scrutiny. *Language Learning, 59*(2), 249-306.

Huttenlocher, P. R. (1999). Dendritic and synaptic development in human cerebral cortex: time course and critical periods. *Developmental Neuropsychology, 16*(3), 347-349.

Chechik, G., Meilijson, I., & Ruppin, E. (1998). Synaptic pruning in development: A computational account. *Neural Computation, 10*(7), 1759-1777.

Music Boost for Language Skills

Moreno, S., Marques, C., Santos, A., Santos, M., & Besson, M. (2009). Musical training influences linguistic abilities in 8-year-old children: more evidence for brain plasticity. *Cerebral Cortex, 19*(3), 712-723

Moreno, S., Bialystok, E., Barac, R., Schellenberg, E. G., Cepeda, N. J., & Chau, T. (2011). Short-term music training enhances verbal intelligence and executive function. *Psychological science, 22*(11), 1425-1433.

Piro, J. M., & Ortiz, C. (2009). The effect of piano lessons on the vocabulary and verbal sequencing skills of primary grade students. *Psychology of Music, 37*(3), 325-347.

Hurwitz, I., Wolff, P. H., Bortnick, B. D., & Kokas, K. (1975). Nonmusicol Effects of the Kodaly Music Curriculum in Primary Grade Children. *Journal of learning Disabilities, 8*(3), 167-174.

Marin, M. M. (2009). Effects of early musical training on musical and linguistic syntactic abilities. *Annals of the New York Academy of Sciences, 1169*(1), 187-190.

Schön, D., Magne, C., & Besson, M. (2004). The music of speech: Music training facilitates pitch processing in both music and language. *Psychophysiology, 41*(3), 341-349.

Magne, C., Schön, D., & Besson, M. (2006). Musician children detect pitch violations in both music and language better than nonmusician children: behavioral and electrophysiological approaches. *Journal of Cognitive Neuroscience, 18*(2), 199-211.

Besson, M., Schön, D., Moreno, S., Santos, A., & Magne, C. (2007). Influence of musical expertise and musical training on pitch processing in music and language. *Restorative Neurology and Neuroscience, 25*(3), 399-410.

Schön, D., & François, C. (2011). Musical expertise and statistical learning of musical and linguistic structures. Frontiers in Psychology, 2,167.

Jentschke, S., & Koelsch, S. (2009). Musical training modulates the development of syntax processing in children. *Neuroimage, 47*(2), 735-744.

Francois, C., & Schön, D. (2011). Musical expertise boosts implicit learning of both musical and linguistic structures. *Cerebral Cortex, 21*(10), 2357-2365.

Schön, D., Boyer, M., Moreno, S., Besson, M., Peretz, I., & Kolinsky, R. (2008). Songs as an aid for language acquisition. *Cognition, 106*(2), 975-983.

After Eight: Benefits for pre-and post-teens

Degé, F., Wehrum, S., Stark, R., & Schwarzer, G. (2011). The influence of two years of school music training in secondary school on visual and auditory memory. *European Journal of Developmental Psychology, 8*(5), 608-623.

Brodsky, W., & Sulkin, I. (2011). Handclapping songs: a spontaneous platform for child development among 5–10 year old children. Early Child Development and Care, 181(8), 1111-1136.

Kokotsaki, D., & Hallam, S. (2007). Higher education music students' perceptions of the benefits of participative music making. *Music Education Research, 9*(1), 93-109.

Music Boost for the Elderly

Wan, C. Y., & Schlaug, G. (2010). Music making as a tool for promoting brain plasticity across the life span. *The Neuroscientist, 16*(5), 566-577.

Hanna-Pladdy, B., & MacKay, A. (2011). The relation between instrumental musical activity and cognitive aging. Neuropsychology, 25(3), 378.

Varvarigou, M., Creech, A., Hallam, S., & McQueen, H. (2012). Benefits experienced by older people in group music-making activities. *Journal of Applied Arts & Health, 3*(2), 133-148.

Baker, K. (2011, April 20). Musical Activity May Improve Cognitive Aging. Retrieved from EMORY University: http://shared.web.emory.edu/emory/news/releases/2011/04/musical-activity-may-improve-cognitive-aging.html#.UKPZSRxlbyA

Hanna-Pladdy, B., & Gajewski, B. (2012). Recent and past musical activity predicts cognitive aging variability: direct comparison with general lifestyle activities. *Frontiers in Human Neuroscience, 6*, 198.

Kraus, N. (2011). Musical training gives edge in auditory processing. The Hearing Journal, 64(2), 10.

Bugos, J. A., Perlstein, W. M., McCrae, C. S., Brophy, T. S., & Bedenbaugh, P. H. (2007). Individualized piano instruction enhances executive functioning and working memory in older adults. Aging and Mental Health, 11(4), 464-471.

We Are All Born Musical: The Musicality of Newborn Babies

Winkler, I., Háden, G. P., Ladinig, O., Sziller, I., & Honing, H. (2009). Newborn infants detect the beat in music. Proceedings of the National Academy of Sciences, 106(7), 2468-2471.

Perani, D., Saccuman, M. C., Scifo, P., Spada, D., Andreolli, G., Rovelli, R., & Koelsch, S. (2010). Functional specializations for music processing in the human newborn brain. Proceedings of the National Academy of Sciences, 107(10), 4758-4763.

Malloch, S. N. (2000). Mothers and infants and communicative musicality. Musicae scientiae, 3(1 suppl), 29-57.

Nakata, T., & Trehub, S. E. (2004). Infants' responsiveness to maternal speech and singing. Infant Behavior and Development, 27(4), 455-464.

Trainor, L. J., & Zacharias, C. A. (1998). Infants prefer higher-pitched singing. Infant Behavior and Development, 21(4), 799-805.

Masataka, N. (2005). Preference for consonance over dissonance by hearing newborns of deaf parents and of hearing parents. Developmental science, 9(1), 46-50.

Perani, D. (2012). Functional and structural connectivity for language and music processing at birth. Rendiconti Lincei, 22(3), 1-10.

Brandt, A., Gebrian, M., & Slevc, L. R. (2012). Music and early language acquisition. Frontiers in Psychology, 3, 327.

Hannon, E. E., & Trehub, S. E. (2005). Tuning in to musical rhythms: Infants learn more readily than adults. Proceedings of the National Academy of Sciences of the United States of America, 102(35), 12639-12643.

Trainor, L. J., Tsang, C. D., & Cheung, V. H. (2002). Preference for sensory consonance in 2-and 4-month-old infants. *Music Perception, 20*(2), 187-194.

Zentner, M., & Eerola, T. (2010). Rhythmic engagement with music in infancy. *Proceedings of the National Academy of Sciences, 107*(13), 5768-5773.

Music Boost for the Brain (for a more comprehensive list, see the Boxes 1-3 and their Reference pages)

Schlaug, G., Jäncke, L., Huang, Y., Staiger, J. F., & Steinmetz, H. (1995). Increased corpus callosum size in musicians. Neuropsychologia, 33(8), 1047-1055.

Schlaug, G., Forgeard, M., Zhu, L., Norton, A., Norton, A., & Winner, E. (2009). Training induced Neuroplasticity in Young Children. Annals of the New York Academy of Sciences, 1169(1), 205-208.

Gaser, C., & Schlaug, G. (2003). Brain structures differ between musicians and non-musicians. The Journal of Neuroscience, 23(27), 9240-9245.

Schlaug, G., Norton, A., Overy, K., & Winner, E. (2005). Effects of music training on the child's brain and cognitive development. *Annals of the New York Academy of Sciences, 1060*(1), 219-230.

Paradiso, S., Andreasen, N. C., O'Leary, D. S., Arndt, S., & Robinson, R. G. (1997). Cerebellar size and cognition: correlations with IQ, verbal memory and motor dexterity. *Neuropsychiatry, neuropsychology, and behavioral neurology, 10*(1), 1.

Music Boost for Spatial-visual and Spatial-temporal Intelligence

Rauscher, F. H., & Zupan, M. A. (2000). Classroom keyboard instruction improves kindergarten children's spatial-temporal performance: A field experiment. Early Childhood Research Quarterly, 15(2), 215-228.

Hetland, L. (2000). Learning to make music enhances spatial reasoning. Journal of Aesthetic Education, 34(3/4), 179-238.

Zafranas, N. (2004). Piano keyboard training and the spatial–temporal development of young children attending kindergarten classes in Greece. Early Child Development and Care, 174(2), 199-211.

Rauscher, F. H., Shaw, G. L., Levine, L. J., Wright, E. L., Dennis, W. R., & Newcomb, R. L. (1997). Music training causes long-term enhancement of preschool children's spatial-temporal reasoning. Neurological research, 19(1), 2-8.

Rauscher, F. H., & Zupan, M. A. (2000). Classroom keyboard instruction improves kindergarten children's spatial-temporal performance: A field experiment. Early Childhood Research Quarterly, 15(2), 215-228.

Costa-Giomi, E. (1999). The effects of three years of piano instruction on children's cognitive development. Journal of Research in Music Education, 47(3), 198-212.

Brochard, R., Dufour, A., & Despres, O. (2004). Effect of musical expertise on visuospatial abilities: Evidence from reaction times and mental imagery. *Brain and cognition, 54*(2), 103-109.

Jakobson, L. S., Lewycky, S. T., Kilgour, A. R., & Stoesz, B. M. (2008). Memory for verbal and visual material in highly trained musicians. *Music Perception, 26*(1), 41-55.

Pietsch, S., & Jansen, P. (2011). Different mental rotation performance in students of music, sport and education. *Learning and Individual Differences, 22*(1), 159-163.

Patston, L. L., Kirk, I. J., Rolfe, M. H. S., Corballis, M. C., & Tippett, L. J. (2007). The unusual symmetry of musicians: Musicians have equilateral interhemispheric transfer for visual information. *Neuropsychologia, 45*(9), 2059-2065.

Rauscher, F. H. (2003). Effects of piano, rhythm, and singing instruction on the spatial reasoning of at-risk children. *Proceedings of the European Society for the Cognitive Sciences of Music,* Hannover, Germany: Hannover University Press.

Rauscher, F. H., & Hinton, S. C. (2011). Music instruction and its diverse extra-musical benefits. *Music Perception, 29*(2), 215-226.

Gaser, C., & Schlaug, G. (2003). Brain structures differ between musicians and non-musicians. The Journal of Neuroscience, 23(27), 9240-9245. "Music training enhances gray matter volume in the superior parietal region that is associated with visuospatial abilities."

Music Boost for Reading Skills

Anvari, S. H., Trainor, L. J., Woodside, J., & Levy, B. A. (2002). Relations among musical skills, phonological processing, and early reading ability in preschool children. Journal of experimental child psychology, 83(2), 111-130.

Barwick, J., Valentine, E., West, R., & Wilding, J. (1989). Relations between reading and musical abilities. British Journal of Educational Psychology, 59(2), 253-257.

Lamb, S. J., & Gregory, A. H. (1993). The relationship between music and reading in beginning readers. Educational Psychology, 13(1), 19-27.

Mackenzie-Beck, Janet (2003). Is it possible to predict students' ability to develop skills in practical phonetics? In: Proceedings of the 15th International Congress of Phonetic Sciences. Universitat AutÒnoma de Barcelona, 2833 -2836.

Dankovicová, J., House, J., Crooks, A., & Jones, K. (2007). The relationship between musical skills, music training, and intonation analysis skills. Language and Speech, 50(2), 177-225.

François, C., Chobert, J., Besson, M., & Schön, D. (2012). Music training for the development of speech segmentation. Cerebral Cortex, 22(7), 1473 - 1716.

Murphy, C. F. B., & Schochat, E. (2011). Effect of nonlinguistic auditory training on phonological and reading skills. Folia Phoniatrica et Logopaedica, 63(3), 147-153.

Movsesian, E. A. (1967). The influence of teaching music reading skills on the development of basic reading skills in the primary grades. Unpublished Doctoral dissertation, University of Southern California, Los Angeles, United States.

Nicholson, D. L. (1971). *Music as an aid to learning.* Unpublished Doctoral dissertation, New York University, New York, United States.

Klemish, J. (1973). A review of recent research in elementary music education. *Bulletin of the Council for Research in Music Education, 34*, 23-40.

Hurwitz, I., Wolff, P. H., Bortnick, B. D., & Kokas, K. (1975). Nonmusicol Effects of the Kodaly Music Curriculum in Primary Grade Children. *Journal of learning Disabilities, 8*(3), 167-174.

Butzlaff, R. (2000). Can music be used to teach reading? *Journal of Aesthetic Education, 34*(3/4), 167-178.

Gromko, J. E. (2005). The effect of music instruction on phonemic awareness in beginning readers. *Journal of Research in Music Education, 53*(3), 199-209.

Douglas, S., & Willatts, P. (2005). The relationship between musical ability and literacy skills. *Journal of Research in Reading, 17*(2), 99-107.

Bhide, A., Power, A., & Goswami, U. (2013). A Rhythmic Musical

Intervention for Poor Readers: A Comparison of Efficacy With a Letter Based Intervention. Mind, Brain, and Education, 7(2), 113-123.

Moritz, C., Yampolsky, S., Papadelis, G., Thomson, J., & Wolf, M. (2012). Links between early rhythm skills, musical training, and phonological awareness. Reading and Writing, 1-31.

Music Boost for Mathematics

Harris, M. A. (2007). Differences in mathematics scores between students who receive traditional Montessori instruction and students who receive music enriched Montessori instruction. Journal for Learning through the Arts, 3(1), 1-50.

Hoch, L., & Tillmann, B. (2012). Shared structural and temporal integration resources for music and arithmetic processing. Acta psychologica, 140(3), 230-235. See also Chapter 21.

Kelstrom, J. M. (1998). The untapped power of music: Its role in the curriculum and its effect on academic achievement. NASSP Bulletin, 82(597), 34-43.

Graziano, A. B., Peterson, M., & Shaw, G. L. (1999). Enhanced learning of proportional math through music training and spatial-temporal training. Neurological Research, 21(2), 139.

Music Training Compared with Other Activities

Vs. all other activities, including reading, crossword puzzles and exercise. Hanna-Pladdy, B., & Gajewski, B. (2012). Recent and past musical activity predicts cognitive aging variability: direct comparison with general lifestyle activities. *Frontiers in Human Neuroscience, 6*, 198.

Vs. Educational TV programmes. Register, Dena M. (2003).The Effects of Live Music Groups Versus an Educational Children's Television Program on the Emergent Literacy of Young Children. *Electronic Theses, Treatises and Dissertations.* Paper 1903.

Vs. Science training. Roden, I., Grube, D., Bongard, S., & Kreutz, G. (2013). Does music
training enhance working memory performance? Findings from a quasi-experimental longitudinal study. Psychology of Music.

Vs. Visual art training. Moreno, S., Bialystok, E., Barac, R., Schellenberg, E. G., Cepeda, N. J., & Chau, T. (2011). Short-term music training enhances verbal intelligence and executive function. Psychological science, 22(11), 1425-1433.

Vs. Training in painting. Moreno, S., Marques, C., Santos, A., Santos, M., & Besson, M. (2009). Musical training influences linguistic abilities in 8-year-old children: more evidence for brain plasticity. *Cerebral Cortex, 19*(3), 712-723

Vs. Drama. Schellenberg, E. G. (2004). Music lessons enhance IQ. *Psychological Science, 15*(8), 511-514.

Vs. Free play to classical music. Gerry, D., Unrau, A., & Trainor, L. J. (2012). Active music classes in infancy enhance musical, communicative and social development. *Developmental Science, 15*(3), 398-407.

Vs. Musical but non-educational games. Moyeda, I., Gómez, I. C., & Flores, M. (2006). Implementing a musical program to promote preschool children's vocabulary development. *Early Childhood Research & Practice, 8*(1).

Vs. Play therapy. Hendon, C., & Bohon, L. M. (2008). Hospitalized children's mood differences during play and music therapy. *Child: care, health and development, 34*(2), 141-144.

Vs. Playing. Kim, J., Wigram, T., & Gold, C. (2008). The effects of improvisational music therapy on joint attention behaviors in autistic children: a randomized controlled study. *Journal of autism and developmental disorders, 38*(9), 1758-1766. Vs Play

Vs. Playing. Kim, J., Wigram, T., & Gold, C. (2009). Emotional, motivational and interpersonal responsiveness of children with autism in improvisational music therapy. Autism, 13(4), 389-409. Vs play

Vs. Listening to Music. Dunbar, R. I., Kaskatis, K., MacDonald, I., & Barra, V. (2012). Performance of music elevates pain threshold and positive affect: Implications for the evolutionary function of music. *Evolutionary psychology: an international journal of evolutionary approaches to psychology and behavior, 10*(4), 688.

Vs. Computer Training. Graziano, A. B., Peterson, M., & Shaw, G. L. (1999). Enhanced learning of proportional math through music training and spatial-temporal training. *Neurological Research, 21*(2), 139.

Vs. Other creative activities. Toyoshima, K., Fukui, H., & Kuda, K. (2011). Piano playing reduces stress more than other creative art activities. *International Journal of Music Education, 29*(3), 257-263.

Vs. Other youth activities. Larson, R. (1994). Youth organizations, hobbies, and sports as developmental contexts. *Adolescence in context: The interplay of family, school, peers, and work in adjustment*, 46-65.

Vs. Other extracurricular activities. Eccles, J. S., & Barber, B. L. (1999). Student Council, Volunteering, Basketball, or Marching Band What Kind of Extracurricular Involvement Matters? *Journal of adolescent research*, *14*(1), 10-43.

Music Skills as a Remedy for Learning Disabilities

Njiokiktjien, C., De Sonneville, L., & Vaal, J. (1994). Callosal size in children with learning disabilities. Behavioural brain research, 64(1), 213-218.

Hynd, G. W., Semrud-Clikeman, M., Lorys, A. R., Novey, E. S., Eliopulos, D., & Lyytinen, H. (1991). Corpus callosum morphology in attention deficit-hyperactivity disorder: morphometric analysis of MRI. Journal of Learning Disabilities, 24(3), 141-146.

Badaruddin, D. H., Andrews, G. L., Bölte, S., Schilmoeller, K. J., Schilmoeller, G., Paul, L. K., & Brown, W. S. (2007). Social and behavioral problems of children with agenesis of the corpus callosum. Child Psychiatry & Human Development, 38(4), 287-302.

Waber, D. P., Weiler, M. D., Bellinger, D. C., Marcus, D. J., Forbes, P. W., Wypij, D., & Wolff, P. H. (2000). Diminished motor timing control in children referred for diagnosis of learning problems. *Developmental neuropsychology*, *17*(2), 181-197.

Loui, P., Kroog, K., Zuk, J., Winner, E., & Schlaug, G. (2011). Relating pitch awareness to phonemic awareness in children: implications for tone-deafness and dyslexia. *Frontiers in psychology, 2*,111.

Santos, A., Joly-Pottuz, B., Moreno, S., Habib, M., & Besson, M. (2007). Behavioural and event-related potentials evidence for pitch discrimination deficits in dyslexic children: Improvement after intensive phonic intervention. *Neuropsychologia, 45*(5), 1080-1090.

Krommyda, M., Papadelis, G., Chatzikallia, K., Pastiadis, K., & Kardaras, P. (2008) Does awareness of musical structure relate to general cognitive and literacy profile in children with learning dis-abilities? Conference on Interdisciplinary Musicology (pp. 1-10). Thessaloniki: Aristotle University of Thessaloniki.

Music Training Engages the Whole Brain

Miranda, E. R., & Overy, K. (2009). Preface: The Neuroscience of Music, *Contemporary Music Review, 28*(3), 247-250.
Altenmüller, E. O. (2001). How many music centers are in the brain? *Annals of the New York Academy of Sciences, 930*(1), 273-280.

Alluri, V., Toiviainen, P., Jääskeläinen, I. P., Glerean, E., Sams, M., & Brattico, E. (2011). Large-scale brain networks emerge from dynamic processing of musical timbre, key and rhythm. *NeuroImage, 59*(4), 3677-3689.

Gaser, C., & Schlaug, G. (2003). Brain structures differ between musicians and non-musicians. *The Journal of Neuroscience, 23*(27), 9240-9245.

Gosselin, N., Peretz, I., Johnsen, E., & Adolphs, R. (2007). Amygdala damage impairs emotion recognition from music. *Neuropsychologia, 45*(2), 236-244.

Koelsch, S., Fritz, T., & Schlaug, G. (2008). Amygdala activity can be modulated by unexpected chord functions during music listening. *Neuroreport, 19*(18), 1815-1819.

Munte, T. F., Altenmuller, E., & Jancke, L. (2002). The musician's brain as a model of neuroplasticity. *Nature Reviews Neuroscience, 3*(6), 473-477.

Grahn, J. A. (2009). The role of the basal ganglia in beat perception. *Annals of the New York Academy of Sciences, 1169*(1), 35-45.

Grahn, J. A., & Brett, M. (2007). Rhythm and beat perception in motor areas of the brain. *Journal of Cognitive Neuroscience, 19*(5), 893-906.

Zimmerman, E., & Lahav, A. (2012). The multisensory brain and its ability to learn music. *Annals of the New York Academy of Sciences, 1252*(1), 179-184.

Patston, L. L., Corballis, M. C., Hogg, S. L., & Tippett, L. J. (2006). The Neglect of Musicians Line Bisection Reveals an Opposite Bias. *Psychological Science, 17*(12), 1029-1031.

Patston, L. L., Hogg, S. L., & Tippett, L. J. (2007). Attention in musicians is more bilateral than in non-musicians. *Laterality, 12*(3), 262-272.

Patston, L. L., Kirk, I. J., Rolfe, M. H. S., Corballis, M. C., & Tippett, L. J. (2007). The unusual symmetry of musicians: Musicians have equilateral interhemispheric transfer for visual information. *Neuropsychologia, 45*(9), 2059-2065.

Music Boost for Movement skills (Bodily-kinesthetic intelligence)

Grahn, J. A., & Brett, M. (2007). Rhythm and beat perception in motor areas of the brain. *Journal of Cognitive Neuroscience, 19*(5), 893-906.

Derri, V., Tsapakidou, A., Zachopoulou, E., & Kioumourtzoglou, E. (2001). Effect of a music and movement programme on development of locomotor skills by children 4 to 6 years of age. *European journal of physical education, 6*(1), 16-25.

Brown, J., Sherrill, C., & Gench, B. (1981). EFFECTS OF AN INTEGRATED PHYSICAL EDUCATION/MUSIC PROGRAM IN CHANGING EARLY CHILDHOOD PERCEPTUAL-MOTOR PERFORMANCE.*** *Perceptual and Motor Skills, 53*(1), 151-154.

Zachopoulou, E., Tsapakidou, A., & Derri, V. (2004). The effects of a developmentally appropriate music and movement program on motor performance. *Early Childhood Research Quarterly, 19*(4), 631-642.

Klein, S. A., & Winkelstein, M. L. (1996). Enhancing pediatric health care with music. Journal of pediatric health care, 10(2), 74-81.

Early Music Training: a Gift for Life

Hanna-Pladdy, D. (2011, April 20). Childhood Music Lessons May Provide Lifelong Boost in Brain Functioning. Retrieved from American Psychological Association: http://www.apa.org/news/press/releases/2011/04/music-lessons.aspx

Moffitt, T. E., Arseneault, L., Belsky, D., Dickson, N., Hancox, R. J., Harrington, H., & Caspi, A. (2011). A gradient of childhood self-control predicts health, wealth, and public safety. Proceedings of the National Academy of Sciences, 108(7), 2693-2698.

Hanna-Pladdy, B., & Gajewski, B. (2012). Recent and past musical activity predicts cognitive aging variability: direct comparison with general lifestyle activities. Frontiers in Human Neuroscience, 6, 198.

Kraus, N. (2011). Musical training gives edge in auditory processing. The Hearing Journal, 64(2), 10.

Casey, B. J., Somerville, L. H., Gotlib, I. H., Ayduk, O., Franklin, N. T., Askren, M. K., & Shoda, Y. (2011). Behavioral and neural correlates of delay of gratification 40 years later. Proceedings of the National Academy of Sciences, 108(36), 14998-15003.

Benefits of a higher IQ

Batty, G. D., Deary, I. J., & Gottfredson, L. S. (2007). Premorbid (early life) IQ and later mortality risk: systematic review. *Annals of epidemiology, 17*(4), 278-288.

Batty, G. D., Wennerstad, K. M., Smith, G. D., Gunnell, D., Deary, I. J., Tynelius, P., & Rasmussen, F. (2009). IQ in early adulthood and mortality by middle age: cohort study of 1 million Swedish men. Epidemiology, 20(1), 100-109.

Gottfredson, L. S., & Deary, I. J. (2004). Intelligence predicts health and longevity, but why? *Current Directions in Psychological Science, 13*(1), 1-4.

Zagorsky, J. L. (2007). Do you have to be smart to be rich? The impact of IQ on wealth, income and financial distress. *Intelligence, 35*(5), 489-501.

Chicken and egg

Norton, A., Winner, E., Cronin, K., Overy, K., Lee, D. J., & Schlaug, G. (2005). Are there pre-existing neural, cognitive, or motoric markers for musical ability? Brain and cognition, 59(2), 124-134

Schlaug, G., Forgeard, M., Zhu, L., Norton, A., Norton, A., & Winner, E. (2009). Training induced Neuroplasticity in Young Children. Annals of the New York Academy of Sciences, 1169(1), 205-208.

Haimson, J., Swain, D., & Winner, E. (2011). Do Mathematicians Have Above Average Musical Skill? Music Perception, 29(2), 203-213.

Conway, C. M., Pisoni, D. B., & Kronenberger, W. G. (2009). The importance of sound for cognitive sequencing abilities the auditory scaffolding hypothesis. Current Directions in Psychological Science, 18(5), 275-279.

Learning disabilities remedy

First There Was Sound: The importance of auditory abilities to general cognitive functioning

Conway, C. M., Pisoni, D. B., & Kronenberger, W. G. (2009). The Importance of Sound for Cognitive Sequencing Abilities: The Auditory Scaffolding Hypothesis. Current directions in psychological science, 18(5), 275-279.

Dmitrieva, E. S., Gel'man, V. Y., Zaitseva, K. A., & Lan'ko, S. V. (2008). Age-related features of the interaction of learning success and characteristics of auditory operative memory. Neuroscience and behavioral physiology, 38(4), 393-398.

Pantev, C., Oostenveld, R., Engelien, A., Ross, B., Roberts, L. E., & Hoke, M. (1998). Increased auditory cortical representation in musicians. Nature, 392(6678), 811-814.

Musacchia, G., Strait, D., & Kraus, N. (2008). Relationships between behavior, brainstem and cortical encoding of seen and heard speech in musicians and non-musicians. Hearing research, 241(1-2), 34.

Kraus, N. (2011). Musical training gives edge in auditory processing. The Hearing Journal, 64(2), 10.

Rabbitt, P. (1991). Mild hearing loss can cause apparent memory failures which increase with age and reduce with IQ. Acta Oto-laryngologica, 111(S476), 167-176.

Parent wellbeing

Nicholson, J. M., Berthelsen, D., Abad, V., Williams, K., & Bradley, J. (2008). Impact of music therapy to promote positive parenting and child development. Journal of Health Psychology, 13(2), 226-238.

Walworth, D. D. (2007). The Effect of Developmental Music Groups for Parents and Premature Or Typical Infants Under Two Years On Parental responsiveness And Infant Social Development. Ann Arbor: ProQuest LCC.

Mozart Myth

Thompson, W. F., Schellenberg, E. G., & Husain, G. (2001). Arousal, mood, and the Mozart effect. Psychological Science, 12(3), 248-251. Steele, K. M., Bass, K. E., & Crook, M. D. (1999). The mystery of the Mozart effect: Failure to replicate. *Psychological Science, 10*(4), 366-369.

McKelvie, P., & Low, J. (2002). Listening to Mozart does not improve children's spatial ability: Final curtains for the Mozart effect. *British Journal of Developmental Psychology, 20*(2), 241-258.

McCutcheon, L. E. (2000). Another failure to generalize the Mozart effect.Psychological reports, 87(1), 325-330.

Schellenberg, E. G. (2005). Music and cognitive abilities. *Current Directions in Psychological Science, 14*(6), 317-320.

Schellenberg, E. G., & Hallam, S. (2005). Music Listening and Cognitive Abilities in 10 and 11 Year Olds: The Blur Effect. *Annals of the New York Academy of Sciences, 1060*(1), 202-209.

Schellenberg, E. G., Nakata, T., Hunter, P. G., & Tamoto, S. (2007). Exposure to music and cognitive performance: Tests of children and adults. *Psychology of Music, 35*(1), 5-19.

Rauscher, F. (2002). Mozart and the mind:Factual and fictional effects of musical enrichment. In J. M. Aronson, *Improving Academic Achievement: Impact of Psychological Factors on Education* (pp. 267-278). New York: Emerald Group Publishing.

Nantais, K. M., & Schellenberg, E. G. (1999). The Mozart effect: An artifact of preference. *Psychological Science, 10*(4), 370-373.
1. Husain, G., Thompson, W. F., & Schellenberg, E. G. (2002). Effects of musical tempo and mode on arousal, mood, and spatial abilities. *Music Perception, 20*(2), 151-171.

Pietschnig, J., Voracek, M., & Formann, A. K. (2010). Mozart effect–Shmozart effect: A meta-analysis. Intelligence, 38(3), 314-323.

Songs as learning tools

Medina, S. L. (1990).The Effects of Music upon Second Language Vocabulary Acquisition. San Francisco.

Schön, D., Boyer, M., Moreno, S., Besson, M., Peretz, I., & Kolinsky, R. (2008). Songs as an aid for language acquisition. Cognition, 106(2), 975-983.

Šišková, D. (2008). Teaching Vocabulary through Music. Unpublished Diploma's Thesis, Masaryk University,Brno, Czech Republic.

Campabello, N., De Carlo, M. J., O'Neil, J., & Vacek, M. J. (2002). Music Enhances Learning. Unpublished Master's Theses, Chicago, Saint Xavier University.

Recommended reading (in alphabetical order)

A music learning theory for newborn and young children by Edwin E. Gordon. Published in 2003 by Gia Publications. Exactly what it says on the title - a thought-provoking and well-argumented theory on how music is learned in the early years, with highly relevant practical implications for music educators as well as parents wishing to understand their child's musical development.

The power of music: its impact on the intellectual, social and personal development of children and young people by Susan Hallam. Published in 2010 in the International Journal of Music Education. A comprehensive yet concise academic paper that reviews the research on various extra-musical benefits of music training, from the academic to the social. An important as well as a quick read for any parent wishing to further their understanding on the benefits of music training.

The Developmental Psychology of Music by David J. Hargreaves. Published in 1986 by Cambridge University Press. This is the definitive book on investigating children's musical development from the point of view of Psychology and it is as relevant today as ever. This book set the way for a whole new area of research, investigating music learning not as a separate phenomenon but as one that is an essential part of child development.

What do young children learn in and through music? by David J.

Hargreaves. Lecture notes for the keynote speech at the MERYC EU (European Network of Music Educators and Researchers of Young Children) conference in Hague in July 2013. These lecture notes summarize the core aspects of the various aspects and benefits of music learning for children and is thus a very quick but important read for the time-challenged parent. These notes also feature the first academic reference to my book in its unpublished manuscript form. These lecture notes are freely available at http://www.meryc.eu/Documents/Conference2013/MERYC2013%20The%20Hague%20Keynote%20Prof%20David%20Hargreaves.pdf

How Popular Musicians Learn: A Way Ahead for Music Education by Lucy Green. Published in 2002 by Ashgate. A trailbrazing read for anyone wishing to understand the processses of learning to play and create popular music - a journey that is commonly taken informally, and based on self-teaching.

Music, Informal Learning and the School: A New Classroom Pedagogy by Lucy Green. Published in 2008 by Ashgate. This is an excellent book regarding how adolescents can learn infinitely better by guiding them to teach themselves and letting them tap into their own interests. Many children who have studied music since childhood start to lack motivation in adolescence and this book will help the parents of such adolescents in conquering these obstacles. Although aimed at teachers of adolescents, this book also opens up important prospects for music educators who teach younger, pre-adolescent children.

Is music important? by Adrian C. North and David J. Hargreaves. An article published in The Psychologist in 2003. A concise yet highly relevant read on the power of music, busting many commonly held myths regarding the very question 'is music important?'. This article is free to read online at http://www.thepsychologist.org.uk/archive/archive_home.cfm/volumeID_16-editionID_97-ArticleID_586-getfile_getPDF/thepsychologist%5C0803nort.pdf

Infant Musicality: New Research for Educators and Parents by Johannella Tafuri. Published in 2008 by Ashgate. A great, comprehensive read on how musical children really are - even before their moment of birth! This book also details the incredible effects of early music training on bringing out the various musical skills of babies and young children.

How is music learning celebrated and developed? by Graham Welch and Pauline Adams. A Professional User Review of UK and related international research undertaken for the British Educational Research Association, 2003. A concise read based on extensive research and offering very clear practical instructions on how to help children develop musically. Despite being aimed at educators, this paper is an enlightening and enjoyable read to any parent wishing to understand their children's musical needs.

The misunderstanding of music (Inaugural Professorial Lecture) by Graham Welch. Published in 2001 by the Institute of Education, University of London. This vastly enlightening yet concise read should be compulsory reading to anyone dealing with children in either professionally or through parenting. Let's not believe the 'musicality myth' that musical ability is reserved for the special few - this book hammers home the fact that 'we are all musical; we just need the opportunity', armed with extensive research and clarity of argumentation.

Note from Liisa: I am always keen to learn more - if you have a recommendation of a book, article or research paper that you feel I should read, please email me your recommendation via info@moosicology.com .